Contesting Femicide

Focusing on femicide, this book provides a contemporary re-evaluation of Carol Smart's innovative approach to the law question as first outlined in her groundbreaking book, *Feminism and the Power of Law* (Routledge 1989). Smart advocated turning to the legal domain not so much for demanding law reforms as construing it as a site on which to contest gender and more particularly, gendered constructions of women's experiences. Over the last 30 to 40 years, feminist law scholars and activists have launched scathing trans-jurisdictional critiques of the operation of provocation defences in hundreds of femicide cases. The evidence unearthed by feminist scholars that these defences operate in profoundly sexed ways is unequivocal. Accordingly, femicide cases have become critically important sites for feminist engagement and intervention across numerous jurisdictions. Exploring an area of criminal law that was not one of Smart's own focal concerns, this book both honours and extends Smart's work by approaching femicide as a site of engagement and counter-discourse that calls into question hegemonic representations of gendered relationships. Femicide cases thus provide a way to continue the endlessly valuable discursive work Smart advocated and practiced in other fields of law: both in articulating alternative accounts of gendered relationships and in challenging law's power to disqualify women's experiences of violence while privileging men's feelings and rights.

Adrian Howe is an associate lecturer, Law School, Birkbeck University, London, UK where she also has a visiting post. She has published widely in the field of sexed violence and is currently developing a Theatre in Education project based on her research on intimate partner femicide cases. The project's first play, *Othello on Trial*, has been performed in Melbourne, Australia and London, UK.

Daniela Alaattinoğlu is a doctoral candidate at the European University Institute, Italy. She has taught criminal law at the Finnish Police University College and published within the fields of femicide, gender and law, gender violence and human rights. Her LLM thesis was awarded with the annual award for excellence by the Finnish Lawyers' Association in 2014.

Porta Santo Stefano, Bologna, July 2014

Photo by Adrian Howe

a GlassHouse Book

Contesting Femicide

Feminism and the Power of Law Revisited

Edited by Adrian Howe and Daniela Alaattinoğlu

Routledge
Taylor & Francis Group
a GlassHouse Book

First published 2019
by Routledge
2 Park Square, Milton Park, Abingdon, Oxon OX14 4RN

and by Routledge
52 Vanderbilt Avenue, New York, NY 10017

First issued in paperback 2020

A GlassHouse book

Routledge is an imprint of the Taylor & Francis Group, an informa business

British Library Cataloguing-in-Publication Data
A catalogue record for this book is available from the British Library

Library of Congress Cataloging-in-Publication Data
Names: Howe, Adrian, editor. | Alaattinoglu, Daniela, editor.
Title: Contesting femicide : feminism and the power of law revisited / edited by Adrian Howe and Daniela Alaattinoglu.
Description: Abingdon, Oxon ; New York, NY : Routledge, 2019. | Includes bibliographical references and index.
Identifiers: LCCN 2018021782 | ISBN 9781138478626 (hbk)
Subjects: LCSH: Women—Crimes against. | Homicide. | Sociological jurisprudence. | Feminist jurisprudence. | Smart, Carol. Feminism and the power of law.
Classification: LCC K5191.W65 C66 2019 | DDC 345/.0252082—dc23
LC record available at https://lccn.loc.gov/2018021782

ISBN 13: 978-0-367-66571-5 (pbk)
ISBN 13: 978-1-138-47862-6 (hbk)

Typeset in Galliard
by Apex CoVantage, LLC

Contents

Contributors

Daniela Alaattinoğlu is a PhD candidate at the Department of Law at the European University Institute, Italy. She has dealt with femicide and violence against women in her research and work, particularly in her former teaching at the Police College of Finland.

Cemre Baytok works as the Sexual Harassment Prevention Office Coordinator at Boğaziçi University in Istanbul, Turkey. A feminist activist, she joined the Socialist Feminist Collective in 2008 and has taken part in feminist femicide watches since 2009.

Ilaria Boiano has worked as a women's rights lawyer at the NGO *Differenza Donna* since 2008. She has written many publications on gender-based violence and feminist legal practice and is one of the founders of the Atelier of Legal Feminism, an organisation researching legal feminism and feminist practices of law, with a focus on violence against women and femicide.

Anna Butler commenced her work as the inaugural Manager of the Domestic Violence Death Review Team (New South Wales, Australia) in 2011. She is responsible for developing and implementing the Team's executive function, operational framework and domestic violence reform agenda.

Emma Buxton-Namisnyk is a doctoral researcher at the University of Oxford and the inaugural Research Analyst on the Domestic Violence Death Review Team, New South Wales, Australia. In the latter role, she has designed and implemented research examining domestic and family violence context homicides and suicides.

Myrna Dawson is professor of sociology and Director of the Centre for the Study of Social and Legal Responses to Violence at the University of Guelph, Ontario, Canada. She leads the recently launched Canadian Femicide Observatory for Justice and Accountability and is the Co-Director of the Canadian Domestic Homicide Prevention Initiative with Vulnerable Populations and has spent the past 20 years researching social and legal responses to violence with an emphasis on violence against women and femicide.

Adrian Howe was foundation professor at the University of Central Lancashire, UK. Her first book, *Punish and Critique: Towards a Feminist Analysis of Penality*, was published in Maureen Cain's and Carol Smart's Sociology of Law and Crime series, the first book of which was *Feminism and the Power of Law*. Her continuing debt to Smart's work is also registered in a subsequent book, *Sex, Violence and Crime – Foucault and the 'Man' Question*.

Bronwyn Naylor is professor in the Graduate School of Business and Law, RMIT University, Melbourne, Australia. She has consulted to law reform bodies over many years on reforming laws addressing gendered violence and has carried out grant-funded research on killings of women by their intimate partners and the effect of recent reforms to the law and defences.

Johanna Niemi (Niemi-Kiesiläinen) is a professor at the Faculty of Law at the University of Turku, Finland. Writing a book on criminal procedure and violence in intimate partnerships in the early 2000s, she realised that criminal law doctrines are based on gendered assumptions about violence, more specifically on men killing other men.

Marjo Rantala is a PhD candidate in gender and law at the University of Helsinki, Finland and a Senior Officer at the Finnish Office of the Ombudsman for Equality. Involved with women's rights issues since 2010, including violence against women and femicide, she has participated as a representative of Finland in the negotiations of the Istanbul Convention.

Carol Smart is emerita professor of sociology at the University of Manchester, UK. Her most recent publications include *Personal Life: New Directions in Sociological Thinking*; *Same-Sex Marriages: New Generations, New Relationships* (with B. Heaphy and A. Einarsdottir) and *Relative Strangers: Family Life, Genes and Donor Conception* (with P. Nordqvist). She is now retired and living in Leeds, UK.

Patsilí Toledo is an adjunct lecturer at the Autonomous University of Barcelona, Spain. Her published PhD focused on the processes of criminalisation of femicide/feminicide in Latin American countries and she has collaborated with international entities and local NGOs on the topic since 2009.

Danielle Tyson is senior lecturer in criminology in the School of Humanities and Social Sciences at Deakin University, Victoria, Australia. Her research examining intimate partner femicide cases post-abolition of the controversial partial defence of provocation has sought both to challenge provocation's victim-blaming narratives and ensure more just outcomes for women who kill an abusive male partner.

Preface

Carol Smart

Feminism and the Power of Law was published in 1989 and, although I regard it as one of my most significant monographs, I now find it quite discomfiting to read. So much has changed. Matters which were of great importance in terms of feminist legal debate now seem irrelevant. Other critical matters such as rape and the sexual exploitation of children are perhaps treated more seriously than they were thirty years ago, but we must acknowledge that both the continuing prevalence and the inadequate institutional response to these offences have still hardly been addressed. So in rereading the text I experience a mixture of embarrassment that some of it feels so dated coupled with a sense of despair that so much is so slow to change. It was therefore with somewhat mixed emotions that I greeted the plan put forward by Adrian and Daniela to resurrect my book and subject it to a contemporary appraisal. But of course *Feminism and the Power of Law* is, in fact, no longer 'mine'. As soon as a book is published it becomes public property, available to all, and subject to all kinds of readings far beyond the control of the author. Indeed, this is the point I most want to address in this Preface, but before I do I wish to make it clear that, in spite of my mixed emotions, the predominant feeling I had was one of delight that feminist scholars might still find value in the text and that they were prepared to apply truly critical thinking to ideas and ideals over which I laboured so hard all those years ago. I feel enormously honoured.

Adrian and Daniela point out in their Introduction that in several central ways, *Feminism and the Power of Law* has been misconstrued or misinterpreted. This, they argue, is in spite of the fact that I tried very hard to correct misunderstandings. In truth I was taken aback by some of the criticisms which I felt were misplaced or based on very careless readings of the text. But, of course, I am hardly alone in being 'misunderstood' so I won't dwell on that. Instead what now interests me most is the question of why my attempt to reframe law's place in feminist politics seemed to cause so much anger and confusion. Why has this resentment persisted? Why was feminist engagement with law taken to be above critical comment? Why was it so heretical to suggest that there may be different ways of engaging with law? Or to propose that law might be used as a complex site of discursive struggle rather a simple pragmatic tool of the good? What was the insistence that I was wilfully advocating a retreat from law (which I did not!) really about?

To get to the core of this problem it is important to have some knowledge of the moment in which the book appeared. Second Wave Feminism may have started in the late 1960s, but it was only reaching the taught syllabus of universities in countries like the UK, USA, Canada and Australia in the 1980s. Some of the most exciting and engaged work was appearing in law schools partly because law, unlike disciplines such as sociology or history, seemed to offer both theoretical and practical solutions to newly identified problems. At that time there was a very strong commitment in academic circles to finding and operationalising feminist principles and policies. So in many ways law was the perfect place for feminist interventions as it appeared to provide the immediate, practical tools that other disciplines mostly could not.

Second Wave Feminism also brought with it (rightly or wrongly) the assurance that this time the new women's movement would get it right and would succeed where previous movements had failed. The First Wave Movement was revered but it seemed obvious to the new band of activists that it had not gone far enough and that it had not been sufficiently radical or wide-ranging. Thus, in spite of truly daunting odds, there was an energy and optimism in the new movement. Feminists in law schools may have been few in number but they were profoundly committed to using the law as the best available tool to effect change. Given this context it is perhaps not too surprising that my intervention seemed like a bucket of cold water thrown on the fire of bright determination. I appeared in the guise of the thief of hope.

I was of course aware of this perception. However, my intention was not to kill hope, but to identify different spaces for, and modes of, intervention which would preserve a slower burning hope which would not be extinguished by the force of realpolitik. I was by then acutely aware of the problems that could arise from unrealizable hopes being dashed or unfulfilled and the sudden disillusionment that could follow. I was more interested in inculcating the stamina needed for a long haul, peppered with minor victories and major disappointments. And so, for me, the idea that law was a site of struggle rather than a solution to struggle was crucial. This understanding did not come solely from Foucault although he eloquently propounded this political point of view. Rather his framing of the issues gave clarity to my personal experiences (of campaigning) and my socio-historical study of law undertaken as a postgraduate student. I had immersed myself in the early feminist campaigns of the nineteenth and early twentieth centuries. In particular I studied feminist engagement with issues of wife-killing (as it was then called), marriage, divorce and the 'custody' of children, the sexual abuse of girls, prostitution and so-called contagious diseases. Early feminists had also placed their faith in legal reform as the solution to the problems they perceived and, in many ways, they were pretty successful in getting new laws onto the statute book. Often they rallied support precisely because they had a clear goal, namely getting a new law through Parliament. And they also garnered effort by proclaiming that one final, mighty push would achieve the necessary solution. Hence Mary Lowndes, a feminist campaigner against the sexual abuse of girls in the 1920s, called upon those women who had recently won the vote to use their new power to force the men in government to act:

> But in very truth a new day has dawned, though the sun has not broken through the clouds. In former years we might have said: 'Surely ten righteous men in higher places might arise and remedy these horrors'. They have not arisen. Now we say: 'Ten million women voters can deal with these questions'. As *knowledge of the true situation* grows, more and more they will stand behind Lady Astor, Mrs Wintringham and their supporters, in the House urging the Home Secretary 'to look into this matter and to act'. If he would act quickly and strongly, he would have the whole of the *awakened public conscience* behind him.[1]

I think this passage sums up the problem neatly, namely the idea that an Act of Parliament can remedy 'these horrors'. The point at which a new piece of legislation in the UK gets what is called Royal Assent can be seen as a very clear marker of success for a campaign. It makes all the effort seem worthwhile and there is a tangible outcome. The fact that very little may change as far as victims are concerned is much less tangible and often only discovered many years later. It is even seen as curmudgeonly to point out that the promise of law reform has not been fulfilled. More importantly, the feminist voices that called for change could be readily silenced after the reform precisely because they had been given what they asked for and so had no legitimate reason to continue their complaint.

My postgraduate research showed clearly how, by analogy, the optimistic crest of a wave of reform was followed by a deep trough of silence and passivity. Put simply it is really hard to keep banging on about a thing if you appear to have got what you asked for. This was an important lesson for me and it made me think about other ways of avoiding these peaks of enthusiasm followed by troughs of inactivity and amnesia. The recent 'Me Too' campaign is an example of this. While I welcome the campaign I feel baffled by the collective amnesia that suggests that women did not mind being sexually harassed twenty or thirty years ago. There seems to be an assumption that we have developed a new sensibility and will not accept behaviour that everyone thought was perfectly fine a few decades (or more) ago. But I still have my dog-eared copy of *Sexual Harassment at Work* published in 1982 at the height of the then campaign by feminists in the National Council for Civil Liberties determined to put a stop to such behaviour.[2] How have we come to forget this (and all the other books and articles published on this topic)? Why is the current campaign thought of as 'new' when I remember so well standing up against sexual harassment myself in the 1980s only to find the permanent job I applied for in the law department where I worked went to a man (who went on to teach my course on feminism and law!).

There is a continuous struggle going on; there is progress and regress. I am reminded of the important work of Juliet Mitchell which I found so important when I was formulating the ideas which later appeared in *Feminism and the Power*

1 Lowndes (1923: 11) (emphasis added).
2 Sedley and Benn (1982).

of Law. In 1971 when she was influenced by Marxist scholarship she developed the ideas of 'complex unity' and 'uneven development'.[3] Women's condition, she argued, was not a simple structure but was comprised of different elements which could change over time and which could be realigned. Thus she recognised that while one aspect of women's lives might improve (for example, a law against domestic violence), unless women also gained economic independence or better social welfare provision they would hardly benefit from it. Added to this idea of the complex unity was the idea of uneven development. This referred to the way in which wider social and economic conditions could change and flux, creating an unstable, unpredictable landscape for women's lives and making it impossible to foresee the course of events. I went on to argue that law itself was a complex unity, being made up from different elements which do not necessarily all work in unison or harmony. This complex unity of law was in turn itself subject to processes of uneven development. I suggested that this overall perspective might make one cautious of seeing law reform as a simple solution to a straightforward problem, although even then I was clearly arguing that law could be an important catalyst for change or important site of intervention.[4]

As I said at the beginning of this short preface, political activism and legal campaigns thrive on hope and I was seen as damaging this vital element in the movement for progressive change. Yet I think I was actually trying to protect hope in order to enable the women's movement to keep pressing forwards, rather than waxing and waning. I was, even then, weary of the cycles of remembering and forgetting and saddened by the idea that each new wave of feminism thought their elder sisters had got it all wrong because progress seemed so minimal. The context of this new book is, of course, quite different to the one facing *Feminism and the Power of Law*. For a start I think we are really grasping the reality of regress and the worsening of women's (and other minorities') position. There is, I suspect, less political optimism around and a greater need for resilience. The things that motivated me to write the book thirty years ago may no longer be relevant and the ideas I was working with undoubtedly call for revision and re-framing. This is why I so welcome this collection of feminist essays and I remain deeply appreciative that all the contributors have treated *Feminism and the Power of Law* so seriously.

References

Lowndes, M. 1923 *Child Assault in England* London: Women's Printing Society.
Mitchell, J. 1971 *Women's Estate* Harmondsworth: Penguin Books.
Sedley, A. and Benn, M. 1982 *Sexual Harassment at Work* London: Hyperion Books.
Smart, C. 1995 'Feminism and Law: Some Problems of Analysis and Strategy' in *Law, Crime and Sexuality: Essays in Feminism* London: Sage Publications.

3 Mitchell (1971).
4 Smart (1995).

Acknowledgments

Adrian would like to acknowledge the commitment and outstanding work of her co-editor, Daniela. It is beyond my comprehension how anyone could manage to give this book her full attention while completing a doctorate. But Daniela did. I would also like to thank Hava Dayan, a participant at the Fighting Femicide Conference which Daniela and I organised at Queen Mary University of London in 2015. It was Hava's idea to produce a book based on the papers presented there. While other commitments prevented her from continuing to work on the book project, her ongoing support for it is much appreciated. Karen Ingala Smith's influential research on femicides committed in the UK since 2012 cannot go unacknowledged. Her 'Counting Dead Women' social media campaign reporting these homicides provides the research base for my chapters in this book and for other recent and forthcoming publications. More importantly, Karen's work has been instrumental in elevating femicide into a widely recognised social and political issue in the UK.

Daniela would like to thank Adrian, the main editor, for her tireless determination, excellent and sharp editing and her incredibly hard work as the primary brain and heart behind this book project. I am extremely happy to have met her in 2014, and since then, becoming familiarised with her insightful and original scholarship. I cannot emphasise enough how much I have learned from reading her work, watching her play *Othello on Trial*, and not least, working alongside her with this book. I would also like to join Adrian in thanking Hava, whose participation in brainstorming and nailing down the scope and focus of this book has been invaluable. Apart from sharing her important research with us, Hava has also consistently contributed to this project with her positive energy.

We thank all our contributors for their papers and finally, we thank Carol Smart for writing *Feminism and the Power of Law* which continues to inspire us to this day.

Introduction

Adrian Howe and Daniela Alaattinoğlu

This book is both a celebration of the profound significance of Carol Smart's innovative approach to the law question as outlined in her ground-breaking book, *Feminism and the Power of Law*, and a testimonial to its enduring legacy. But while *Contesting Femicide:* Feminism and the Power of Law *Revisited* honours Smart's approach to thinking strategically about feminist engagement with law, it does so with a twist. Smart famously advised feminists against placing all their energy in demanding law reforms, instead encouraging us to construe the legal domain as a discursive site on which to expose and contest gendered constructions of women's experiences. In short, she advocated reading law as discourse, a methodology she followed with reference to law's constitution of the harms of rape, child abuse and pornography. She also explored law's relationship to women's bodies, examined the problem of rights in relation to feminist goals and querying the pursuit of a feminist jurisprudence. Our book has more modest goals. It explores law's handling of wife-killing – now 'intimate partner femicide' (or 'intimate femicide' as it is called in North America) – a field of inquiry that was not one of Smart's focal concerns but that nevertheless provides golden opportunities for exploring local laws as discursive sites of engagement and counter-discourse *and* for achieving feminist law reform agendas.

The idea for writing this book came out of the international conference *Fighting Femicide: Cultural and Legal Interventions* which we organised and was held at Queen Mary University of London in November 2015. Our call for papers explained that we were interested in receiving proposals that analysed the most prevalent form of femicide in western countries, namely intimate partner femicides. It emphasised that the conference would be concerned primarily with charting the cultural understanding and legal reception of these homicides within dominant cultural communities. Keeping the focus on the deeply gendered constitution of intimate partner homicide within dominant cultures remains a huge challenge for researchers who refuse still pervasive othering practices that locate culturally inscribed excuses for violence against women – and the violence itself – in minority communities. While not all feminist researchers share our commitment to targeting femicide and excuses for it within dominant communities, it is clear that coining the term 'femicide' to refer to the political nature of killings of women has in itself been a significant political intervention in many countries.[1] What emerged from the conference was that intimate partner femicide cases have become critically important sites for feminist engagement and intervention across numerous jurisdictions. Here then was stunning confirmation of the view Carol Smart put forward thirty years ago that however difficult it is for feminist law reformers to achieve substantive or even symbolic victories for women, law itself remains an invaluable site for contesting hegemonic representations of gendered relationships. More particularly, it provides an immensely valuable site for challenging historically mandated excuses for killing women.

While *Feminism and the Power of Law* ranks high in the list of influential late twentieth century feminist socio-legal texts, it is also one of the most misunderstood, coming in as it has for sustained criticism that continues to this day. The sticking point has ever been Smart's warning to feminist researchers and activists not to get too caught up in law reform, a warning frequently misread as advocating a retreat from law and feminist legal activism, notwithstanding her many assurances to the contrary. Time and again Smart has reasserted her conviction that law must remain a 'site of struggle' for feminists because it provides a 'forum for articulating alternative visions and accounts'.[2] Even after uncovering the resistance of the English legal profession to recognising child abuse as harmful, she never wavered from the conviction that law 'understood in its widest meaning, is still one of the most important sites of engagement and counter-discourse'. Ten years after she wrote *Feminism and the Power of Law*, the criminal justice system and legal practice were still for her important, albeit problematic – indeed 'the most problematic' – sites for feminist interventions.[3] She has repeatedly reaffirming this view on the continuing importance of engaging with law, most recently in her essay 'Reflection', published in *Feminist Legal Studies* in 2012. Here she explains again that her counsel to decentre law was 'never meant to mean' that feminists should refuse to engage with law. For despite her misgivings about feminists investing too much in law reform, she was always of the view that law is 'an invaluable site of discursive struggle', for 'endlessly valuable' discursive work.[4]

Smart's numerous clarifications notwithstanding, feminist critics of *Feminism and the Power of Law* continue to interpret it as 'a call for inaction' while making unsupported claims that she urged feminists to 'avoid' the criminal justice system.[5] Whether such claims are attributable to the deleterious lingering effects of the anti-postmodern animus that spawned misinformed criticism of Smart's work in the first place, it is clear that it's past time to set the record straight. Accordingly, this book provides a re-evaluation of Smart's socio-legal conceptualisation of the power of law with a view to demonstrating how her Foucauldian feminist

1 Corradi et al. (2016: 3). See also the seminal book Radford and Russell (1992).
2 Smart (1989: 88).
3 Smart (1999: 392, 407).
4 Smart (2012: 162–164).
5 Smart (1993: 46–47).

method of reading law as discourse still has much to offer feminist socio-legal studies and legal activism.

We begin with a clear statement of Smart's argument in *Feminism and the Power of Law* and whose could be more lucid than her own? Four years after it was published she provided this summary:

> Put briefly, my argument was that we have misunderstood the power of law and that we should recognise that in using law to pursue certain goals we might be contributing to the legalisation of everyday life, which currently seems to give legitimacy to a specific hierarchy of knowledge, which subjugates alternative discourses, for example, feminism. *However, I also argued that certain matters were already in the legal domain and thus could not be abandoned.* I also argued that we might attempt some kind of calculus of harms and decide that although deploying law was problematic that in certain circumstances it might be the best resource available. Finally, I also argued that we might use the legal domain less for achieving law reforms than as a site on which to contest meanings about gender.[6]

It could not be emphasised enough: 'certain matters' were already in the legal domain and needed to be tackled there. In any calculus of harms to women that are already in that domain we would argue that intimate partner femicide must be placed at the top of the list. Not only does this crime violate the most fundamental human right – the right to life – but by construing this type of killing as a lesser form of homicide, one, moreover, that a woman brings upon herself by upsetting a man, criminal courts harm all women. Indeed, if victim-blaming defences to intimate partner femicide and centuries of trial outcomes are any guide, intimate partner femicide is the victim-blaming crime *par excellence* – she 'asked for it' by provoking a man to kill her.

And here is where the twist in this book's honouring of Smart's approach to law occurs. For in challenging law's handling of femicide cases, feminists have used the legal domain not only as a site on which to contest meanings about gender; they have also continued to press for law reforms aimed at curtailing victim-blaming narratives and have met with some success. For example, over the last 30 to 40 years, feminist law scholars and activists have launched scathing critiques of the operation of defences to murder, especially provocation defences, in intimate partner femicide cases in anglophone jurisdictions. The evidence they have unearthed that these defences operate in profoundly sexed ways is unequivocal – for centuries and still today, the law of provocation has facilitated men's claims that sexual infidelity provides a moral warrant for murdering 'unfaithful' wives. It is notable that feminists have been at the forefront of reform movements to abolish provocation, most successfully in several Australian jurisdictions which have banned the defence outright and in England and Wales where it has been replaced with a new

6 Smart (1993: 47) (our emphasis).

defence that expressly excluded sexual infidelity as a trigger for loss of control. Post-reform cases provide opportunities not only for assessing the effectiveness of the reforms in preventing men from getting away with murder but also for continuing the endlessly valuable discursive work that Smart advocated and practiced in other fields of law. That is, they are ideal sites for continuing the work of articulating alternative accounts of gendered relationships, challenging law's power to disqualify women's experiences of violence while privileging men's feelings and rights. Conceived of in this way, the cases are transformed into what Adrian Howe has described as 'a critical, pedagogical means of mobilising consciousness about emotional excuses for violence against women'.[7]

Since the publication of *Feminism and the Power of Law*, there have also been significant developments in international law that have implications for the prevention of femicide. The Inter-American Convention on the Prevention, Punishment and Eradication of Violence against Women (the so-called Belém do Pará Convention) adopted in 1994, was the world's first binding treaty to recognise that violence against women constitutes a violation of human rights. Combined with other human rights instruments, it has provided a framework for women's human rights and gender equality in the Americas, thereby helping to raise awareness of the pervasive problem of violence against women. Importantly, it outlines states' obligations to prevent and eliminate this violence, including obligations to ensure that educational programmes counteract gender prejudices and hierarchies; to promote education on violence against women for justice and law enforcement systems; to promote specialised services for victims, including shelters; to develop awareness-raising programmes on violence against women; to provide victims with readjustment programmes and to encourage the media to develop ethical reporting guidelines.[8] Similar preventive measures are emphasised in the more recent Council of Europe Convention on Preventing and Combating Violence against Women and Domestic Violence (the so-called Istanbul Convention) adopted in 2011. An important step in the creation of a legal framework at a pan-European level to eliminate all forms of violence against women, inclduing domestic violence, this treaty emphasises states' obligation to allocate appropriate and financial resources for prevention programmes.[9] Thanks to these feminist-initiated legal initiatives, femicide is increasingly being perceived as a global problem in legal terms.

Reporting on feminist legal strategies in a range of different jurisdictions, participants in the Fighting Femicide Conference highlighted how feminists globally are working tirelessly to get intimate partner femicide recognised as a first-order

7 Howe (2013: 143). Smart's influence extends beyond her critique of law. Her critique of criminology is channelled in Howe (2008). For Howe's most recent celebration of Smart's work see Howe (2016).

8 The Inter-American Convention on the Prevention, Punishment and Eradication of Violence against Women. 33 ILM 1534 (1994), Article 8.

9 Council of Europe Convention on Preventing and Combating Violence against Women and Domestic Violence. CETS 210 (2011), Article 8 and Chapter 3.

political problem and to reform outmoded laws that have enabled men to get away with murdering their women partners. Inspired by their contributions, we decided to embark on a book project that was at once an exploration of law's power and of feminist engagements with law that registered the influence of Smart's work on socio-legal research on intimate partner femicide. We invited researchers who were already familiar with Smart's Foucauldian method of reading law as discourse and those who were new to it with a view to demonstrating how much it can bring to feminist socio-legal studies and feminist legal activism. In short, we welcomed papers from anyone wishing to contribute to a book planned as a testimonial to the enduring legacy of *Feminism and the Power of Law*. We believe the result to be an engaging insight into transnational feminist engagement with femicide and law.

****

The book is divided into two parts. Part 1 focuses on feminist-inspired criminal law reforms. In Chapter 1 **Adrian Howe** investigates how intimate partner femicide cases have unfolded in the courts in England and Wales after a reform expressly excluding sexual infidelity as a trigger for loss of control. Has the reform had its intended effect of preventing wife-killers getting away with murder? Through analysing these cases, Howe argues that Smart's key insight that law is an important site of engagement with hegemonic constructions of gendered relationships and, crucially, of 'counter-discourse' is still valid today. In Chapter 2 **Danielle Tyson** and **Bronwyn Naylor** assess the feminist-led criminal law reforms in the Australian state of Victoria. Focusing on intentional homicide, and particularly the provocation defence, they investigate how courts are narrating intimate partner femicides in the post-reform era. In Chapter 3 **Patsilí Toledo** analyses the introduction of 'femicide' as a new crime in Latin American countries. This transfer of feminist terminology first used by activists and scholars to address the widespread problem of gender-based killings of women into national criminal laws might seem like a feminist victory. But looking closely at the outcomes of the reforms, Toledo discovers a complex reality that brings her into conversation with Smart's critique of feminists putting too much faith in legal reform.

While the three chapters in Part 1 offer a range of perspectives on how Smart's caution about feminists investing their energies into law reform reads today, the chapters in Part 2 move beyond the question of law reform to explore proliferating sites of feminist legal intervention. In Chapter 4 **Adrian Howe** continues channeling Smart's view of law as a 'discursive field' and a 'site of struggle' in her analysis of intimate partner femicides in England and Wales where the perpetrator has taken his own life or has pleaded diminished responsibility after killing his wife or partner. She also explores how drama and more particularly *Othello on Trial*, the first play in a Theatre in Education project exploring the potential of the creative arts to engage with feminist anti-violence campaigns, provides yet another productive site on which to continue the never-ending feminist project of contesting law's truth.

In Chapter 5 **Daniela Alaattinoğlu** and **Cemre Baytok** investigate feminist litigation and feminist watches as a Smart-inspired way to engage with law in practice and raise awareness about intimate partner femicide and court practice in Turkey. Focusing on one case monitored and litigated by feminists, they demonstrate how feminist discursive engagement with law in practice can be successful. In Chapter 6 **Myrna Dawson** discusses the establishment of the Canadian Femicide Observatory for Justice and Accountability. In the light of national initiatives in law and policy to prevent femicide and violence against women, she highlights the importance of feminists critically engaging with what Smart referred to as law in practice.

In Chapter 7 **Emma Buxton-Namisnyk** and **Anna Butler** analyse how intimate partner femicide cases are being put into discourse in New South Wales, Australia today, comparing judicial sentencing remarks with in-depth qualitative information obtained through the New South Wales Domestic Violence Death Review Team. They ask whether judges are still excusing and normalising violence against women and whether, by contrast, domestic violence death reviews can provide an alternative feminist discourse that more effectively tackles the problem of intimate partner femicide. In Chapter 8 **Ilaria Boiano** explains that Carol Smart's *Feminism and the Power of Law* has been a key reference for Italian feminists and for some a pillar around which Italian feminism continues to question law. Investigating how law plays an important role in reinforcing hegemonic understandings of intimate partner violence but also has potential as a tool of change, she explores judgments made in Italian criminal courts in femicide cases with a view to suggesting how feminist legal practice can contest and subvert the dominant legal culture.

The final two chapters are concerned with Finland, a Nordic country often internationally praised for its gender equality. In Chapter 9 **Daniela Alaattinoğlu** and **Johanna Niemi** engage in a discourse analysis of Finnish criminal law textbooks to find out whether – and how – feminist legal research has been mainstreamed or marginalised in Finnish legal education. Legal education is key to how future lawyers learn to construct the world into the legally relevant and irrelevant, a construction which Smart herself criticised. Looking closely at how this division is made, the authors critique the traditionally context-deprived Finnish criminal law. In Chapter 10 **Marjo Rantala** discusses a case of intimate partner femicide in Finland which she and two other feminist legal scholars have presented before the CEDAW Committee. Given Smart's criticism of rights-based strategies in *Feminism and the Power of Law*, Rantala ponders how deploying rights in a supranational legal forum might contribute to making femicide and gender-based violence political priorities in Finland today.

References

Corradi, C. et al. 2016 'Theories of Femicide and Their Significance for Social Research' 1 *Current Sociology* 21.

Howe, A. 2008 *Sex, Violence and Crime: Foucault and the 'Man' Question* Abingdon, Oxon: Routledge.

——— 2013 'Mastering Emotions or Still Losing Control? Seeking Public Engagement with "Sexual Infidelity" Homicide' 21 *Feminist Legal Studies* 141.
——— 2016 'Feminist Methods and Sources in Criminology and Criminal Justice' 16(2) *Legal Information Management* 102.
Radford, J. and Russell, D.E.H. (eds.) 1992 *Femicide: The Politics of Woman Killing* Boston: Twayne.
Smart, C. 1989 *Feminism and the Power of Law* London: Routledge.
——— 1993 'Proscription, Prescription and the Desire for Certainty?' 13 *Studies in Law, Politics and Society* 37.
——— 1999 'A History of Ambivalence and Conflict in the Discursive Construction of the "Child Victim" of Sexual Abuse' 8(3) *Social & Legal Studies* 391.
——— 2012 'Reflection' 20 *Feminist Legal Studies* 65.

Part 1

Criminal law reform case studies

1 Provocation by sexual infidelity – diminishing returns?

Adrian Howe

Introduction

Carol Smart's warning not to put too much faith in law and law reform notwithstanding, feminist legal scholars and activists have continued to invest time in campaigns to reform the law of murder that commenced before the publication of *Feminism and the Power of Law*. Highlighting the differential treatment of men and women facing murder charges in intimate partner homicides, they have fought for changes that ensure defences operate more equitably. In Anglophone jurisdictions reformers have focused predominantly on the operation of the partial defence of provocation. Opinions differ as to what form reforms should take. Some call for provocation to be retained but reformed to take account of the different circumstances in which women kill, others for an expanded understanding of self-defence. By contrast, those focusing on intimate partner femicide cases advocate limiting or even abolishing victim-blaming provocation defences outright. After decades of campaigning, abolitionists have had some success. As discussed in Chapter 2, the provocation defence has been abolished in several Australian jurisdictions. In others it has been severely restricted, for example, in England and Wales where reformers took the unusual step of abolishing provocation as a defence but replacing it with a loss of control defence that expressly excludes sexual infidelity as a trigger for loss of control. Leading the reform movement's challenge to what she characterised as 'our own version of honour killing', Solicitor General Harriet Harman explained why they decided on this particular course:

> It is a terrible thing to lose a sister or a daughter, but to then have her killer blame her and say he is the victim of her infidelity is totally unacceptable. The relatives say 'he got away with murder' and they're right.[1]

The reformers were determined to stop these killers getting away with murder.

I have discussed this controversial reform and the furor it generated in legal circles elsewhere.[2] This chapter provides an analysis of post-reform intimate part-

1 Quoted in Hinsliff (2008).
2 Howe (2012, 2013).

ner femicides committed in England and Wales between 2012 and 2016. What has become of the traditional provocation by sexual infidelity narrative that Englishmen have resorted to for centuries? How successful has the reform banning that excusatory tale been? Are men still getting away with murder? Reading law as Smart advocated as a discursive field, the chapter celebrates once again her conviction that for all the difficulties it raises for feminists, 'law, understood in its widest meaning', remains 'one of the most important sites of engagement and counter-discourse'.[3] The law of murder, not one of Smart's focal concerns, nevertheless provides golden opportunities for conceptualising law as a discursive site of engagement *and* for pursuing a feminist law reform agenda – one aimed at revolutionising the law of murder.

Contesting provocation by sexual infidelity

Over the centuries English courts have waxed and waned in their approach to wife-killing – now intimate partner femicide – clamping down heavily on defendants in some periods, showing mercy in others.[4] But what has not been fully recognised is that the Homicide Act 1957's expansion of the provocation defence to include provocation by the victim's words or deeds ushered in a golden age for wife-killers. Since then, blaming 'nagging and shagging' women for provoking their own deaths has usually guaranteed an acquittal of murder and a conviction for the lesser offence of manslaughter.

But not always. In one early twenty-first-century case, a man killed his 72-year-old wife with a weighted sock he had packed 'by accident' on their first wedding anniversary. He claimed he had 'exploded' when she told him she had 'feelings' for a former partner but was found guilty of murder by majority verdict.[5] Another man claiming provocation had recorded his estranged wife having sex with another man. Accidently leaving the dictaphone on, he recorded the fatal attack and his last words to his wife: 'you are the weakest link – goodbye'. After six hours of deliberation, the jury unanimously found him guilty of murder.[6] Contrast his fate with that of a man who had smashed his wife's skull, inflicting more than 70 injuries, after she provoked him, he said, by taunting him about an affair with a colleague.[7] The jury took only three and a half hours to clear him of murder. He was sentenced to six years for manslaughter. It was, however, another widely publicised case that galvanised the reform movement, setting it on the path of abolishing sexual infidelity as excuse for murder.

The *Humes* case and its contentious aftermath has been told elsewhere.[8] Suffice it to say that in December 2001, a man described by the court as an 'overworked'

3 Smart (1999: 392).
4 See Weiner (2004).
5 Payne (2002a).
6 BBC (2002).
7 Payne (2002b).
8 Howe (2013) and Burton (2003).

solicitor, knifed his wife to death in front of their four children. He found himself 'in a red mist' and had 'lost it totally' on learning that Maddie Humes wanted to leave him for another man.[9] Or so he said. There was no trial, the prosecution having accepted his plea of guilty to manslaughter on the basis of provocation. He received a seven-year sentence, leaving the victim's family furious that he was seen as the victim while 'Maddie wasn't heard at all'.[10] In December 2002, the Attorney General appealed against Humes' sentence and two others on the grounds that it was unduly lenient. In one a man had killed a woman who had left him, the court noting he had found this 'difficult to accept'. He 'just boiled over', fell into a 'red haze' and choked her to death. Acquitted of murder, he was sentenced to four years imprisonment for manslaughter. The Court of Appeal declined to interfere in any of the sentences. It was unmoved even by argument that sentences were much longer in attempted murder cases than in cases of manslaughter by reason of provocation. As the court explained this anomaly, 'certain assumptions' had to be made in the offender's favour in provocation cases, namely, that the loss of control was reasonable and that the circumstances were such as to make the loss of self-control sufficiently excusable to reduce the gravity of the defendant's offence from murder to manslaughter.[11] Being distressed by a woman who discloses, as Maddie Humes allegedly had, that she had been unfaithful and that she wanted to leave the marriage met this test.

It was time for legislative action. In the face of strenuous opposition from the judiciary, the House of Lords and a wide cross section of the legal fraternity, the reform bill abolishing provocation by infidelity as a defence to murder was finally passed. Set out in sections 54–56 of the *Coroners and Justice Act 2009*, the new defence of loss of control came into force in October 2010.[12] Fast track now to the 2012 case of *Clinton*, conjoined appeals by three men convicted of murdering wives who wanted to leave them and the first post-reform femicide cases to come before the Court of Appeal. Defying the reformers, the court unanimously determined that 'infidelity' – broadly construed to encompass relationship breakdown – may properly be taken into consideration for the purposes of the new partial defence of loss of control when such behaviour was 'integral to the facts as a whole'.[13] So how has this panned out in post-*Clinton* cases?

From manslaughter to murder?

This chapter provides an analysis, based exclusively on newspaper reports, of intimate partner femicides committed in England and Wales over the five-year period from January 1 2012 to December 31 2016. The findings are drawn

9 *R v Suratan, R v Humes and R v Wilkinson* (Attorney General's Reference No 74 of 2002, No. 95 of 2002 and No 118 of 2002) [2002] EWCA Crim 2982 at 285–6.

10 Hinsliff (2003).

11 *R v Suratan, R v Humes and R v Wilkinson* at 274. See also Burton (2003).

12 See Reed and Bohlander (2011).

13 *R v Clinton, Parker and Evans* [2012] 1 Cr App R 26 at 37. See Howe (2012, 2013).

from a wider study of media reports of 400 cases identified from Karen Ingala Smith's 'Counting Dead Women' lists, all compiled from newspaper reports, of over 680 men 'known or suspected' to have killed women in the UK over that period.[14] Confining the analysis to men who faced trial in the reform jurisdiction of England and Wales, I identified 317 defendants who were charged with murder, 240 (75 per cent) of whom pleaded guilty to that offence or were found guilty by a jury.[15] Their ages ranged from 17 to 85 years, their victims' from 15 to 87 years. Many victims are named here by way of memorialising their lives. Their killers are not. Who they are, whatever their class, race and ethnic identity is immaterial to an analysis of law's discursive constitution – as it is reported in the media – of intimate partner femicide today. What matters is how killers and courts are putting its perpetrators, victims and excusatory context into discourse in the post-reform age.

Ninety defendants admitted murder from the start or did so when it became clear during the trial that they had no viable defence. Their victims included Leslie Caile, stabbed to death by a partner plagued by an unfounded suspicion that she was having an affair and Christine Baker who was throttled by her husband when he discovered her infidelity. Seventeen-year-old Sophie Smith, killed by her 18-year-old boyfriend who believed she had cheated on him, was subjected to a four-hour beating to elicit a false confession. Her injuries were likened to those sustained in a serious road crash.[16] What immediately becomes clear from the guilty pleas is not only that allegations of sexual infidelity are losing their excusatory force, but that these 'red mist' cases can now be more readily identified as departure cases – where the victim was estranged, in the process of leaving a relationship or seeking a divorce. Jade Riley-Ward was stabbed 83 times with four different knives by a jealous boyfriend. Her text message saying she 'wanted space' convinced him she was having an affair.[17] Kerry Power's estranged partner strangled her when she rejected his demands for a reconciliation. Lisa Winn's estranged husband could not accept his 25-year marriage was over: 'he couldn't face the thought of her having a life without him'.[18] Helen Lancaster's husband was angry she was having an affair and had sent him divorce papers. Jackie Abbott's husband launched a ferocious attack when she decided to end their relationship. Sarah Pollock was strangled by her former partner who scrawled 'that's the price you pay for having four affairs' on the wall of her flat when she started a new relationship and tried to end all contact with him.[19] Unable to accept her decision to end their relationship and jealous of her new one, Sally Campion's

14 Ingala Smith (2012–2016). Her lists are not confined to intimate partner femicide. For an earlier analysis of these lists see Howe (2014).
15 Seventy-eight cases in which men committed suicide after killing partners or died in prison before their court appearance are discussed in Chapter 4.
16 Moore (2017). Newspaper reports are cited only where there are direct quotations or where a case is described in detail.
17 Pleasance (2013).
18 BBC (2015a).
19 BBC (2015b).

former boyfriend used a claw hammer to inflict 41 separate injuries on her at her home. Sentencing him to life with a 22-year minimum term, the judge said he was 'firmly of the view' that the killer posed 'a very great danger to women with whom you may form relationships in the future'.[20]

In another revealing case, Angela Best's former partner killed her when she started seeing another man after her relationship broke down. He admitted murder as his trial began, his chances of avoiding a conviction for murder negligible given that he had already two killed women partners at a time when defences to murder were more readily available for wife-killers. When he killed his wife by throwing her off a balcony in 1981 he was convicted of manslaughter by provocation, the judge describing him as a 'battered husband' who had suffered violence at the hands of his wife. In 1993 he successfully pleaded guilty to manslaughter by diminished responsibility after strangling a partner who had an affair. He was sent to a secure psychiatric hospital, only to be discharged four years later. Sentencing him to life with a minimum of 26 years for Angela Best's murder, the judge said: 'Such repeated offending, resulting in three separate court cases, must be almost unprecedented'.[21]

Unprecedented though it may have been to kill three women partners, manslaughter convictions were common in the pre-reform period. Now however, the chances of a man avoiding a murder conviction for killing an unfaithful partner appear to be diminishing. Of the 36 defendants running the new loss of control defence, only nine did so successfully. The rest were found guilty of murder. Akua Agyuman's husband stabbed her repeatedly then ran her over with his car. He thought she was having an affair with a neighbour. The prosecutor told the jury there must be evidence that the defendant had 'excusably lost control' but the 'plain truth' was that any loss of self-control here was 'borne entirely of anger and jealousy at what he perceived to be his wife's sexual infidelity'.[22] Shamim Gabriel's husband, who stabbed her more than 30 times in a jealous rage believing she was having affairs, failed to convince the jury that he had lost control fearing an immediate threat of violence from his wife. A consideration of the whole context of his frenzied attack did not save Fozia Ahmed's husband from a murder conviction. He claimed to be under extreme pressure because his young children had serious health problems that triggered financial worries and his wife was not only having an affair but threatened him to take the children away and even to kill them. It was not enough to satisfy the jury. He was however, a recipient of one of the lowest minimum terms set for murder in the five-year period covered by this study – 11 years.[23]

Sophie McDonald's estranged husband began with the stock 'loss of control' excusatory tale, alleging she had '100 secret lovers' during their 15-year long marriage. He also claimed that she had threatened to stop him seeing their

20 BBC (2015c).
21 BBC (2018).
22 Gye (2013).
23 Loweth (2012).

children and would bankrupt if he did not agree to her terms for divorce. But once the trial started, he changed his plea to murder.[24] It took only two hours for a jury to unanimously reject the loss of control defence raised by Rosemary Gill's husband who battered her to death after discovering she was having an affair. Loss of control defences also failed for Heather Arthur's husband who stabbed her after learning of her affair and her desire to leave him; for Assia Newton's husband who killed her over her holiday romance and request for a divorce after a 23-year marriage and for 20-year-old Lauren Masters' former partner who stabbed her 23 times because she wished to end the relationship. Juries rejected the defence for Jade Watson's former partner who strangled her for starting a new relationship; for Anne Birch's estranged husband who killed her on being told their marriage was over and for Charlotte Smith's husband who struck her with force 'off-the-scale in its ferocity' during an argument about her request for a divorce.[25] A jury also rejected the loss of control defence run by Janee Parson's husband after hearing the fatal attack and his final words – 'you lying cow Janee, you're dead' and 'I can't believe you're going straight from me to this guy' recorded on a dictation machine left under a bed to spy on her. Sentencing him to life imprisonment with a 20-year minimum term for murder, the judge explained the new legal status quo thus: one may be 'heartbroken' at a break-up, but the 'failure of a marriage and disappointment at being left for another man is relatively slight mitigation'.[26] It could no longer found a defence.

With provocation by sexual infidelity now off the table as a defence, some defendants opted for a diminished responsibility defence, almost all without success.[27] Others denied all criminal responsibility, some conjuring up increasingly far-fetched scenarios in which they had acted in self-defence. One claimed his wife had impaled herself on a knife, another that she had burnt herself to death. Following a retrial, Dawn Rhodes' estranged husband became the only defendant in this study to walk free. He said he acted in self-defence when he cut her throat during a row in which she 'flipped like the Hulk' as she came at him with a kitchen knife to confront him about his new relationship. After 36 hours of deliberation, the jury found him not guilty despite expert evidence disputing his account of a frontal attack by the victim as 'highly unlikely'. More plausibly, her injuries had been inflicted from behind.[28] The others claiming self-defence were all convicted of murder. Chantelle Barnsdale-Quean's husband claimed his wife attacked him with a kitchen knife and used a ligature to kill herself. Scientific evidence showed she could not have strangled herself in such a way.[29] Leanne McNuff's former partner determined to 'make her life hell' when they broke up a month before he killed her yet claimed she lunged at him with the knife.[30] Laura

24 BBC (2015d).
25 BBC (2013a).
26 Arkell (2013).
27 These cases are discussed in Chapter 4.
28 BBC (2017a).
29 Rush (2013a).
30 Preece (2012).

Davies' boyfriend stabbed her 80 times moments after she ended their relationship. Miriam Nyazema's former partner 'lay in wait' for her at her home. When she returned with a male friend, he attacked her with such ferocity that the knife's blade was left protruding from her back.[31] Combining a self-defence claim with a loss of control defence, Joanna Trojniak's partner said he 'lost control completely' when she threatened him with a knife and taunted him about his distress at the relationship ending. The jury unanimously found him guilty of murder.[32]

No defendant claiming the fatality was an accident escaped a murder conviction and once again, the context of these killings was a recent or impending separation. Sally Lawrence's estranged husband killed her by crashing his car into a tree after the passenger airbag had been disabled. She had instigated divorce months earlier although he insisted he knew nothing of his wife's affair until after her death. The jury accepted the prosecution's case that unable to accept that his wife had moved on, he killed her 'out of greed, anger and possibly jealousy'.[33] When Julie Beattie told her partner she was leaving, he doused her in petrol and set her alight, but claimed it was an accident. Alice Ruggles' former partner broke into her flat when he realised she was moving on after their relationship ended. He then cut her throat but claimed she had fallen on a carving knife during an argument. Leeann Foley's boyfriend claimed he accidently shot her in the face when he only meant to shoot himself. The jury preferred the prosecution's account that he murdered her in a rage after discovering she had spent the evening with another man. Luan Leigh's former partner claimed she had accidently overdosed. The prosecution case was that he had harboured thoughts of a reconciliation but drugged and strangled her when he saw she had removed all his photos. The judge explained law's new understanding of relationship breakdown's depleted excusatory force in a murder trial: feeling 'hurt and puzzled' when your wife asks for a separation or removes your photos is no excuse for murder. Wanting to 'move on with her life' even if he 'harboured thoughts that there would be some sort of reconciliation' was something a woman was 'entitled to do'.[34] In the post-reform cases, her newly recognised entitlement is cancelling out his traditional entitlement to a conviction for manslaughter, all of these 'accidental' killers receiving life sentences for murder with minimum terms ranging between 22 and 25 years.

Finally, how did suicidal killers fare in the courts? Zofia Sadowska's former partner, jealous that she had started dating his childhood friend, stalked and killed her, claiming he did so as part of a lovers' suicide pact. A unanimous jury found him guilty of murder. Verdict: life with a 24-year-minimum. Some got off more lightly. Laura Holden's long-term partner attempted suicide after killing her because she wanted to end the relationship and had met someone else. He admitted murder and was sentenced to life with a minimum of 15 years. Susan

31 Storey (2016).
32 Mahony (2016).
33 Britten (2014).
34 McCarthy (2004).

Cole's husband also pleaded guilty to murder and was given a life sentence with a 12-year minimum. He was said to be overcome by 'chronic feelings of hopelessness': the couple having lost their jobs faced the prospect of losing their home. After failing to convince her to make a suicide pact, he killed her anyway. In mitigation his lawyer said they 'both felt their lives had no worth', overlooking the fact that a woman who refused to make a suicide pact evidently felt that her life had some worth.[35]

Infidelity's diminishing returns?

The last woman to be killed in the five-year period covered by this study was Nicola Woodman, stabbed 20 times by her partner on Christmas day, 2016. Repeated denials of her supposed infidelity had enraged him. 'People just snap, you know what I mean', he told the police. With the historically mandated 'snapping' defence now banned as a trigger for loss of control, he pleaded guilty to murder and was sentenced to life imprisonment with a minimum sentence of 23 years. The police hoped this gave the family some satisfaction that justice has been done.[36] Recall the outcome in the infamous pre-reform 'red mist' case of *Humes* – a seven-year sentence for manslaughter for a man who said he had 'lost it totally' over his wife's supposed infidelity, a sentence that outraged the victim's family and precipitated the reform movement to stop men getting away with murder. Are they still? How effective has the reform been?

Court dispositions in post-femicide cases suggest that defendants who were once characterised as impassioned killers deserving of sympathy now tend to be condemned as irrationally jealous murderers. Of the 240 convicted of murder, three received a whole life sentence, including two who had killed previous partners. The rest were given life sentences with minimum terms ranging from 11 to 38 years. They included Naudel Turner's partner who stabbed her to death when she ended their relationship. The prosecutor told the jury that sexual jealously 'can't excuse an unlawful killing. However humiliated and upset he felt, there was no justification for killing her in broad daylight, and we say this is murder'. Life with a 20-year minimum term.[37] Nor did pleading guilty to murder save Esther Arogundale's former partner from a long sentence: life with a minimum term of 20 years and 6 months. The judge regarded the 'considerable emotional strain' he was under as 'significant' but being 'understandably upset' about the relationship ending did not warrant stabbing her 13 times. After all:

> Many men and women have to endure the discovery that the husband, wife or partner is no longer content with the relationship they have . . . . Many are jealous or unhappy. But what the law cannot and will not permit is the use of violence.[38]

35 Duffin (2013).
36 BBC (2017b).
37 Murdermap (2013a).
38 Osuh (2012).

The new law also applied to younger offenders. A teenager who had become 'irrationally concerned' that Kayleigh-Anne Palmer, his 16-year-old pregnant girlfriend, would leave him for another boy, strangled her to make her 'be quiet'. He received a life sentence with a 14-year minimum.[39] Another jealous teenager who stabbed his 15-year-old girlfriend Megan-Leigh Peat 60 times was convicted of murder and had his minimum term of ten years increased by five years, the Court of Appeal agreeing with submissions made on behalf of the Attorney General that a ten-year term was too low and did not adequately reflect the seriousness of the crime.[40]

If the number of convictions and long sentences for murder are any guide, a victim's 'innocence' or, more commonly, lack thereof – central to the traditional provocation defence – appears to be losing its currency with the growing recognition of a woman's right to leave a relationship notwithstanding the stress it might cause her partner. But not always. Sometimes juries accepted loss of control defences, resulting in convictions for manslaughter and sentences ranging from as low as six years, reminiscent of the pre-reform era. Amongst other troubling cases, a jury sympathised with Susan Davenport's estranged husband who killed her when she made the 'bombshell' revelation that he was not the father of their eldest son. He said she made the revelation during an argument when she arrived with papers relating to the sale of the house, taunting him with 'You aren't half the man you think you are' and the new man was 'a lot better man than you'.[41] The jury unanimously acquitted him of murder. He received a six-year sentence for manslaughter. Another jury took only four hours to clear Carol Bland's killer of murder. He said she had cheated on him, 'rubbed his face in it', constantly nagged, bullied him and spent extravagantly during their 44-year marriage and he just 'snapped'. The jury was perhaps swayed by evidence given by the victim's mother who described her daughter's behaviour as 'wicked'.[42] His six-year sentence for manslaughter indicates jury and judge were in sync as they seemed to be for Pauline Butler's killer. The jury unanimously accepted his account of losing control when she threatened him with a knife as their relationship deteriorated. The judge's pronouncement – 'People who wish to end relationships and live alone without their former partner are entitled to do that without being killed for it' – suggested a longer sentence than the seven and a half years imposed.[43]

At other times though, there was a disjunction between the sentence imposed and jury verdicts evincing residual sympathy for men upset by a departing woman. Running a combined defence of self-defence and loss of control worked for Elife Beqa's killer. Becoming increasingly jealous of his wife's friendship with another man, he had monitored her phone, stopped her from using Facebook, insisted she leave her job and finally strangled her. The jury cleared him of murder after hearing that she had threatened to kill herself and the children if he left her and

39 Best (2014).
40 *R v Hall* (Attorney General's Reference No 56 of 2012) [2012] EWCA Crim 2911.
41 Robinson (2015).
42 Roughly (2015).
43 BBC (2014).

the marriage ended. While the judge found the evidence that the defendant had not acted in reasonable self-defence 'in truth, overwhelming', he had to accept that the jury thought that what the victim had said and done made him lose his self-control. He sentenced him to ten and a half years.[44] In another telling case, Mariola Cudsworth's husband said he 'snapped' when she admitted having sex with a lover and was planning to leave him. The jury was told that legally, his claim that his wife had admitted having sex with another man was not a defence to murder. But if they believed she had threatened to leave and that was the trigger for him to snap, they could acquit him of murder. Might someone, the defence asked, who 'realised both the deception he has been subjected to and the fact his life was about to be utterly shattered, snap, as he did?' After three days of deliberation, the jury agreed – killing an unfaithful woman who 'threatened' to leave was not murder.[45] But the 15-year sentence was one of the longest handed down for manslaughter.

As for victims' families, Charmaine Macmuiris' felt her jealous boyfriend's life sentence for murder with a minimum term of 14 years failed to reflect the severity of what was described in court as a 'vicious attack on an entirely innocent victim' whom he falsely believed was seeing another man.[46] Angela Crompton's family was 'deeply disappointed' that the jury accepted her husband's claim of having lost control when he hammered her to death. He had been worried that she would not stay in the marriage. That he would serve only half of his sentence for manslaughter was 'merely salt in the wound'. At the trial, the family felt as if 'Angela herself was on trial, and in many ways that has been the hardest part for us'. They felt they had all been 'let down in this case by the justice system'.[47] So did Pamela Jackson's family. Their outrage at the jury clearing her partner of murder was reported under the heading: 'Manslaughter Injustice'. Aware that the killer would serve only half of his 18-year term, her son despaired: 'Nine years for a man that's capable of killing someone and burying them on the moors – there's no justice'.[48]

Christine Henderson's family also felt let down by the jury. The prosecution said the stabbing by her former partner was a 'brutal and sustained attack' in revenge for rejecting him. The defence claimed she had taunted him about a previous partner, causing him to lose control. Family members were reported to have rushed distraught from the court when the jury foreman announced a unanimous verdict of not guilty to murder after two days' deliberation. An incredulous family friend was 'disgusted' at the outcome. They were 'not expecting that at all'. But the family thanked the judge 'for coming to the only sentence suitable for this crime' – life with a minimum term of seven and a half years, not to be released until he was considered he was no longer a danger to

44 Murdermap (2013b).
45 Calderwood (2016).
46 Turner (2013).
47 BBC (2013b).
48 Rush (2013b).

the public. As for the family friend, she remained perplexed: 'I'm just wondering, what is murder?'[49]

What indeed? Residual resistance to depriving distraught wife-killers of a defence can be found even in a case where the defendant admitted murder. Having stabbed her 51 times in front of a witness whom he also attacked, Claire Monro's husband pleaded guilty to murder. His lawyer then convinced him to apply to withdraw his guilty plea, indicating – as the prosecution observed – 'a clear dichotomy' between the defendant's and his lawyer's accounts of the fatal attack. The application was rejected. At the sentencing hearing, the prosecution argued that there was no loss of control over his wife's affair which he had known about for some weeks. Instead, the attack marked the end of weeks of 'intolerable intrusion' into his wife's life, a 'campaign of surveillance' no less. It was a murder 'committed out of jealousy, pride and anger' at his wife's announcement that the marriage was over. According to the defence, 'the reality' was 'more nuanced' than that. The stress caused by the deteriorating marriage and his wife's affair was surely a mitigating factor. The judge agreed, taking three years from the sentence in mitigation.[50]

Why being stressed in such circumstances should mitigate at all is surely inconsistent with judicial pronouncements that a woman is entitled to leave a relationship 'without being killed for it' as the judge put it in the Butler case. Nevertheless, life with a minimum term of 26 years was still far higher than sentences imposed in pre-reform departure cases and nearly four times the sentence imposed for manslaughter in *Humes*. For the prosecutor, the judge and even the defendant initially, Claire Monro's killing was clearly murder. Only the defence lawyer thought otherwise. Having failed to show it could be defended, all that remained was a plea in mitigation for a client who was light years removed from the easily defended impassioned wife-killer of old.

Conclusion

When leading the movement to reform the English law of murder, Solicitor General Harman was said to have favoured abolishing provocation outright, the preferred option in Australian jurisdictions.[51] Might that have been more effective in curtailing residual sympathy for men killing unfaithful or departing women? While conclusive findings must await more extensive comparative studies of pre-and post-reform cases across reform jurisdictions, we can at least make a preliminary assessment of the English reformers' predictions that they were implementing 'an important law change that will end the culture of excuses'; that changing it would 'end the injustice of women being killed by their husband then being blamed' and that 'the days of sexual jealousy as a defence are over'.[52]

49 Passant (2015).
50 Humphries (2015).
51 Hinsliff (2003). Australian feminists have long advocated abolishing provocation outright. See for example Howe (1998, 1999, 2002, 2004) and Tyson (2013).
52 Scoop Independent News (2008).

Are those days over? Not quite. Loss of control defences succeeded for nine defendants, including one due to fear of violence, a defence introduced to assist battered women who kill men. A few were given sentences for manslaughter of between four to seven years, on a par with the pre-reform sentences that had so outraged families and reformers. Just as concerning was the judge's direction – in the Cudsworth case – that the jury could accept a loss of control defence if they believed her 'threat' to leave was the trigger making him snap. By reinforcing the pre-reform notion that a man provoked to kill a departing woman is guilty of manslaughter only, such a direction highlights the limitations of a reform confined to excluding sexual infidelity as trigger for loss of control. Yet while residual jury sympathy for some enraged killers and occasional risibly short sentences remain causes for concern, the English reform appears to be working in most cases to curtail both unfaithfulness and departure as excuses for murder. So many guilty pleas and convictions for murder are testimony to that. The historically mandated provocation by infidelity script followed in so-called 'crimes of passion' is finally losing its purchase, now exposed as code for a man's murderous rage at being abandoned by a woman who, as criminal courts are increasingly recognising, is entitled to leave a relationship without fatal consequence. Law's traditional wife-killer, reproduced over the centuries as an impassioned man provoked to kill an unruly and unfaithful wife in a spur-of-the-moment 'red mist' frenzy, is a shadow of his former self. That legendary *criminel passsionel* emerges from the post-reform cases discursively depleted, a man incapable of coping with relationship breakdown who kills 'his' woman in a frequently planned, far from spontaneous attack only to find that alleging loss of control in the face of such adversity no longer has much excusatory force. The reform is having its intended effect – men, at least most of them, are no longer 'getting away with it'.

So it seems the English reformers were right not to heed Carol Smart's caution against feminist investment in law reform. After all, the criminal law has not been deaf to this feminist core concern. The English law of murder is one area of law that no longer disqualifies feminist knowledge. Not that Smart would think it wasn't worth the effort. She recognised that feminist law reform work can be useful and that as crimes such as rape were 'already in the legal domain', they must be addressed there.[53] Moreover, when she warned that feminists can be too easily 'seduced by law', that they tended to cling to the naive hope 'that new law or more law might be better than the old law', that indeed, in exercising law, they may 'produce effects that make conditions worse' for women, she was referring specifically to reforms that extended law into 'new terrains'.[54] Reforms to defences to murder do no such thing. They actually work in the way that Smart advocated, decentring and retracting law, disqualifying its age-old truths about the excusatory force of men's emotional turmoil. Far from deploying law 'in the cause of women', or extending 'law's imperialist reach', this has been an

53 Smart (1989: 2, 49).
54 Smart (1989: 160–162).

exercise in withdrawing law from the cause of men.[55] It's been a mostly successful challenge to law's power to define 'the truth' of intimate partner femicide, one furthermore, that reads law as Smart counselled, as a site of discursive struggle and a forum for articulating an alternative feminist account, this time of so-called 'crimes of passion'.[56] Had she turned her mind to these crimes, I feel sure she would have endorsed the reform movement. After all, even if one takes a less favourable view of the reform's impact, the post-reform cases – perhaps especially the problematic ones – continue to supply rich discursive sites for that endlessly valuable feminist work of contesting law's truths.

References

Burton, M. 2003 'Case Note: Sentencing Domestic Homicide upon Provocation: Still "Getting Away with Murder"' 11 *Feminist Legal Studies* 279.

Howe, A. 1998 'The Provocation Defence: Finally Provoking Its Own Demise?' 22 *Melbourne University Law Review* 466.

——— 1999 'Reforming Provocation (More or Less)' 12 *Australian Feminist Law Journal* 127.

——— 2002 'Provoking Polemic: Provoked Killings and the Ethical Paradoxes of the Postmodern Feminist Condition' 10 *Feminist Legal Studies* 39.

——— 2004 'Provocation in Crisis: Law's Passion at the Crossroads? New Directions for Feminist Strategists' 21 *Australian Feminist Law Journal* 55.

——— 2012 'Enduring Fictions of Possession: Sexual Infidelity and Homicidal Rage in Shakespeare and Late Modernity (Glossing *Othello*)' 21 *Griffith Law Review* 772.

——— 2013 '"Red Mist" Homicide: Sexual Infidelity and the English Law of Murder (Glossing *Titus Andronicus*)' 3 *Legal Studies* 407.

——— 2014 'Fatal Love' 2(1) *Griffith Journal of Law and Human Dignity* 4.

Ingala Smith, K. 2012–2016 'Counting Dead Women' https://kareningalasmith.com/counting-dead-women

Reed, A. and Bohlander, M. (eds.) 2011 *Loss of Control and Diminished Responsibility* Farnham, Surrey: Ashgate.

Smart, C. 1989 *Feminism and the Power of Law* London: Routledge.

——— 1992 'The Woman of Legal Discourse' 1(1) *Social and Legal Studies* 29.

——— 1999 'A History of Ambivalence and Conflict in the Discursive Construction of the "Child Victim" of Sexual Abuse' 8(3) *Social and Legal Studies* 391.

Tyson, D. 2013 *Sex, Culpability and the Defence of Provocation* London: Routledge.

Weiner, M.J. 2004 *Men of Blood: Violence, Manliness and Criminal Justice in Victorian England* Cambridge: Cambridge University Press.

Newspapers (all accessed March 15 2018)

Arkell, H. 2013 'Father-of-two "Stabbed Adulterous Wife to Death in Front of Their Young Son in Attack Which Was Recorded on Dictaphone He Used to Spy on

55 Smart (1992: 30).
56 Smart (1989: 88, 164).

Her"' *Daily Mail* www.dailymail.co.uk/news/article-2323868/Andrew-Parsons-stabbed-adulterous-wife-death-young-son-attack-recorded-spy-dictaphone.html

BBC 2002 'Life for "Weakest Link" Killer' news.bbc.co.uk/2/hi/uk_news/england/1795846.stm

——— 2013a 'Devendra Singh Jailed for Murder of Wife Charlotte Smith' www.bbc.com/news/uk-england-stoke-staffordshire-23044637

——— 2013b 'Sculptor Thomas Crompton Jailed for Seven and a Half Years for Killing Wife' www.bbc.com/news/uk-england-norfolk-21198156

——— 2014 'Leeds Businessman Jailed for Seven Years for Killing Ex-Partner' www.bbc.com/news/uk-england-leeds-29742419

——— 2015a 'Man Jailed for Murdering Wife in Somerset Garden' www.bbc.com/news/uk-england-somerset-33470711

——— 2015b 'Colin Dymond Jailed for Murdering Ex-Partner over "Affairs"' www.bbc.com/news/uk-england-dorset-34149904

——— 2015c 'Sally Campion Hammer Murderer Matthew Keough Jailed for Life' www.bbc.com/news/uk-england-beds-bucks-herts-33048278

——— 2015d 'Dawlish Killer James McDonald "Laughed at Abduction Question"' www.bbc.com/news/uk-england-devon-34660078

——— 2017a 'Robert Rhodes Cleared of Killing Wife during Row' www.bbc.com/news/uk-england-surrey-40096106

——— 2017b 'Pregnant Woman's Christmas Day Murderer James Hutchinson Jailed' www.bbc.com/news/uk-england-leeds-40409428

——— 2018 'Triple killer Theodore Johnson Jailed for 26 Years' www.bbc.com/news/uk-42583114

Best, J. 2014 'Teenager Who Murdered Pregnant Girlfriend Wrote Letter to Her Devastated Mum Saying "LOL"' *Mirror* www.mirror.co.uk/news/uk-news/teenager-who-murdered-pregnant-girlfriend-4374173

Britten, N. 2013 'Husband "Drove Wife" into Tree with Airbag Switched Off' *Telegraph* www.telegraph.co.uk/news/uknews/crime/10104640/Husband-drove-wife-into-tree-with-airbag-switched-off.html

Calderwood, I. 2016 'Jealous Husband Who Stabbed Wife to Death Is Cleared of Murder because She Said She Had a New Lover and Was Leaving Him' *Daily Mail* www.dailymail.co.uk/news/article-3401586/Jealous-husband-stabbed-wife-death-cleared-murder-said-new-lover-leaving-him.html

Duffin, C. 2013 'Man Living on Benefits Killed Wife of 32 Years after Being Overcome by "Hopelessness"' *Telegraph* www.telegraph.co.uk/news/uknews/law-and-order/10091962/Man-living-on-benefits-killed-wife-of-32-years-after-being-overcome-by-hopelessness.html

Gye, H. 2013 'Jealous Husband Stabbed Wife 15 Times' *Daily Mail* www.dailymail.co.uk/news/article-2524723/Jealous-husband-stabbed-wife-15-times-ran-sent-Christmas-card-lay-dying-hospital.html

Hinsliff, G. 2003 '"Crime of Passion" Is No Defence' *The Guardian* www.theguardian.com/politics/2003/jan/19/ukcrime.prisonsandprobation

——— 2008 'Harman and Law Lord Clash over Wife Killers' *The Guardian* www.theguardian.com/politics/2008/nov/09/harriet-harman-defence-of-provocation

Humphries, J. 2015 'Andrew Munro Jailed for 26 Years after Stabbing His Wife to Death' *Liverpool Echo* www.liverpoolecho.co.uk/news/liverpool-news/andrew-munro-jailed-26-years-10390754

Loweth, J. 2012 'Life Term for Man who Killed Wife in Row' *Telegraph & Argus* www.thetelegraphandargus.co.uk/news/local/localbrad/9855657.Police_welcome_verdict_after_Cottingley_husband_guilty_of_murdering_wife/

Mahony, D. 2016 'Pawel Sroka "Lost Control Completely and Stabbed His Girlfriend Joanna Trojniak to Death at Their Home in Addiscombe after She Called Him a Cry Baby"' *Your Local Guardian* www.yourlocalguardian.co.uk/news/local/14753886.Man__stabbed_his_girlfriend_to_death_after_she_called_him_a_cry_baby_/

McCarthy, R. 2014 'Luan Leigh Murder: Obsessed Husband Killed Wife after She Removed His Photos from Her Bedroom' *Birmingham Mail* www.birminghammail.co.uk/news/midlands-news/luan-leigh-murder-husband-killed-8317195

Moore, C. 2017 'Teenager, 18, Is Jailed for Life for Murdering His 17-Year-Old Girlfriend Six Weeks after She Gave Birth Because He Wrongly Thought She'd Cheated on Him' *Daily Mail* www.dailymail.co.uk/news/article-4279386/Teenager-18-jailed-life-murdering-girlfriend.html

Murdermap 2013a 'Stabbed by a Former Lover: Naudel Turner' www.murdermap.co.uk/pages/cases/case.asp?CID=85901908&VID=1050&Case=Stabbed-by-a-former-lover:-Naudel-Turner

——— 2013b 'Strangled by Her Husband: Elife Beqa' www.murdermap.co.uk/pages/cases/case.asp?CID=465650601&Case=Southall-death:-Elife-Beqa

Osuh, C. 2012 'Jailed for Life: Man Who Knifed Mother of His Child to Death at Their Salford Home' *Manchester Evening News* www.manchestereveningnews.co.uk/news/local-news/jailed-for-life-man-who-knifed-698798

Passant, A. 2015 'Friend's Disgust at Christine Henderson Murder Trial Verdict' *Gazette-Live* www.gazettelive.co.uk/news/local-news/friends-disgust-christine-henderson-murder-3670131

Payne, S. 2002a 'Murder Charge Pensioner Says Marriage Led to Rows' *Telegraph* www.telegraph.co.uk/news/uknews/1381735/Murder-charge-pensioner-says-marriage-led-to-rows.html

——— 2002b 'Six Years for Teacher Who Beat to Death His Unfaithful Wife' www.telegraph.co.uk/news/uknews/1381196/Six-years-for-teacher-who-beat-to-death-his-unfaithful-wife.html

Pleasance, C. 2013 'Jealous Boyfriend Who Stabbed Ex-Girlfriend 83 Times after Wrongly Accusing Her of Having an Affair Is Jailed for Life' *Daily Mail* www.dailymail.co.uk/news/article-2527984/Jealous-boyfriend-stabbed-ex-girlfriend-83-times-wrongly-accusing-having-affair-jailed-life.html

Preece, R. 2012 'Soldier "Stabbed Ex-Girlfriend to Death after He Hacked Her Facebook Account and Discovered She'd Had an Abortion"' *Daily Mail* www.dailymail.co.uk/news/article-2197796/Leanne-McNuff-murder-Soldier-stabbed-ex-death-hacked-Facebook-discovered-abortion.html

Robinson, J. 2015 'Husband Stabbed His Ex-Wife to Death after She Made the "Bombshell Revelation" That He Was Not the Father of Their Eldest Son' *Daily Mail* www.dailymail.co.uk/news/article-3309252/Husband-stabbed-ex-wife-death-bombshell-revelation-not-father-eldest-son.html

Roughly, L. 2015 'Husband Who Stabbed Cheating Wife Carole Bland to Death Is Cleared of Murder' *The Bolton News* www.theboltonnews.co.uk/news/11839940.UPDATED__Husband_who_stabbed_cheating_wife_to_death_is_cleared_of_murder/

Rush, R. 2013a 'Husband "Strangled Wife Then Stabbed Himself to Make It Look Like She Attacked Him with Kitchen Knife before She Committed Suicide"' *Daily Mail* www.dailymail.co.uk/news/article-2409667/Darfield-man-Stephen-Barnsdale-Quean-strangled-wife-stabbed-himself.html

——— 2013b 'Nine Years for a Man That's Capable of Killing Someone' www.dailymail.co.uk/news/article-2439304/Adrian-Muir-Pamela-Jacksons-sons-anger-unjust-sentence-given-manslaughter.html

Scoop Independent News 2008 'UK Murder Law Reforms: Provocation Not an Excuse' www.scoop.co.nz/stories/WO0807/S00844/uk-murder-law-reforms-provocation-not-an-excuse.html

Storey, K. 2016 'Jilted Lover Accused of Murder "Lay in Wait" for Ex-Partner before Threatening Her with Gun, Court Hears' *Manchester Evening News* www.manchestereveningnews.co.uk/news/greater-manchester-news/jilted-lover-accused-murder-lay-11347423

Turner, R. 2013 'David O'Sullivan Jailed for Life for Christmas Day Murder of Charmaine Macmuiris' *Wales Online* www.walesonline.co.uk/news/wales-news/david-osullivan-pleads-guilty-christmas-4288041

2 Reforming defences to murder, an Australian case study

Danielle Tyson and Bronwyn Naylor

Carol Smart was firmly of the view that law in general and criminal justice and legal practice in particular are critically important, albeit 'problematic', sites for feminist intervention.[1] But in *Feminism and the Power of Law*, she warns that 'the main dilemma for any feminist engagement with law is the certain knowledge that, once enacted, legislation is in the hands of individuals and agencies far removed from the values and politics of the women's movement'.[2] Was that only then, or does it remain true today? This chapter assesses the effectiveness of feminist-led reforms to the law of murder introduced in the Australian state of Victoria over the period 2000–2014. Have the reforms, enacted to address feminist concerns about the gendered operation of defences to murder in intimate partner homicides, been a waste of feminist time? How have courts implemented the reforms? To what extent have they enabled courts to challenge gendered narratives? The following analysis of post-reform defence narrative and sentencing provides an opportunity to continue the 'endlessly valuable' discursive work that Smart advocated and practised in other fields of law.[3] Intimate partner femicide cases are, we suggest, ideal sites for continuing the work of challenging law's power to disqualify women's experiences of violence while privileging men's feelings and rights and also for articulating alternative accounts of gendered relationships.

Beware law reform!

Since the late twentieth century, feminist legal scholars and activists in Australia and other anglophone jurisdictions have criticised the gendered operation of defences to murder in intimate partner homicides cases. More broadly, they have challenged the previously unquestioned 'normality' of men's violence and controlling behaviours towards women. But was law reform the best strategy? As Smart observed, frustration over the ways in which legal reforms get translated into measures which only slightly improved women's lives led many feminist activists to regard law reforms as 'a waste of time'. Others saw these failures as opportunities

1 Smart (1989: 382, 407).
2 Smart (1989: 164).
3 Smart (1989: 164). See also Howe (2012, 2016: 105).

to renew their engagement with law. Either way, it was clear that 'different strategies' were needed if the same failures were 'not simply to be repeated'.[4]

By the late 1980s, two lines of feminist critique of the operation of defence to murder in intimate partner homicides had emerged. One focused on women who killed their violent partners.[5] Drawing attention to high profile cases,[6] these studies showed how women's fatal attacks on men did not readily fall within the traditional legal narratives of provocation or self-defence. Some feminists argued for law reforms that would extend the concept of self-defence or adapt provocation to situations in which women killed violent partners. The other line of critique focused on the operation of victim-blaming provocation defences in intimate partner femicides, some arguing that the defence should be abolished in as much as it let men get away with murder.[7]

By the turn of the twenty-first century these gender-based critiques were well established. They were instrumental in the Victorian Law Reform Commission (VLRC) receiving a reference to review defences to homicide.[8] The ensuing *Crimes (Homicide) Act 2005* addressed the long-standing feminist argument that the provocation defence be abolished. Now provocation as mitigation would only be dealt with at sentencing. Other key changes included the codification of self-defence to better accommodate the experiences of women who kill their abusive male partners in 'non-confrontational' circumstances. In addition, a new offence of defensive homicide was created to give women and others who kill in response to family violence a possible partial defence should they be unable to successfully raise self-defence. Finally, a key new provision in the homicide legislation was introduced to provide for the admission of evidence highlighting the relationship and social context of family violence to be admitted in cases of homicide.

These have all been important reforms that expressly recognise the gendered operation of defences to homicide by removing provocation's narratives of excuse for femicide, making the defences more accessible to women who kill abusive partners and assisting jurors to understand the dynamics of family violence. How successful have they been? The first post-reform cases appeared to suggest while the reforms were largely working for women defendants who killed violent abusers, they were not working as intended in intimate partner femicide cases. The most critical issue was that provocation's exculpatory narrative of excuse was reappearing under the guise of defensive homicide, the defence that had been devised

4 Smart (1989: 67).

5 Kirkwood (2003); Maguigan (1998); O'Donovan (1993); Schneider (2000); and Sheehy (1994).

6 Eg *Osland v R* (1998) 197 CLR 316; *Ahluwalia* [1992] 4 All ER 889; *Thornton* [1992] 1 All ER 306; *Thornton (No 2)* [1996] 2 All ER 1023; *R v Lavallée* [1990] 1 SCR 852. See also Sheehy et al. (1992).

7 See Edwards (1987); Bandalli (1995); Horder (1992); Howe (1994, 2002, 2004); and Morgan (1997) for critiques of provocation defences. For an overview of these critiques see Tyson (2013).

8 See Victorian Law Reform Commission (VLRC) 2004.

for women who killed violent male partners.[9] Concerns – shared by some feminist groups – about the apparent 'misuse' of the new offence led to two Department of Justice reviews which found that there was 'clear evidence' that defensive homicide

> inappropriately provides a partial excuse for men who kill. Defensive homicide is primarily relied upon by men who kill. In many of these cases, men have killed in circumstances which are very similar to those where provocation previously applied.[10]

Accordingly, the department proposed that the partial defence of defensive homicide be abolished inasmuch as the 'price of having defensive homicide for the comparatively small number of women who kill is substantially outweighed by the cost of inappropriately excusing men who kill'.[11] While some feminists argued for the retention of defensive homicide, the offence was abolished by the *Crimes Amendment (Abolition of Defensive Homicide) Act 2014*.[12]

These concerns, shared by some feminists about the effectiveness of this law reform, serve as a reminder of Smart's warning about the limits of law reform and her advice to feminists to not be 'too easily "seduced" by law'. Too often attempts to use it pragmatically produced unintended effects.[13] Beware unintended effects indeed! But she also said, and we agree, that law should remain an important focus for feminist research, not necessarily in order to produce more law reform, but precisely because of the potential of feminist knowledge and research 'to challenge law as an important signifier' of what she called 'masculine power'.[14] To that end we have joined with other researchers in undertaking a review of legal responses in post-reform cases of intimate partner homicides.[15] In the following analysis we explore how the reforms have impacted on defence narratives and the sentencing process in intimate partner femicides. More particularly, to what extent have the reforms enabled courts to achieve the feminist goal of challenging the victim-blaming narratives that prevailed in pre-reform intimate partner femicides?

Post-reform defence narratives

We have identified a total of 51 men prosecuted in Victoria for killing a current or former partner or perceived male rival over the period 23 November 2005

9 Tyson et al. (2010); Domestic Violence Resource Centre Victoria (2010); and Tyson (2013: 132–137). See also Maher (2014) and Ulbrick et al. (2016).
10 Department of Justice Victoria (2013: viii).
11 Department of Justice Victoria (2013: ix).
12 The Act also reframed self-defence and made a clearer link between the elements of the defence and family violence where a victim of family violence kills their abuser in a context of self-defence. For a detailed overview of the 2014 Victorian reforms see Naylor and Tyson (2017). See also Domestic Violence Resource Centre Victoria (DVRCV) et al. (2015).
13 See Smart (1989: 160).
14 See Smart (1989: 2).
15 The authors collaborated with Deborah Kirkwood and Mandy McKenzie, both formerly with the DVRCV.

to 31 December 2014.[16] Forty-three killed a woman partner or ex-partner, one killed a male sexual partner and seven killed an actual or perceived male sexual rival. Of the 45 charged with murder, 23 pleaded guilty and 36 (or 71 per cent) were found guilty by juries. Six were charged with manslaughter. Of these, three pleaded guilty, and three were found guilty. Most of the killings were committed in the context of separation, with 29 cases (57 per cent) having been committed in the context of actual, pending or previous relationship breakdown. The accused had previously been violent or abusive towards his partner in 27 cases (53 per cent).[17]

What defence arguments are being mobilised in post-reform cases now that provocation has been abolished? Significantly, one was anticipated by the Law Reform Commission when it considered the merits of abolishing that defence. It noted that a possible consequence of abolition was that defence lawyers could argue instead that defendants were so angry and out of control that 'they did not know what they were doing'. In this way, rage could ground a lack of intention defence, thereby undermining the whole purpose of abolishing provocation.[18] That prediction appears to be coming true.

In interviews with police, 15 men said they had killed their women partners after losing control.[19] Three who pleaded guilty to murder said they had 'snapped', 'saw red' or 'lost it' in the moments prior to the killing. One had woken up on the morning of the killing feeling like a 'pressure cooker'.[20] Another was described by a defence psychiatrist as a 'vulnerable man' who was 'undoubtedly very upset about the state of the relationship and in the context of an argument "just lost it"'.[21] During an argument with his wife over her desire to sell the house as part of a divorce settlement, yet another said that her threat to take 'everything' had driven him 'crazy', making him feel 'out of' his 'mind' and he just 'lost it'. He could not remember anything else.[22] As in the provocation cases of old, the victim's words and behaviour were at the centre of these narratives.

16 Cases were identified via the Australasian Legal Information Institute (Austlii) database, which is a comprehensive online database of Australian legislation and case law. In addition to sentencing remarks, we also obtained a number of transcripts of trials and plea hearings from the Victorian Government Reporting Service (VGRS).

17 This is likely to be an underestimate because it is now well established in the national and international literature that family violence is under-reported Buckingham (2010: 125–126).

18 Victorian Law Reform Commission (VLRC) (2003: 104) citing the National Association for Women and the Law cited by the VLRC (2003: 104). See also Buckingham (2010: 145).

19 See *R v Diver* [2008] VSC 399; *R v Piper* [2008] VSC 569; *DPP v Sherna* [2009] VSC 4; *R v Baxter* [2009] VSC 180; *R v Foster* [2009] VSC 124; *R v Robinson* [2010] VSC 10; *R v Felicite* [2010] VSC 245; *R v Bayram* [2011] VSC 10; *R v Ahmadi* [2013] VSC 293; *R v Delich* [2013] VSC 309; *R v Grant* [2013] VSC 13; *R v McPhee* [2013] VSC 581; *DPP v Borthwick* [2010] VSC 613; *DPP v Kelly* [2012] VSC 398; *R v Neacsu* [2012]. *R v Sengoz* [2011] VSC 652.

20 See *R v Felicite* [2010] VSC 245.

21 *R v Diver* [2008] VSC 399 para 47. Glenn Diver pleaded guilty to murder and was sentenced to 17 years' imprisonment with a minimum non-parole period of 14 years.

22 *R v Bayram* [2011] VSC 210 para 9. Omer Bayram, Transcript of plea, 17 January 2011: 23.

Even when loss of control was not a key feature of a defence narrative about a gun going off accidently, the defendant told the police he 'saw red' and 'just lost it'.[23] Loss of control tales were also central to what feminist analysts refer to as 'departure' cases where a man kills his partner when she attempted to leave or had left. The day before her murder, Wendy Chow had asked her partner to move out. At his plea hearing, his defence counsel relied on the evidence of a forensic psychologist to show that at the time of the 'final confrontation' he was 'stressed at the prospect of losing the relationship and by the practical consequences of being put out on the streets with limited resources'. He also submitted that his early experiences had 'left him deeply troubled and flawed. He faced rejection and abandonment on this particular day by the woman that he loved' and 'faced with the loss of that relationship and the loss of control over his life', he just 'snapped'.[24] Another said he killed his wife because she had rejected his attempt to be affectionate. When she rejected his attempt to kiss her he saw 'red, grabbed the knife and stabbed her'.[25]

Several defendants claimed that the killing was accidental. One claimed he was defending himself when his partner slipped and accidentally fell onto the knife, stabbing herself in the throat.[26] Another said he did not know the gun he fired at his ex-partner was loaded.[27] Several strangulation cases were claimed to be accidental. Others argued self-defence, with two claiming that they had been the primary victims of family violence. In one case, the defence presented evidence that the accused's partner had previously perpetrated psychological and physical family violence towards him. He argued that he shot her in self-defence after she confronted him in a public street. He was acquitted on the grounds of self-defence.[28] Another claimed his partner had been extremely controlling, domineering and verbally abusive during their relationship. So he had 'lost control' and strangled her after she taunted him during an argument, a cumulative effect of 'years of abuse' from her.[29] At trial he argued both lack of intent and self-defence. The jury, convinced of these arguments, cleared him of murder, finding him guilty of manslaughter.

Five men claimed they were defending themselves during a verbal or physical confrontation initiated by the victim, and accidentally killed them. Four either

23 *R v Robinson* [2010] VSC 10.

24 *R v Piper* [2008] VSC 569 paras 41 and 53. David Piper pleaded guilty to murder and was sentenced to 16 years' imprisonment with a minimum non-parole period of 15 years.

25 *The Queen v McPhee* [2013] VSC 581 paras 6 and 8. McPhee's 'good character' was accepted as a mitigating factor by the sentencing judge and he was sentenced to 20 years' imprisonment with a minimum non-parole period of 16 years. See: *The Queen v McPhee* [2013] VSC 581 para 25. His sentence was further reduced following an appeal, to take greater account of his 'unblemished and honourable life', as well as other mitigating factors. See *McPhee v The Queen* [2014] VSCA 156 paras. 3, 6 and 14.

26 *R v Lubik* [2011] VSC 137.

27 *R v Torun* [2014] VSC 146.

28 *R v Bracken* [2014] VSC 94.

29 *DPP v Sherna* [2009] VSC 526 para 2.

pleaded guilty to, or were convicted of, manslaughter and one was convicted of defensive homicide. Even though none argued they were the primary victim of family violence, several said the violence was 'mutual' despite evidence showing the accused had made previous threats to kill or that the victim had sought police protection because she was afraid of the accused.[30] Not that this kind of defence strategy is unique to Victoria. A New Zealand study found that while intimate partner homicides are frequently committed by men with a history of family violence and 'red flags' for dangerousness, defence lawyers misrepresent the parties as 'equally matched'. Repeat victimisation is constructed as 'mundane or unremarkable' while the women's deaths are 'unlucky' rather than intentional or foreseeable events.[31]

In many cases, the stress, anxiety or depression experienced by the accused formed a key part of the defence narrative leading up to and framing the killing. True, only one defendant raised a mental impairment defence, his defence counsel submitting that he was a 'mentally ill, emotionally vulnerable man, who, under ongoing and increasing stresses, lost his grip on reality to the point where he ended up doing things without comprehending what it was he was actually doing'.[32] The defence failed, the jury convicting him of murder. But it is notable that in at least half the cases we studied, the defendant's poor mental state was highlighted and frequently depicted as having resulted from relationship breakdown or other relationship 'difficulties'. In some cases it was said to be compounded by negative experiences in childhood or adulthood. Here the defence counsel relied on the expert opinion of one or more forensic psychologists or psychiatrists to support the contention that the offender suffered a loss of control after a build-up of stress due to behaviour by the victim, and that the offender's mental condition at the time of the homicide should be accepted as mitigating the sentence imposed in over half the cases. In 12 cases (approximately a quarter of the total in the study), the sentencing judge accepted that the offender's mental illness or disorder was causally linked to his offending to some extent, thereby reducing his moral culpability.

In one case, a man killed his wife by stabbing her multiple times in the neck. The day before the killing she had called the police to their home after an argument about her communicating online with another man. She told the police that he had threatened her with a knife, but when the police arrived both denied that he had done this.[33] During the plea hearing, the defence described the killing as 'a spontaneous outburst' in response to his wife's desire to separate. Citing the report of a forensic psychiatrist, the defence described him as having 'anger management issues'. He was 'vulnerable to stressors' and the depression he was suffering at the time impaired his judgment and 'made him more prone

30 *R v Middendorp* [2010] VSC 202; *DPP v Pennisi* [2008] VSC 498; *R v Ahmadi* [2013] VSC 293.

31 Buckingham (2010: 125–126). See also McKenzie et al. (2016).

32 *R v Baxter* [2009] VSC 180; Robert Baxter, Transcript of trial, 18 February 2009: 65.

33 *R v Felicite* [2010] VSC 245 para 12.

to losing his temper'.[34] In contrast, the prosecution argued that the defendant's resort to aggression and abuse was not an isolated incident and that his earlier attempts to address his 'anger management issues' were only 'frugal'.[35] However, the sentencing judge, found that there was 'no suggestion' that he had ever been physically violent to his wife 'before this event'. Accepting the defence plea for mitigation on the ground of mental stress, the judge commented that he regarded the defendant's prospects of rehabilitation 'as reasonably good', citing his good 'work ethic', lack of prior convictions, his 'passive and caring nature' and 'concern for his immediate and extended family' as further mitigating the sentence imposed.[36] He pleaded guilty to murder and was sentenced to 19 years' imprisonment with a minimum term of 16 years.

In a final case, a man lured his ex-girlfriend away from a party and drove her to a river, where he fatally stabbed her once in the neck, after she ended the relationship. There was considerable evidence of his controlling behaviour which included monitoring her social media accounts and her contact with other people. But at his plea hearing, the defence counsel relied on the evidence of a forensic psychiatrist who reported that he had never been physically violent towards the victim and that, 'prior to and at the time of the offending', he was 'both immature and in the grips of a major depressive disorder of severe intensity with psychotic features'. He was described by the defence counsel as a 'confused young man who got a mental illness and committed a terrible crime'. Sentencing him, the judge said that while 'a history of violent to controlling behaviour in the context of a relationship break-up' was potentially a relevant factor in establishing the 'seriousness of the murder', the defendant had never been physically violent towards the deceased. As far as the judge was concerned, the deceased was 'an intelligent, strong-willed and independent young woman well capable of dealing with such behaviour'.[37] Consequently, when considering all the circumstances, including his plea of guilty, his remorse, his mental state prior to and at the time of offending, his prior good character, his youth and his 'good prospects of rehabilitation', the judge sentenced him to 19-years' imprisonment with a minimum non-parole period of 14 and a half years.[38]

Post-reform sentencing

Gendered narratives resurfaced in sentencing pleas in post-reform cases, particularly where the defence counsel argued that the killing was the result of a 'loss of control' in response to his partner or ex-partner's actions or that it occurred in the context of the defendant's emotional stress. So while the defence counsel rarely explicitly argued that provocation should be a mitigating factor at

34 Ron Felicite, Transcript of plea, 2 May 2010: 4, 59, 60.
35 Ron Felicite, Transcript of plea, 2 May 2010: 66–68.
36 *R v Felicite* [2010] VSC 245 para 20, 25.
37 *R v Stoneham* [2013] VSC 661 paras 50–51.
38 *R v Stoneham* [2013] VSC 661.

sentencing, they frequently argued something very similar, notably that the loss of self-control occurred after a cumulative build-up of mental stress due to the victim's behaviour over a period of time.

Occasionally, the defence counsel did directly propose that provocation should be a mitigating factor. Encouragingly, a handful of judges stated that separation and infidelity were not conduct that could justify homicide. In these cases, the sentencing judge decided that the evidence did not demonstrate a genuine loss of control because the killing took several minutes or multiple blows, or because the behaviour that was supposed to have triggered it was not sudden but had occurred at some time prior to the killing. For example, one judge observed that the defendant had been aware for several days that his wife wanted to leave him, so the murder was not a 'spontaneous' loss of control.[39] Another said that the termination of a relationship was 'an experience of a kind undergone by many, many adults. It was not a situation justifying or encouraging violence'.[40] In other cases, judges rejected any implication that the victim women's actions had been 'provocative' or otherwise unreasonable. For example, in *R v Mocenigo*, the judge stated 'I am not able to say whether provocation played any part in your resorting to fatal violence. On such evidence as there is, there is nothing mitigating about the circumstances in which the jury have found that Ms Hall died'.[41]

However, we also found that in some cases, an explanatory defence narrative for a man's fatal attack on his partner often linked his mental disorder to the victim's behaviour, thereby evoking the traditional victim-blaming narrative of the abolished provocation defence.[42] While some judges questioned the offender's claim to have lost control in individual cases, they rarely questioned or challenged the notion that an offender could 'lose control' of their actions in the context of high emotion. In these narratives, separation or infidelity by the offender's partner was framed as having contributed to or as triggering his mental illness or disorder, leading him to act in a way that he would not normally act. A specific and very revealing example can be found in a case where the defendant was convicted of murder for killing a male sexual rival. When assessing the weight to be given to the conduct of the victim and the defendant's wife in provoking the killing, the sentencing judge said he accepted that the defendant was 'in some sense provoked by the victim's association' with his wife and 'the deceitful way' in which they had 'concealed their affair'. This had

39 *R v Neacsu* [2012] VSC 388 paras 40, 42.

40 *R v Piper* [2008] VSC 569 para 39.

41 *R v Mocenigo* [2012] VSC 599 para 10. Our findings are similar to those identified in Hunter and Tyson's study of post-provocation sentencing in Victoria for the period 2005 to 2015. Hunter and Tyson found that the language of provocation was explicitly raised in 13 of the 61 sentencing judgments they analysed, only to be summarily dismissed by the presiding judge in nine of these cases. See Hunter and Tyson (2016: 141–142). Likewise, Freiberg et al. (2015: 59) could only find a small number of cases where provocation was overtly discussed.

42 See also Hall et al. (2015) and Burman (2010).

contributed to the defendant's 'compromised' mental state. However, the judge further remarked that while this reduced his moral culpability, the reduction was not 'large' in as much as there is

> no longer much scope for the recognition of a reduction in moral culpability in crimes resulting from idiosyncratic (even if, in some quarters, still entrenched) psycho-social attitudes to the rights and roles of women.[43]

While that was a very clear statement of judicial recognition of a woman's right to life, other judges still struggled to see it. For example, a judge in another case thought there was 'no causal connection' between the defendant's mental state and the offence other than that posed by his history, one that included difficulties he had 'endured since arriving in this country'. Then there was his 'depression and anxiety, all of which would have contributed' to his ability to cope 'when confronted with a situation of conflict', namely, his wife's desire to separate.[44]

That said, it is significant that a few judges are challenging any suggestion that the victim's conduct had been provocative, some making implicit or explicit statements affirming the women's right to leave a relationship, to commence a new relationship or to otherwise act autonomously. Moreover, in nine of the cases in our study, judges went beyond simply rejecting provocation-type arguments to condemn men's violence towards their intimate or former partners. For example, in *R v Azizi*, the judge found that the defendant had treated his wife 'as a person lacking in individual rights, and a person that must do what she was told to do by you'.[45] She continued:

> It is clear that you were unable to accept that your wife had rights, which rights included the ability to leave you, if that was what she desired, to seek an intervention order against you, if that was what she required and to be supported to live separately and apart, if that was what she required.[46]

She made similar remarks in *R v Neacsu*:

> Our community, parliament and the courts have repeatedly said that women are not chattels, they are not something that is owned by a man, any man. Your wife was entitled to leave you. You may not have liked that, but she had the right to do so. She did not have to tell you where she was going, or if she was pursuing a relationship with another man. You had no right to know this, and you had no right to control what she did.[47]

43 *R v Budimir* [2013] VSC 149 paras 41, 55–56.
44 *The Queen v Ahmadi* [2013] VSC 293 para 22.
45 *R v Azizi* [2010] VSC 112 para 18.
46 *R v Azizi* [2010] VSC 112 para 21.
47 *R v Neacsu* [2012] VSC 388 para 43.

And in *R v Singh*, another judge remarked:

> You murdered someone you professed to love. . . . Despite feeling betrayed, you murdered someone who was completely entitled to end her marriage to you and form a relationship with someone else if she wished to.[48]

Although traditional victim-blaming narratives appear to be alive and well in some of the cases we analysed, it was also evident that post-provocation sentencing provides an opportunity for some judges to mobilise a counter-discourse challenging the gendered narratives prevalent in pre-reform cases of intimate partner femicide.[49]

Conclusion

As Carol Smart counselled, feminists cannot ignore the law 'precisely because of its power to define'.[50] So: how is law's power to define manifest in post-reform cases in Victoria? Our study has showed that it is common for defence counsel to explain intimate partner femicide in terms of accident or loss of self-control, as a response to the victim's attack, or as a result of mental illness or emotional distress. These factors were frequently intertwined, with the victim woman's actions – ending a relationship or beginning a new one or arguing with the offender – at the centre of the explanatory framework. As analysts have observed in other anglophone jurisdictions, such courtroom narratives tend to 'mirror batterers' beliefs that women of all ages provoke men's violence'.[51] They are 'common denial or minimisation tactics'.[52] Although the partial defence of provocation has been abolished in Victoria, elements of the provocation narrative underscored the explanatory narratives about intimate partner femicide in the cases we analysed. We identified a greater emphasis by defence counsel and some judges on mental illness or distress as an avenue for offenders to argue for reduced culpability or as mitigation in sentence. Some judges were sceptical about some of these claims, a small number explicitly rejecting any suggestion by the offender that the victim had in some way 'provoked' her own demise. Nonetheless the use of mental illness as the primary explanatory narrative in these cases reveals defendants' felt sense of entitlement to use lethal violence against a woman asserting her autonomy.

In conclusion, the reforms have had some success in challenging the gendered assumptions underpinning these provocation-like victim-blaming narratives. However, there is also evidence that in the absence of the provocation defence, these assumptions may be redeployed as part of the defendant's mental health

48 *R v Singh* [2015] VSC 738 para 40.
49 See also Freiberg et al. (2015) and Hunter and Tyson (2017).
50 See Smart (1989: 165).
51 See Buckingham (2010: 148).
52 See Hartley (2001: 534).

narrative in which the intimate partner victim is blamed for exacerbating his existing mental illness or fragile state of mind. Neverthelesss, as we hope our findings have demonstrated, the power of feminism lies in its ability to challenge legal discourse's insidious narratives of excuse for men's violence. To this extent at least, the Victorian reforms have achieved a successful decentring of law's truth about the excusatory force of men's emotions in intimate partner femicides.

References

Bandalli, S. 1995 'Provocation: A Cautionary Note' 22 *Journal of Law and Society* 398.

Buckingham, J. 2010 'Romantic and "Real Life" Relationships in Criminal Law: Reconstructing Red Flags for Dangerousness/Lethality' 1 *New Zealand Law Review* 93.

Burman, M. 2010 'The Ability of Criminal Law to Produce Gender Equality: Judicial Discourses in the Swedish Criminal Justice System' 16 *Violence against Women* 173.

Department of Justice Victoria

2013 *Defensive Homicide: Proposals for Legislative Reform: Consultation Paper-Criminal Law Review* Melbourne: Department of Justice Victoria.

Domestic Violence Resource Centre Victoria 2010 *Defensive Homicide: Too Soon to Say?* Collingwood: DVRCV Publications www.dvrcv.org.au/knowledge-centre/our-blog/defensive-homicide-too-soon-say

Domestic Violence Resource Centre Victoria et al. 2015 *Submission on the Victorian Department of Justice's Defensive Homicide: Proposals for Legislative Reform: Consultation Paper 2013* Collingwood: DVRCV Publications.

Edwards, S.S.M. 1987 '"Provoking Her Own Demise": From Common Assault to Homicide' in J. Hanmer and M. Maynard (eds.) *Women, Violence and Control* Hampshire: The MacMillan Press.

Freiberg, A. et al. 2015 'Homicide Law Reform, Provocation and Sentencing' in K. Fitz-Gibbon and A. Freiberg (eds.) *Homicide Law Reform in Victoria: Retrospect and Prospects* Leichardt, Victoria: The Federation Press.

Hall, G. et al. 2015 'Themes in Judges' Sentencing Remarks for Male and Female Domestic Murders' 23(3) *Psychiatry, Psychology and Law* 395.

Hartley, C. 2001 '"He Said, She Said" the Defence Attack of Credibility in Domestic Violence Felony Trials' 7(5) *Violence against Women* 510.

Horder, J. 1992 *Provocation and Responsibility* Oxford: Clarendon Press.

Howe, A. 1994 'Provoking Comment: The Question of Gender Bias in the Provocation Defence' in N. Grieve and A. Burns (eds.) *Australian Women: Contemporary Feminist Thought* Melbourne: Oxford University Press.

——— 2002 'Provoking Polemic: Provoked Killings and the Ethical Paradoxes of the Postmodern Feminist Condition' 10 *Feminist Legal Studies* 39.

——— 2004 'Provocation in Crisis: Law's Passion at the Crossroads? New Directions for Feminist Strategists' 21 *The Australian Feminist Law Journal* 53.

——— 2012 '"Red Mist" Homicide: Sexual Infidelity and the English Law of Murder (Glossing Titus Andronicus)' 33(3) *Legal Studies* 407

——— 2016 'Feminist Methods and Sources in Criminology and Criminal Justice' 16 *Legal Information Management* 102.

Hunter, R. and Tyson, D. 2016 'The Implementation of Feminist Reforms: The Case of Post-Provocation Sentencing' 26(2) *Social & Legal Studies* 129.

——— 2017 'Justice Betty King: A Study of Feminist Judging in Action' 40(2) *University of New South Wales Law Journal* 778.

Kirkwood, D. 2003 'Female Perpetrated Homicide in Victoria Between 1985 and 1995' 36(2) *Australian and New Zealand Journal of Criminology* 152.

Maguigan, H. 1998 'More Than Victims: Battered Women, the Syndrome Society, and the Law [Review]' 17 *Criminal Justice Ethics* 50.

Maher, J. 2014 'Commentary on R v Middendorp', in H. Douglas et al. (eds.) *Australian Feminist Judgments: Righting and Rewriting Law* Oxford and Portland: Hart Publishing.

McKenzie, M. et al. 2016 *Out of Character? Legal Responses to Intimate Partner Homicides by Men in Victoria 2005–2014* Collingwood: DVRCV Publications.

Morgan, J. 1997 'Provocation Law and Facts: Dead Women Tell No Tales, Tales Are Told about Them' 21 *Melbourne University Law Review* 237.

Naylor, B. and Tyson, D. 2017 'Reforming Defences to Homicide in Victoria: Another Attempt to Address the Gender Question' 6(3) *International Journal for Crime, Justice and Social Democracy* 72.

O'Donovan, K. 1993 'Law's Knowledge: The Judge, the Expert, the Battered Woman, and Her Syndrome' 20 *Journal of Law and Society* 427.

Schneider, E.M. 2000 *Battered Women and Feminist Law-Making* New Haven: Yale University Press.

Sheehy, E. 1994 'Developments in Canadian Law after *R. v. Lavallee*' in J. Stubbs (ed.) *Women, Male Violence and the Law* Sydney: Institute of Criminology.

Sheehy, E. et al. 1992 'Defending Battered Women on Trial: The Battered Woman Syndrome and Its Limitations' 16 *Criminal Law Journal* 369.

Smart, C. 1989 *Feminism and the Power of Law* London: Routledge.

Tyson, D. 2013 *Sex, Culpability and the Defence of Provocation* Abingdon, Oxon: Routledge.

Tyson, D. et al. 2010 *Review of the Offence of Defensive Homicide: Submission to the Department of Justice, Victoria* http://artsonline.monash.edu.au/wp-content/arts-files/womens-and-gender-studies/Tyson%20Kirkwood%20&%20Capper%202010.pdf

Ulbrick, M. et al. 2016 'Abolishing Defensive Homicide: A Step Forward for Populist Punitiveness at the Expense of Mentally Impaired Offenders' 40(1) *Melbourne University Law Review* 324.

Victorian Law Reform Commission (VLRC) 2003 *Defences to Homicide: Options Paper* Melbourne: VLRC Publications.

——— 2004 *Defences to Homicide: Final Report* Melbourne: VLRC Publications.

3 Criminalising femicide in Latin American countries – legal power working for women?

Patsilí Toledo

Introduction

It took just ten years for the words 'femicide' and 'feminicide' to go from being neologisms used mostly by Latin American feminist activists and academics to becoming legislated as a new crime in more than a dozen countries.[1] Since 2007, a wave of criminal reforms has echoed feminist campaigns to raise awareness about the pervasiveness of gender-based killings of women in the region and the lack of adequate response from the state authorities. The criminalisation of feminicide acknowledges the gravity of these crimes and also the feminist conceptual elaboration and tireless activism. From this perspective, many feminists consider the criminalisation to be a triumph. However, a closer analysis reveals a much greater complexity behind this legal phenomenon.

Reflecting retrospectively on why she wrote *Feminism and the Power of Law*, Carol Smart singled out the commitment of young feminists in campaigning for law reform.[2] This commitment clearly remains strong in Latin America where in the last decade a significant number of feminists have been fully committed to campaigning for law reform in relation to gender-based killings of women. How successful have they been? Should they have heeded Smart's warning that law is 'so deaf to core concerns of feminism that feminists should be extremely cautious of how and whether they resort to law'?[3] This chapter assesses the achievements of the Latin American feminist law reform campaigns against femicide with reference to the reservations Smart expressed three decades ago about turning to law for solutions.

Femicide, feminicide, feminists and the role of the state

The Latin American feminist movement has had a long engagement with law, mostly with international human rights law as a tool to promote legal reform

1 Argentina, Bolivia, Brazil, Chile, Colombia, Costa Rica, Ecuador, El Salvador, Guatemala, Honduras, Mexico, Nicaragua, Panama, Peru, Dominican Republic and Venezuela. All translations in this chapter are the author's own.

2 Smart (2012: 162).

3 Smart (1989: 2).

at the domestic level. This engagement was clearly crystallised in the adoption of the Convention of Belém do Pará in 1994 which also showed the strength and coordination of the Latin American feminist movement. A shared colonial history and language in most of the region as well as the regular continental feminist meetings since the 1980s and the work of diverse continental feminist networks (on women's health, popular education and violence against women) has provided feminists in the continent with a high level of organisation.[4] After decades of dictatorships and armed conflicts in the continent, feminist and human rights activists were confident in the ability of international law to impact national laws and exercised a huge influence in the mostly democratic governments in place at the beginning of 1990 to promote the adoption of the Convention.[5]

As expected, the Convention, the first binding international instrument on violence against women, became a legal tool that fostered the adoption of many domestic laws against this violence. After Belém do Pará, many Latin American states adopted their first laws on domestic or family violence but mostly in gender-neutral terms that prioritised civil remedies. In sharp contrast, the Convention's definition of violence against women – as 'any act or conduct, based on gender, which causes *death* or physical, sexual or psychological harm or suffering to women, whether in the public or the private sphere' – had always included gender-based killings of women.[6] In fact, gender-based killings of women were not socially or politically visible until about a decade later, when the use of the expressions 'femicide' used by feminists in some Latin American countries and 'feminicide', used in others, became frequent beyond feminist activism.

The Convention highlighted state responsibility for dealing with gender-based violence against women, including its prevention, investigation, punishment and eradication. Since the early 1990s, state failure to meet these obligations was clear in relation to the abduction and killings of hundreds of women publicly denounced in Ciudad Juárez, Mexico and later in other countries such as Guatemala.[7] Those crimes were not only characterised by exceptional brutality and sexual violence, but also by public authorities failing to investigate or punish them. Victims' families faced frequent obstacles when trying to access justice, not least the all too familiar narrative of victim-blaming based on gender stereotypes regarding women's behaviour.

4 The Latin American and Caribbean Feminist *Encuentros* have taken place in diverse countries every three years since 1981. The 14th *Encuentro* was celebrated in Montevideo in 2017.

5 Toledo (2015).

6 Article 1, emphasis added. The Convention in 1994 was more specific than the 1993 UN Declaration on the Elimination of Violence Against Women, which did not expressly mention the death of women among the consequences of this violence.

7 A database by sociologist Julia Monárrez identified 382 killed women and girls in Ciudad Juárez between 1993 and 2004, more than a hundred of which had suffered torture or rape, including mutilation and incineration, as well as an undetermined number of women and girls missing in the same period, who are believed to have had the same end. Monárrez (2009: 9–10).

The work of feminist activists and networks was crucial in bringing international attention to these murders, reflected in hundreds of recommendations to the Mexican state – and later to other Central American countries – from diverse international human rights bodies.[8] Years later, the Inter-American Court of Human Rights (IACtHR) expressly condemned Mexico for the inaction of state agents in the emblematic 'Cotton Field' (*Campo Algodonero*) case. More recently, it condemned Guatemala in the case of Claudina Isabel Velásquez Paiz. In these cases, the IACtHR ruled that the states had violated not only the American Convention on Human Rights but also the Convention of Belém do Pará by not guaranteeing the right of the victims to life, integrity and freedom. They were also condemned for their negligence, failing to take effective steps to address gender-based violence against women.[9]

According to Mexican feminist anthropologist and politician Marcela Lagarde, that impunity was the central element differentiating 'femicide' from 'feminicide'. She took the notion of femicide from the work of Diana Russell and Jane Caputi who had defined femicide as the 'murder of women by men motivated by hatred, contempt, pleasure, or a sense of woman ownership'.[10] Lagarde defined 'feminicide' ('feminicidio' in Spanish) as gender-based killings of women committed due to states' failures to prevent and punish them, becoming – in her words – a 'state crime'.[11] The human rights framing implicates governments' failures to act with due diligence and take reasonable steps to prevent, investigate and prosecute gender-based violence against women. Although other Latin American feminists have kept using the original term 'femicide' – simply translated as 'femicidio' – with no express reference to impunity or state responsibility, states' obligations are still a key element in feminist demands for the criminalisation of femicide.[12]

Political factors behind the reforms

Laws criminalising 'femicide' and 'feminicide' in Latin America have now removed the conceptual and political difference between both terms. In fact, those laws have been successful in deleting any reference to state responsibility,

8 Toledo (2017b).

9 Inter-American Court of Human Rights, *González Banda et al ('Cotton Field') v. Mexico* Series C 205 (2009) and *Velasquez Paiz et al v Guatemala* Series C 307 (2015).

10 Russell and Caputi (1990: 35).

11 Lagarde (2005). Interestingly, some European countries have also adopted this definition. The Statement by Germany presented to the UNODC Open-ended Intergovernmental Expert Group Meeting on gender-related killing of women and girls, 11–13 November 2014, stated that 'Femicide (understood as the killing of women simply because of their gender and to which there is little or no state reaction) is not a phenomenon which can be found in Germany'. UNODC (2014b: 1) and Lagarde (2010: xxiii).

12 Others such as sociologist Julia Monárrez use *feminicidio* as the correct linguistic translation into Spanish of femicide. While the expression 'feminicide' is used by the feminist movement in countries such as Mexico, Bolivia, El Salvador, Dominican Republic, Peru, Colombia and Brazil, 'femicide' is the expression used in Costa Rica, Guatemala, Honduras, Nicaragua, Venezuela, Chile and Argentina. Monárrez (2006).

negligence or disregard of these crimes or their victims. In Guatemala, where femicide was criminalised in 2008, legislators decided to use the word 'femicide' instead of 'feminicide' to avoid the latter's political focus on state responsibility.[13] In most countries there has been no reference to state agents' action or inaction, so the crime – although called feminicide – has been criminalised just as any other crime with no reference to public authorities' responsibility or negligence.[14]

Recalling Smart's concerns about the impossibility of predicting the outcomes of law reforms, it comes as no surprise to learn that feminists have not been able to control how laws on femicide are enacted in Latin American countries.[15] The influence of women's movements and feminist activism during these legislative proceedings varied hugely across the continent. In many cases women's demands have not been heard, for instance, regarding the importance of punishing public authority negligence and abuses in investigations and prosecutions. State authorities have been able to shift the political focus from their responsibility to adequately prevent and investigate these crimes to perpetrators and their punishment. The political focus has shifted from human rights law to criminal law, from state responsibility to individual criminal responsibility. Using criminal law, the last recourse for state action, gives the impression that the strongest action has been taken and that femicides have received the maximum response from the state.

Furthermore, the criminalisation of femicide has been popular and therefore politically convenient. Most of the laws criminalising femicide in Latin America have been passed unanimously with the support of right and left wing parliamentary parties. Legislators and public authorities have taken political advantage of the high media visibility and social mobilisation around femicides, passing laws to show their support for such a popular cause that mobilises so many people in the streets. In some cases, the laws have even been used to clean the public image of authorities that have been criticised in relation to other cases involving women's rights. For instance, in 2010 the Mexican state of Guanajuato was publicly denounced for imprisoning for almost ten years seven peasant women accused of murdering their foetuses when in fact some were stillborn or had miscarried. Following a strong public reaction when the cases were denounced by the Office of the UN High Commissioner for Human Rights, all seven women were released in September 2010. Few months later, the government of Guanajuato promoted and passed legislation criminalising feminicide in May 2011 in order to show a commitment to

13 Toledo (2017a: 231).

14 The only exception is the criminalisation in the Mexican federal penal code, where the same legal reform introduced together with the crime of feminicide, another offence to punish negligence in investigation by prosecutors. However, the Mexican federal penal code has a minimum impact in practice, as most of the crimes committed in Mexico are judged according to the law of some of the 31 Mexican States and the Federal District that integrate the Federation.

15 Smart (1989: 164).

women's rights. Women's organisations, however, protested that they had not been consulted or invited to participate in the law-making process, and called for a rejection what they termed a 'fast track' approval of the criminalisation of feminicide.[16]

While appearing to be important legal reforms on paper, the budgetary enforcement of these laws is often missing with governments reluctant to burden the criminal justice system with additional crimes given that femicide is already punished as homicide. This is another example of how criminal law has become a favourite tool of Latin American governments to deal with social problems in a context of neoliberal politics that precludes other interventions such as public education, social support and healthcare.

Multiple scenarios, multiple meanings, multiple crimes

According to data provided by the last United Nations Office on Drugs and Crime (UNODC) Global Study on Homicide, the Americas have the highest homicide rate in the world and, together with Africa, a rate of family related homicide higher than in all other regions. But although most gender-based killings of women in Latin American countries are committed by their intimate partners or family members – as in most of the world – this varies significantly among different subregions and countries.[17] Latin American feminist movements have traditionally included and emphasised the role of non-intimate violence within the scope of gender-based violence against women.[18] The traditional distinction between intimate and non-intimate lethal violence against women – not taking into account diverse contexts such as transnational organised crime or human trafficking – might however be insufficient to analyse and comprehend the phenomenon of femicide.[19]

The diversity of the contexts in which women are killed is also reflected in how femicide has been criminalised in Latin American countries. What counts as a femicide in one country might not be considered as such in another. For example, Chile and the Dominican Republic confine femicide to the killing of women by their current or former intimate partners. Costa Rica is even more restrictive, reducing femicide to homicides committed by current partners.[20] In these countries, the killings of women committed by strangers – such as the emblematic cases of rape, torture and murder of women in Ciudad Juárez – do not constitute femicide.[21]

16 Torres (2011).

17 UNODC (2014a).

18 This idea was present in the Declaration of 25 November as the International Day for the Elimination of Violence against Women, introduced by Latin American feminists in 1981, commemorating the date of the 1960 assassination of the three Mirabal sisters, political activists killed by the Dominican Trujillo dictatorship.

19 See for example Carcedo et al. (2010).

20 From 2011 to 2013, a similar provision was included in the Penal Code of Peru, based on Law No. 29819, adopted 5 December 2011, published 27 December 2011.

21 Inter-American Court of Human Rights, *González Banda et al ('Cotton Field') vs. Mexico*, 16 November 2009.

These restrictive laws fit in a criminal law system that traditionally has criminalised the killing of women committed by their husbands or intimate partners. *Uxoricide* (a wife killed by her husband) has historically been a crime with a specific legal status, being either justified in cases of the wife's infidelity (as 'honour' homicide) or punished more severely as a form of parricide or aggravated by kinship.[22] Moreover, crimes committed by intimate partners are often much easier for law enforcement to investigate and to prosecute than those related to organised crime or criminal gang activities.[23]

These laws have also been criticised by feminist activists for their reductionist view of gender-based violence and killings of women. Costa Rica was the first country where femicide became a specific crime in 2007. However, the legislative procedure took almost seven years. The original bill, written by the women's movement, underwent so many modifications that the law ended up limiting gender-based violence and killings of women to those committed by their current intimate partners, causing some feminist activists to wonder if it had been worth the effort.[24] But this is hardly surprising. As Carol Smart pointed out in *Feminism and the Power of Law*:

> It is a dilemma that all radical political movements face, namely the problem of challenging a form of power without accepting its own terms of reference and hence losing the battle before it has begun. Put simply, in accepting law's terms in order to challenge law, feminism always concedes too much.[25]

Feminist activists promoting femicide law reform in Latin America have faced precisely this dilemma as they struggle to translate 'femicide'/'feminicide', socio-political concepts developed by feminist anthropologists and sociologists, into the language of criminal law. While the expressions 'killing a woman because she is a woman' and 'misogynistic killing of women' are often used as short definitions of femicide by feminist activists and academics and in international human rights law documents, they have not translated into criminal law, at least in practice. In 2008 for instance, Colombia introduced the killing of a woman 'because she is a woman' as an aggravated form of homicide. That provision, considered at the time to constitute the criminalisation of femicide, has rarely been applied as most prosecutors and judges believe men kill women because of jealousy or anger, not because the victim is a woman.[26] Argentinian judge and legal scholar Eugenio Zaffaroni, currently a judge of the Inter-American Court of Human

22 'Honour homicide' provisions remained in force in some Mexican states and were criticised by the CEDAW Committee in 2012. CEDAW Committee (2012). Most European countries removed the crime of parricide during the twentieth century. It existed in Spain until 1995.

23 UNODC (2014a).

24 Toledo (2014: 207ff).

25 Smart (1989: 5).

26 Defensoría del Pueblo de Colombia (2011: 199). This led to a reform of the penal code and the criminalisation of feminicide as an autonomous offence in 2014.

Rights, took this position when the criminalisation of femicide was approved by the Argentinian parliament in 2012. A member of the Supreme Court at the time, he declared that nobody kills a woman because she is a woman, and that accordingly, this legislation would not have any effect.[27]

Laws criminalising femicide often use words or expressions that are very difficult for legal practitioners, prosecutors and the judiciary to interpret and apply. Some laws refer to a certain, specific mental state of the perpetrator, such as misogyny. Some say the crime is committed for gender-related reasons or because the victim is a woman. Some refer – as an element of the crime – to the context of unequal power relations between men and women.[28] But all these expressions lead to serious problems of interpretation as they lack legal definitions and may not fulfil the precision required by the principle of legality. In practice, these difficulties may result in the laws not being implemented.

To classify a woman's killing as femicide, the laws generally include different elements. These elements are that the killing is committed by an intimate partner (common to most laws) or perpetrated under certain circumstances or through certain acts. The most frequent circumstances include: a relationship between victim and perpetrator, such as family relationships or other relations in which there is subordination or dependence; previous violence by the perpetrator; and circumstances related to characteristics of the victim, such as physical or psychological vulnerability, pregnancy or young age.[29] Other circumstances are related to the manner of killing and often reflect country-specific phenomena or trends. These include whether the killing was particularly cruel or violent, including mutilation or other forms of degrading injuries inflicted to the victim's body before and after death, or exhibiting the body of the victim in public.[30] In several countries, it is also considered to be a gender-related circumstance if the killing was committed in front of the children or relatives of the victim.[31]

Amongst all this diversity, there have also been cases in Mexico in which the newly introduced legislation is disregarded in practice, effectively reducing the scope and numbers of feminicide. This explains why, although more than 10,000 women have been murdered in Mexico since 2012, less than 20 per cent of the cases have been judged as feminicides.[32] In Mexico, where the expression 'feminicide' itself has been used as an accusation against the state, several authorities

27 Minuto Uno (2012).

28 Misogyny: Guatemala and Nicaragua. Gender-related reasons: Honduras and Mexican federal penal code and the penal codes of several Mexican states. Victim is a woman: Ecuador, Guatemala and Peru. Context of unequal power relations between men and women: Panama, Ecuador, Guatemala and Nicaragua.

29 Toledo (2014: 226ff).

30 Defamatory or degrading injuries to the victim's body: El Salvador, Guatemala, Honduras, Mexican federal penal code, Nicaragua, Panama. Defamatory or degrading injuries to the victim's body after the killing: Honduras. Exhibiting the body of the victim in public: Mexican federal penal code and the penal codes of several Mexican states.

31 Ecuador, El Salvador, Guatemala, Nicaragua, Panama.

32 Durán (2017).

have argued that in their jurisdictions there were no feminicides but only homicides of women (for example, related to drug-trafficking or organised crime). In some states, the criminalisation of feminicide, while carrying the same punishment as aggravated homicide, contains elements that are in practice hard to prove – often harder than elements of aggravated homicides. Therefore, there is no incentive for prosecutors to prosecute these cases. Instead, they prosecute the crimes as aggravated homicide, leading to distorted data that hides the gendered traits of many of the killings. In Guanajuato, for instance, although 124 women were killed between January and October 2017, only 19 cases were considered as feminicides.[33] Because of their restrictive or inadequate scope, some feminist activists have tried to prevent these laws from being passed.[34]

In short, the huge variety of definitions of femicide across Latin America makes it impossible to compare data from one country to another or even within one country, as in Mexico. This result is paradoxical, since advocates of criminalisation of femicide were convinced this would be a tool to obtain comparable data on femicide across the continent.

Challenges of the practical application of a new crime

Some legal academics have expressed concern about the strategy of criminalising femicide. The main criticism, beyond the question of how to define femicide, is that it could constitute a form of discrimination or a 'presumption of guilt' against men. This criticism has been made of other gender-specific offences that criminalise different violent crimes against women more severely than similar crimes committed against men.[35] However, in several countries, the punishment for femicide is equivalent to that for other aggravated homicides, including for example, when women kill men in intimate partner homicides in Chile and Costa Rica. This option, although rejected by some feminist groups, answers the criticism that femicide laws allegedly discriminate against men.

Minimum punishments for femicide have increased compared to other aggravated homicides in some Latin American countries.[36] Penalties vary between countries, ranging from a 12-year minimum in Brazil to life imprisonment in Argentina and Chile with numerous countries having a minimum of 20 years of imprisonment. But impunity remains a problem in many cases. In the Mexican state of Puebla, the crime of feminicide was introduced into the penal code in late 2012. Between then and September 2017, there have been 324 killings of

33 García (2017).
34 Toledo (2014: 267ff).
35 This was the focus of the constitutional actions against the *Bill on Criminalisation of Violence against Women*, before the Costa Rican Constitutional Court (Sala Constitucional) between 2001 and 2004, and a similar constitutional debate was held in Spain regarding the Spanish Organic Law 1/2004 on Comprehensive Protection Measures against Gender-based Violence. Toledo (2014).
36 Mexican Federal Penal Code, Panama, Honduras and El Salvador.

women, but convictions in only six cases.[37] Also, there is still a wide application of mitigating circumstances in these crimes. In Peru, for example, there is a general rule in criminal proceedings that allows the punishment of the accused to be reduced to below the legal minimum whenever there is a sincere confession and repentance. This rule is habitually applied in cases of feminicide, often when committed by an intimate partner.[38] In Mexico, more than a dozen criminal codes still consider 'violent emotion' a mitigating circumstance, one often related to the very gender-related factors that the crime of femicide has brought to light. In a case of attempted femicide in Chile, an appellate court confirmed a decision where the woman's infidelity was considered to have caused a violent emotion or emotional outburst in the accused and this constituted a 'mitigating circumstance'.[39] The lower court had established that on the basis of witness evidence and police collaboration, his wife's infidelity had been revealed 'in the moment prior to the assault'. Therefore it could be said that the defendant had acted irrationally under the influence of 'stimuli so powerful' that he did not even bother to disguise the attack when police arrived.[40]

Once again, this trend brings to mind Carol Smart's warning about the 'backlash' that can follow women's resort to law, one that can take the form of 'a counter-use of law to re-establish traditional rights'.[41] She provides by way of example, juror reluctance to convict men for 'doing "natural" manly things' if penalties are seen as unreasonably severe.[42] Three decades later, this might be happening in Latin America. Consider, for example, a recent study of 144 sentences in Argentinian intimate partner killings showing that judges tend to apply mitigating circumstances more often to men than to women.[43] Could it be that Latin American judges are acting similarly to Smart's reluctant juries, by using the mitigation provision to reduce punishments they consider to be too tough?

Another particularly complex issue is that only a few of the new provisions explicitly envisage the perpetrator as a man. Therefore, women can also be convicted of these crimes in several Latin American countries. This has serious consequences when femicides have a harsher punishment than other similar killings, and as a result, intimate partner killings in lesbian couples automatically qualify as aggravated, while the same is not true for homosexual men. Furthermore, in a comparison of the first ten convictions for feminicide in Mexico, the two highest convictions were in fact imposed on the only two women accused. In the case of one who had killed her mother, the prosecutor considered her declaration that she hated her mother to be a clear example of hatred towards women.[44] It is also

37 Camacho (2017).
38 Meléndez and Sarmiento (2008: 19).
39 Chile, Appeals Court of La Serena, Case No 227–2016 (2016).
40 Chile, Criminal Court of Ovalle, Case No. 28–2016 (2016).
41 Smart (1989: 138).
42 Smart (1989: 45).
43 Rodríguez and Chejter (2014).
44 Bolaños (2012).

a clear example of Smart's recognition that in engaging with law to produce law reforms, the women's movement is 'tacitly accepting . . . the idea that law is the means to resolve social problems', when in fact it may produce effects that make conditions worse.[45] Persistent stereotyping of victims occurs not only in acquittals but also in some convictions for femicide. For instance, in Argentina, a judge made a victim-blaming ruling that the crime took place because the victim had not terminated the relationship with the perpetrator.[46]

> Both the accounts of Ms R and her children and the accounts of the neighbours clearly prove a situation of family violence over a long time which are validated by the authority records . . . the violence was increasingly aggravated over the years, mainly because of the indecision of the aforementioned woman to put an end to it, for whatever reason.[47]

In some cases, judges have insisted that to prove gender-based violence against a woman, the victim needs to be in a situation of dependence and vulnerability. If the woman was empowered or there was not an asymmetric relationship, these judges do not consider the killing as gender-based violence as can be illustrated in this 2015 Argentinian case:

> But let us not forget that for 'gender violence' to exist, as we have seen, the presence of a 'vulnerable female victim' is required and the existence of 'asymmetric relations of inequality and power between the sexes, which subordinate the woman'. These conditions do not exist in the present case. There was no unequal power relationship. On the contrary . . . she showed herself as a person determined to defend her rights and those of her daughter.[48]

In other cases, a power imbalance is clearly established. For example, one judge noted that between the accused and the victim there was undoubtedly a clear unequal power relationship based on the idea of the victim being inferior because she was a woman. There had been physical violence, psychological violence and economic violence, all of which was testament to that. In short, 'the existence of gender-based violence between the defendant Quiroga and María Rita Valdez has been thoroughly proven, leading to the death of the victim in a gender context'.[49] In another case, the judge noted that the woman had been 'the victim of gender-based violence by her partner' by way of referencing the killer's 'acts of absolute contempt for the life of the woman' as expressed in his verbal and

45 Smart (1989: 161).
46 Toledo (2017a: 255).
47 Argentina, Fourth Chamber in the Criminal Court of Salta, Case CAM No. 2.337/14 (2014).
48 Argentina, Eleventh Chamber in the Criminal Court of Córdoba, Case L-2015401/2015 (2015).
49 Argentina, First Chamber in the Criminal Court of Catamarca, Case No 22/2014 (2014).

physical aggression against her 'without expressing any interest in the injury that could result, ultimately ending his partner's life'.[50]

Which women? What rights?

As Marcela Lagarde argues:

> in the cause to eradicate violence against women and girls and to construct their human rights, legislating is part of an all-encompassing process that involves social movements, activism, study and awareness-building, as well as the possibility of theoretically naming, from a feminist gender perspective, those facts that are made invisible, irrelevant, or considered normal.[51]

The criminalisation of femicide has brought attention to the gender-related nature of men's fatal attacks on women. An important component of a feminist perspective has nevertheless gone missing – the political power of pointing to states' gender-biased negligence with regards to these crimes. With these neologisms becoming common currency globally – for example, in United Nations' documents – it should be kept in mind that many women are still disappearing and being killed in Ciudad Juárez and other places in Latin America.[52] While the levels of violence in Latin American countries in the last decades are increasing, the killing of mostly poor women do not have the international media and political attention they once had.[53]

It should not be assumed that the strong impact of feminist activism and mobilisation in the adoption of these laws is evidence of the power of feminist influence in politics or law in general in this continent. In fact, it should be remembered that more than 97 per cent of women of childbearing age in Latin America and the Caribbean live in countries where abortion is restricted or banned altogether.[54] Some of the most severe laws on abortion have been passed in countries that have criminalised femicide, supported by politicians in the whole

50 Argentina, Court of Instruction No. 3 of Corrientes, Case 97877/13, Bill of Indictment (2013).

51 Lagarde (2010: xxiii–xxiv).

52 For instance, the UN Special Rapporteur on Violence against Women and the United Nations Office on Drugs and Crime (UNODC) call for States to establish a 'Femicide Watch'. UNODC (2017).

53 The region has increasing homicide rates, an increase related to the action of organised crime. UNODC (2014a). For example, 68 per cent of the international recommendations from human rights bodies to Mexico regarding the situation of feminicide in Ciudad Juárez were issued between 2005 and 2010, and have decreased significantly since then. This information is compiled from the *Recomendaciones Internacionales a México en materia de Derechos Humanos* database in 2018, upheld by the Secretaría de Relaciones Exteriores, (SRE), Oficina en México del Alto Comisionado de Naciones Unidas para los Derechos Humanos (ONU-DH) and Centro de Investigación y Docencia Económicas (CIDE).

54 Sedgh et al. (2016).

political spectrum, including religious and conservative parties.[55] So it seems that women's demands are heard much more readily when they lack agency and are seen as victims, especially dead victims.

Have the new laws against femicide made conditions worse for women as Smart warned they could all those years ago?[56] Perhaps not, but there are worrying tendencies. The diversity of laws prevents coherent data collection and general conclusions. In some places feminists consider criminalisation of femicide worth the effort. In others, they do not. Certainly, the depolitisation of the concept and the symbolic disappearance of state responsibility through the use of criminal law is deeply worrying. So is the low level of prosecutions and convictions for femicide. Other problems are the worsening conditions experienced by lesbian women convicted for killing an intimate partner to an aggravated punishment and the pervasiveness of the stereotyped understanding of gender-based violence and its victims, even in judgments applying the new laws. But in my view, the most worrying are the symbolic and concrete consequences of laws and policies only focusing on 'the tip of the iceberg' of gender-based violence against women, namely femicide. These policies and laws forget the large majority of women who survive gender-based violence. The demand expressed in the recent feminist slogan 'we want ourselves alive' – *nos queremos vivas* – is, no doubt, placing the threshold too low.

References

Bolaños, C. 2012 'PGJDF: Lidera odio en los feminicidios' *El Universal* mujeres. especial.eluniversal.com.mx/2012/03/08/pgjdf-lidera-odio-en-los-feminicidios/

Camacho, M. 2017 'Quedan impunes 98 de cada 100 feminicidios perpetrados en Puebla: Odesyr' *La Jornada de Oriente* www.lajornadadeoriente.com.mx/2017/09/19/quedan-impunes-98-100-feminicidios-perpetrados-puebla-odesyr/

Committee on the Elimination of Discrimination against Women (CEDAW Committee) 2012 *Concluding Observations of the Committee on the Elimination of Discrimination against Women: Mexico* UN Doc. CEDAW/C/MEX/CO/7-8.

Defensoría del Pueblo de Colombia 2011 *Decimoctavo Informe del Defensor del Pueblo al Congreso de la República, Primera parte* www.defensoria.gov.co/public/pdf/02/18_informe_congreso_I.pdf

Durán, V. 2017 'Las muertas que no se ven: el limbo de los feminicidios' *Aristegui Noticias* https://aristeguinoticias.com/0702/mexico/las-muertas-que-no-se-ven-el-limbo-de-los-feminicidios-reportaje-especial/

García, N. 2017 'Aclarados todos los feminicidios: PGJE' *Periódico Correo* https://periodicocorreo.com.mx/van-19-feminicidios-en-guanajuato-en-2017-afirma-la-pgje/

Lagarde, M. 2005 'El feminicidio, delito contra la humanidad' in Camara de Diputados del H. Congreso de la Unión – LIX Legislatura *Feminicidio, justicia y derecho* Mexico City: Congreso de la Unión 151.

55 As in El Salvador, Nicaragua, Honduras, Guatemala and Chile.
56 Smart (1989: 161).

——— 2010 'Preface: Feminist Keys for Understanding Feminicide: Theoretical, Political and Legal Construction' in R. Fregoso and C. Bejarano (eds.) *Terrorizing Women: Feminicide in the Américas* Durham and London: Duke University Press xi.

Meléndez, L. and Sarmiento, P. 2008 *Feminicidio* DEMUS Lima: Sinco Editores.

Minuto Uno 2012 'Para Zaffaroni, la ley de Femicidio "no tendrá eficacia"' www.minutouno.com/notas/270106-para-zaffaroni-la-ley-femicidio-no-tendra-eficacia

Monárrez, J. 2006 'Las diversas representaciones del feminicidio y los asesinatos de mujeres en Ciudad Juárez, 1993–2005' in El Colegio de la Frontera Norte and Comisión para la Prevención y Erradicación de la Violencia contra las Mujeres en Ciudad Juárez *Sistema Socioeconómico y Geo-referencial sobre la Violencia de Género en Ciudad Juárez, Chihuahua: propuestas para su prevención*, Vol. 2 353 Law Reform Commission.

——— 2009 *Trama de una injusticia. Feminicidio sexual sistémico en Ciudad Juárez* Mexico: El Colegio de la Frontera Norte – Miguel Ángel Porrúa.

Rodríguez, M. and Chejter, S. 2014 *Homicidios conyugales y de otras parejas. La decisión judicial y el sexismo* Buenos Aires: Editores del Puerto.

Russell, D. and Caputi, J. 1990 'Femicide: Speaking the Unspeakable' *Ms.* September/October 34.

Sedgh, G. et al. 2016 'Abortion Incidence between 1990 and 2014: Global, Regional, and Subregional Levels and Trends' 388(10041) *The Lancet* 258.

Smart, C. 1989 *Feminism and the Power of Law* London: Routledge.

——— 2012 'Reflection' 20(2) *Feminist Legal Studies* 161.

Toledo, P. 2014 *Femicidio/Feminicidio* Buenos Aires: Didot.

——— 2015 'Movimiento de mujeres, derechos humanos y tipificación del femicidio/feminicidio en Latinoamérica' in M. Femenías (ed.) *Los ríos subterráneos, IV. violencias cruzadas: miradas y perspectivas* Rosario: Prohistoria Ediciones 25.

——— 2017a 'Femicidio' in J. Di Corleto (ed.) *Género y Justicia Penal* Buenos Aires: Didot 237.

——— 2017b 'El reconocimiento jurídico-penal del femicidio/feminicidio en Latinoamérica desde la perspectiva de los derechos humanos' in O. Parra et al. (eds.) *La lucha por los derechos humanos hoy. Estudios en homenaje a Cecilia Medina Quiroga* Valencia: Tirant lo Blanch 455.

Torres, G. 2011 'Llaman a no aprobar "fast track" ley de feminicidio en Guanajuato' *CIMAC* cimacnoticias.com.mx/node/40447

United Nations Office on Drugs and Crime (UNODC) 2014a *Global Study on Homicide 2013: Trends, Context, Data* Vienna: United Nations Publications.

——— 2014b 'Statement by Germany on the Investigation and Prosecution of Gender-Related Killings of Women and Girls' www.unodc.org/documents/justice-and-prison-reform/IEGM_GRK_BKK/Germany_Annex.pdf

——— 2017 'Femicide Watch Platform Prototype Launched at 2017 UN Crime Commission' www.unodc.org/unodc/en/frontpage/2017/May/femicide-watch-platform-prototype-launched-at-2017-un-crime-commission.html

Part 2

Proliferating sites of feminist legal intervention

4 'Being wrought, perplexed in the extreme' – Othello and his Syndrome

Adrian Howe

Soft you, a word or two before you go.
I have done the state some service, and they know't.
No more of that. I pray you, in your letters,
When you shall these unlucky deeds relate,
Speak of me as I am. Nothing extenuate,
Nor set down aught in malice. Then must you speak
Of one that loved not wisely but too well,
Of one not easily jealous but, being wrought,
Perplexed in the extreme

Othello 5.2.347–355

As far as I recall, it was *Feminism and the Power of Law* that kick-started my poststructuralist, or more specifically, Foucauldian feminist turn. There has never been a turning back. Socio-legal research, criminological teaching, pub brawls with positivists, a Theatre in Education project, all succumbed to the pleasures of unravelling discursive constructions of legal and criminological truths about men and women. What a joy it was then, decades later, to come across a parallel universe, a rich vein of literary studies from the late 1980s extolling the merits of the very same approach Carol Smart advocated way back then. There she was reading law as a 'discursive field', a 'site of struggle', an 'institutionalised and formalised site of power struggles' that provides resources for women, children and men, 'albeit differentially'.[1] Here were North American Shakespeare scholars examining how Shakespearean texts function to 'naturalise interested representations of the real' by producing and reproducing 'historically specific relations of power', gendered ones included. Reading his drama as 'a site of struggle conducted through discourse', Foucauldian discourse no less, theirs was an avowedly political analysis of how 'truth effects are produced through discourse', especially 'authoritative discourses' that delimit what can be recognised as true, including 'what passes as a truthful reading of women'.[2] For them, as for Smart, the

1 Smart (1989: 49, 88, 138).
2 Howard and O'Connor (1987: 3, 6–8) and Howard (1987: 174–175).

analytical starting point was 'the order of discourse' and more particularly, 'the ordering of women in relation to the ordering of discourse itself'.[3] Here then, for those who need it, is backing from on high – (does it get any higher than Shakespeare?) – for discourse analysis, that frequently misunderstood, sometimes maligned poststructuralist methodology that Smart deployed when addressing law questions and that she found herself constantly defending.

Reading law thus, Chapter 1 traced the increasingly attenuated tales of unfaithfulness presented in defences to murder in cases in English and Welsh courts between 2012 and 2016. It was concerned particularly with assessing the effectiveness of the reformed defence excluding sexual infidelity as a trigger for loss of control in post-reform cases. This chapter continues the analysis of femicides committed over that same five-year year period, commencing with cases that did not proceed to court, the killers having suicided. Speculating about their likely fates had they lived to face criminal charges opens up an inquiry into pleas to manslaughter they might have entered in response to a murder charge. Might they have resorted to the new diminished responsibility plea which came into effect in October 2010 at the same time as the new loss of control defence? Unlike the provocation by infidelity defence that so taxed feminist reformers, diminished responsibility pleas had not raised feminist concerns about its scope, no cases having led to a similar outcry that this defence was letting men get away with murder. Nevertheless, the fact that men who kill their women partners frequently plead mental impairment warrants feminist attention. These cases are not only rich sites for challenging the discursive constitution of historically mandated excuses for murdering women; they also touch on another of Smart's focal concerns in *Feminism and the Power of Law* – her Foucauldian-inflected interest in how law interacted with emergent 'psy' professions in the late twentieth. Was law's power being 'overshadowed by medical discourse' as Foucault argued?[4]

While it was the battle between legal and clinical truths that preoccupied Smart, my focus is on how the new diminished responsibility plea is narrating intimate partner femicide today. What is its excusatory purchase? Is it allowing wife-killers to get away with murder if prosecutors accept it or, failing that, juries accept it as a partial defence to murder? Are medicalised explanations for femicide more convincing than loss of self-control tales? Another way of approaching these questions, one I have experimented with in recent years, is to dramatise femicide by putting Shakespeare's Othello on trial for murder at the Old Bailey, loading him up with currently available defences and leaving it the audience as jury to deliver the verdict. *Othello on Trial*, the first play in a Theatre in Education project exploring the potential of the creative arts to engage with feminist anti-violence campaigns, provides yet another productive site on which to continue the never-ending feminist project of contesting law's truth.

3 Parker (1987: 96, 110–111).

4 Smart (1989: 14–19). Smart found no discernible patterns or signposts pointing to 'an inevitable future'.

'Murder'-suicide

I have identified 78 intimate partner femicides committed in England and Wales between January 1 2012 and December 31 2016 by men who then committed suicide or killed themselves while awaiting trial.[5] As in Chapter 1, only the victims are named here. The killers' identities are of no consequence save for one striking demographic that is pertinent to the question of who should play the defendant Othello in *Othello on Trial*. Unlike the cases that proceeded to court where black, Asian and Eastern European appear to have been overrepresented, the men who suicided after committing femicide were overwhelmingly white British as were their victims. For now all we need note is that the media reports of coronial inquests on which this study is based often refer to these cases inaccurately as 'murder-suicides'. As the coroner noted when recording a verdict that 79-year-old Edith Gravener had been unlawfully killed by her husband, the law did not allow coroners to say any more than that. It was for criminal courts not coronial inquests to say 'any party was murdered' let alone to 'give blame' and he for one definitely refused to assign blame in this 'extremely sad case' – there are 'occasions where one party loses one in the family but to lose two, it's extremely sad'.[6]

As with the cases that did proceed to court, the most common trigger for femicide-suicide was relationship breakdown, as it was on New Year's Day, 2012, in the very first case in this five-year study. When Susan McGoldrick tried to leave her partner to start a new life, he killed her along with her sister Alison and Alison's daughter Tanya in front of Susan's daughter Laura. Then he killed himself. Myrna Kirby's husband killed her then hanged himself. After a string of failed marriages he couldn't face another divorce. He told healthcare workers 'life would be perfect if the divorce was not going ahead'.[7] Julie Connaughton's husband bludgeoned her to death with a hammer before killing himself. He had researched murder on the internet by typing 'When someone p . . . you off, is it worth killing them?' into a search engine website when he discovered she was planning to divorce him.[8] Junella Valentine's former partner killed her then hanged himself when she told him their relationship was over and she was seeing someone else. Twenty-nine-year old Haley Stringer was stabbed to death by her estranged husband who then killed himself after she started a new relationship with a younger man. Two days before she was due to move out Nicola Langtree's husband killed himself after strangling her. He had researched 'murder-suicide' online after struggling to cope with the breakdown of their 11-year marriage. Stacey Henderson's initiation of divorce proceedings was the final straw for her husband. He killed her the following day. His brother said that he was 'very

5 Two died of natural causes while awaiting trial. Six children aged between 11 and 19 were also killed. The cases were identified from Karen Ingala Smith's lists, 2012–2016. References are provided only when there is a direct quotation from a newspaper report.

6 Mulligan (2016).

7 Rkaina (2014).

8 For Our Daughters (2013a).

troubled and devastated that his marriage was over'.[9] Jane McCartney's estranged husband felt the same way so he stabbed her with a bread knife before suiciding. The inquest into their deaths heard he 'felt humiliated about the collapse of his marriage and hated the fact that people would know about the break-up'.[10]

Guida Rufino pleaded for her life before she was knifed to death by her estranged partner a day after she finally ended their relationship. Claire Hart's husband killed her and their 19-year-old daughter days after she left him. His son described him as 'a "terrorist" living within our own home' who had subjected the family to years of domestic abuse. Leaving a 12-page suicide note saying 'Revenge is a dish served cold. Karma is a b-h' would surely have ruled out a loss of control defence had this killer survived.[11] Almost certainly a conviction for murder awaited given law's long-standing tradition of distinguishing cold-blooded homicide from partially excusable hot-blooded, spur of the moment, 'red mist' killings. The same outcome could be predicted for Andrea Johnson's husband, the coroner determining he did not kill her 'in a moment of madness or while his ability to control his actions was impaired' – the killing was deliberate.[12] The inquest into Annette Creegan's death came to the same conclusion. There was no evidence her partner was mentally impaired when he killed her. He knew what he was doing. It was a 'carefully executed' killing, the sort that attracts a conviction for murder.[13]

What about less carefully planned, more frenetic femicide-suicides committed by men suspecting, frequently without foundation, that their partners had been unfaithful? Yvonne Davies' husband had a 'fixation' about an affair his wife had in the past and uncovered flirtatious text messages she had sent to a male colleague. So he bludgeoned her with a hammer and then stabbed her to death before hanging himself.[14] Derisa Trenchard's husband thought she was having an affair despite there being no evidence to that effect. He beat her to death with a hammer before stabbing himself with a kitchen knife. The inquest heard they had a seemingly happy marriage until he become 'paranoid', constantly needing reassurance about their relationship.[15] Deborah Morris's husband killed himself while on remand in prison. Believing she was having an affair, he stabbed her 16 times, including a stab wound to the heart in their marital bed. It was not the first time he had entertained unfounded suspicions. The coroner said the couple had 'a pretty normal marriage' except for one 'explosive' incident, an assault on his wife followed by a suicide attempt 'undoubtedly caused' by his 'mental health issues'. There was 'considerable evidence' that the fatal attack was sparked by another 'paranoid incident' where he 'completely lost it for no logical or rational reason'.[16]

9 BBC (2015).
10 BBC (2016).
11 Ward (2017).
12 Walsh (2013).
13 Smith (2013).
14 Scheerhout (2015).
15 BBC (2014a).
16 Isle Of Wight County Press (2013).

Diminished responsibility?

What might have been the likely legal outcomes for these killers? Coronial inquiries as to whether killers were mentally impaired at the time of the homicidal 'incidents'; whether they suffered from fixations, neurotic neediness or experienced 'paranoid incidents' – in short whether they had mental health issues – raise very directly the question of whether these men would have entered diminished responsibility pleas had they lived to face court. As we saw in Chapter 1, law reformers concerned about the operation of provocation by sexual infidelity defences in intimate partner femicide cases replaced them with a new more restrictive loss of control defence to ensure more murder convictions. But what about the defence that medicalises criminal responsibility? The new diminished responsibility plea introduced by Section 52 of the *Coroners and Justice Act 2009* provides that a person not be convicted of murder if suffering from an abnormality of mental functioning that arises from a recognised medical condition and that substantially reduced their responsibility for their actions. This new wording appears to give more scope to the importance of expert psychiatric evidence in determining criminal responsibility but the jury remains the ultimate arbiter.[17]

Seventy-one-year old Hilda Oakland's fiancée hit her with a pole during an argument then strangled her with a rope 'to make sure' she was dead. He told the police 'I suppose I must have wanted her gone', that is, 'to be dead', while remaining calm and matter of fact. Charged with murder, he pleaded guilty to manslaughter by diminished responsibility at his first court appearance but hanged himself in his cell while awaiting trial.[18] Would his plea have succeeded? The coroner conducting the inquest into Margaret Mercati's death was quite certain her husband's would have had he not hanged himself after killing her. Believing she was having an affair, he strangled her. Noting that he suffered from a medical illness, the coroner said she did not think the fatalities were premeditated:

> I think for some reason he became enraged. I'm satisfied he was not suffering from what lawyers call 'insanity'. He was obviously not a well man . . . . He would have been found guilty to manslaughter due to diminished responsibility.[19]

The inquest heard that Mercati suffered from 'Othello Syndrome', a condition said to give him paranoid delusions that made him obsessively accuse his wife of 30 years of infidelity. A consultant psychiatrist who had treated him said he had responded well to anti-psychotic drugs. His fixation was lessening. But the treatment stopped when he was jailed for theft and the delusions continued following his release. Two hours before the couple were found dead, his wife had booked a medical appointment for him after he tried to force his way into their bedroom, believing she was in there with another man.

17 For assessments of the new plea see Reed and Bohlander (2011).
18 BBC (2017).
19 Murdermap (2015a).

Unsurprisingly, the case attracted considerable media attention. Reporting it the headline, 'Diamond thief who killed himself and wife had "Othello syndrome"', *The Telegraph* explained that the syndrome

> also known as morbid jealousy, is named after Shakespeare's tragic hero who kills his wife Desdemona after becoming consumed with jealousy. The condition affects men more than women but is relatively rare in both.[20]

It is indeed rare. To my knowledge 'Othello Syndrome' has never been introduced for a woman defendant in a murder case and I have come across only one English case where it was pleaded for a wife-killer – the 1979 case of *Vinagre*, an appeal against a life sentence imposed after a plea of guilty to manslaughter on the grounds of diminished responsibility.[21] We shall return to this case to consider whether the reformed diminished responsibility defence might provide, as the psychiatric evidence in the Mercati inquest suggests, an opening for the reintroduction of the syndrome.

Post-reform diminished responsibility cases

Moving on from cases where the perpetrator committed suicide, I have identified 75 intimate partner femicide cases in the five-year period from 2012 to 2016 where the defendant pleaded diminished responsibility. Prosecutors accepted 41 pleas of guilty to manslaughter in these cases, almost all from men suffering from psychosis, dementia or delusional disorders.[22] Many were given hospital orders, some indefinite, under the Mental Health Act, including Sandra Boakes' 80-year-old husband who killed her while suffering paranoid psychosis characterised by fears about her relationship with another man. Twenty-three-year-old Melissa Liddle's partner killed her while suffering from delusions that she was having an affair. The judge imposed a restriction order for 'the protection of the public' (read: women in relationships with men).[23] Others, like 24-year-old Gemma Finnigan's schizophrenic partner who was given a 20-year sentence for manslaughter, had to serve their sentence in prison.

At the other end of the scale, a four-year sentence was imposed on Josephine Gilliard's depressed elderly husband. This case attracted criticism, the feminist group *For Our Daughters* noting that 'many people have "moderate" and even severe depression, but very few batter and stab other people to death'. Querying how a man 'so apparently "frail" managed to mount' the prolonged attack on his wife, the group expressed concern about 'the apparently increasing number of elderly men who kill their wives' who are 'viewed with great sympathy by the courts, with the length of their marriages treated as a mitigating factor'. Elderly

20 Silverman (2013).
21 *R v Vinagre* (1979) 69 Cr App R 104.
22 One man was found not guilty by reason of insanity. Two were unfit to plead.
23 Hodgson (2016).

women, after all, are 'among the most vulnerable victims of domestic violence and are far more likely to be killed than elderly men'.[24] One, 83-year-old Josephine Williamson, was killed by her 88-year-old husband because he didn't want her to become a 'decrepit old hag' after her dementia worsened. He 'loved her too much for that'. So he pushed her down the stairs, strangled her and attempted suicide. His lawyer argued that he had 'acted under a depressive illness'. He was handed a two-year prison sentence, suspended for two years, the judge evidently unmoved by that prosecutor's description of the killer as 'a former professional vet who had put down hundreds of pets' yet 'chose to kill his wife in a manner that would have been terrifying and painful for her'.[25]

When a manslaughter plea is rejected the case proceeds to court. Unless there is clear evidence of mental impairment, these defendants are usually convicted of murder, juries evidently unimpressed with psychiatric testimony about medical conditions that allegedly diminish their criminal responsibility. In 30 of the 34 cases that went to court the defendants were found guilty of murder. At least half were departure cases. Lengthy minimum sentences for murder ranging from 20 to 28 years indicate judge and jury were on the same page. Nineteen-year-old Samantha Laney's jealous ex-boyfriend threatened to 'slice her open' after she ended their relationship. He stabbed her to death shortly when she arrived to collect her belongings from their flat, later telling the jury: 'I wanted to hurt her, just to make her feel how I felt'. A consultant forensic psychiatrist said he had an 'adjustment disorder', described as 'a reaction to a stressful life event, such as a bereavement or a separation' which 'fits in between more severe mental illness and a *normal reaction*'. It could, he said, cause 'quite dramatic behaviour'.[26] They jury rejected such fine distinctions, deciding the dramatic behaviour was murder. Sentence: life with a 21-year minimum. Jane Bartholomew's depressed former partner killed her because he could not accept that his 25-year relationship was over. Life with a 22-year minimum. Juries were also unimpressed by psychiatric evidence for two defendants claiming to be suffering from a narcissistic personality disorder which affected their mental functioning. Natalie Esack's estranged husband, a former policeman, stabbed her to death after he failed to come to terms with her new relationship. He had made numerous threats to kill her: 'you are a walking dead woman'.[27] Natasha Wake's former partner stabbed her multiple times in a frenzied attack to 'shut her up' as their children slept upstairs.[28] They received life sentences with 28 and 21-year minimum terms respectively.

Having argued that Samantha Medland's former partner had 'violently overreacted' towards her leaving him, 'lashing out at her in an explosive loss of temper', the prosecution welcomed the jury's verdict that he was not suffering from a recognised medical condition which substantially impaired his responsibility

24 For Our Daughters (2013b).
25 Willgress (2016).
26 McQueeney (2012) (my emphasis).
27 Stretch (2012).
28 Patient (2017).

for his actions when he killed her.[29] Life with a 25-year minimum. The *BBC News* reported Caroline Parry's murder under the banal, matter-of-fact headline 'Christopher Parry shot wife Caroline dead "because she left"'.[30] He said he only meant to shoot himself. Psychiatrists disagreed about his mental health. While two said he was severely depressed and this had substantially impaired his responsibility, a third concluded that his depressive illness before the shooting was 'mild-to-moderate'. The jury must have agreed with the latter opinion. At any rate, it accepted the prosecution account that the shooting was a carefully planned act of murder by a man 'not prepared to let go'.[31] He was sentenced to life with a 26-year minimum term.

Psychiatrists disagreed about whether Denisa Silmen's partner was mentally ill when he stabbed her to death, almost decapitating her. She had also been strangled and hit with an iron. In total there were 62 groups of injuries, many thought to have been inflicted after death. He was finally found fit to plead after a year-long investigation into his mental state. A witness testified he heard him tell the victim: 'If you will leave me, I shall kill you' and 'if I go to prison, I will pretend I'm mad. They will put me in hospital and I will get free from there'. The prosecution's case was that he killed her because he was enraged at the prospect of her finally leaving him and it was no coincidence that she was 'packing her suitcase' when he killed her. It was 'a killing committed in anger and jealousy'. The jury agreed. Sentencing him to life with a 20-year minimum, the judge said the murder was 'the product of narcissistic rage' at her departure and could 'properly be described as the slaughter of an innocent woman' – a victim's innocence evidently remaining a factor to be considered in post-reform cases.[32]

Others convicted of murdering exiting women after juries rejected their diminished responsibility defences received life sentences with minimums ranging from 14 to18 years which was still far higher than pre-reform cases. Michelle Giles' partner killed her because she wanted to end their relationship. He said he did not remember the attack because he had 'alcohol dependency syndrome'.[33] With a history of mental health problems, Clair Parrish's partner flew into a jealous homicidal rage when she attempted to end their relationship. Lorna McCarthy's estranged husband fatally stabbed her in the heart after discovering she had been using dating websites and had no interest in saving their relationship. Natalia Strelchenko had planned her escape from her husband's violence. Days before she was due to leave, he attacked her for the last time. He claimed a combination of severe depression, drink and tranquilisers meant he couldn't remember killing her. Ravinder Jutla's partner stabbed and bludgeoned her to death. He gave 'little indication as to why he killed her', leaving police to speculate that 'he may

29 BBC News (2013).
30 (2014b).
31 (2014c).
32 Murdermap (2015b).
33 McCarthy (2014).

have become aware that she was planning on ending their relationship'.[34] That, after all, is the predominant theme in intimate partner femicides and diminished responsibility cases are no exception. Jury rejections of the psychiatric classification of 'separation bereavement' as a reaction to a 'stressful life event' which fit between more severe mental illness and 'a normal reaction' *is* the new normal. Killing a departing woman, whether due to an alleged loss of self-control or mental impairment of some kind, is being registered as murder in twenty-first-century England and Wales.

Crime of passion's demise?

What though of exit cases complicated by a man learning of his wife's affair around the same time that he hears she is leaving him? That's why Mandy Gallear's husband said he killed her. He stabbed her to death a day after learning that she was planning to live with the new man, alleging she said 'I love him more than you'.[35] Prior to the reforms tightening up partial defences to murder, this was the kind of killing scenario that led to successful provocation by sexuality defences resulting in convictions for manslaughter and sentences ranging between four and seven years. Not now. This jury unanimously found him guilty of murder. As for killings committed in a non-departure context, two 'infidelity' cases resulting in murder convictions and life sentences with minimum terms of 22 and 24 years stand out. Christine Randall's fiancée killed her in a jealous rage mistakenly believing she was having an affair with his cousin. A unanimous jury rejected his claim of temporary insanity. Gemma Stevens' partner killed her over his unfounded suspicions she had been having sex with one of his friends. Psychiatrist evidence was submitted that that he was an alcoholic suffering from depression, anxiety, agoraphobia, suicidal thoughts and fears he would be sectioned. He also had amnesia. The jury was unmoved. In its view this 'most savage attack' was murder.[36]

The high failure rate for mental impairment defences supports the evidence in relation to loss of control defences discussed in Chapter 1 that most juries today have low tolerance for excuses offered by overwrought men who kill 'their' women. That 30 of 34 diminished responsibility defences failed suggests that the new tighter defence – one not part of the feminist law reform agenda – is operating even more effectively than the new loss of control defence that they advocated. Arguably though, the feminist challenge to the partial defence of provocation has had a flow on effect, impacting all intimate partner femicide cases. Read as discursive fields, the cases show that both reformed defences are achieving the feminist goal of preventing men getting away with murder, not least by exposing the 'unfaithful wife' narrative as code for 'separation bereavement' over

34 Murdermap (2015c).
35 Osuh (2017).
36 Derbyshire Times (2016).

a departing one. For the most part, juries are rejecting tales of woe precipitated by either unfaithful or exiting women.

However, there is lingering sympathy for some non-coping killers, notably three who drew on the all too familiar divorce narrative to plead not guilty of murder on the grounds of diminished responsibility due to separation-induced depression. Reihana Rezayi's husband became depressed, sensing her attitude towards him had changed. Was she cheating on him? Five days before he killed her she asked for a divorce. So when she insulted him during an argument he showed her a knife, ostensibly to 'quieten' her, but ended up stabbing her to death. His lawyer likened the offence to 'a crime of passion', the very crime the reformed law of murder was designed to curtail. After hearing a psychiatrist testify he would not have committed the offence but for an 'adjustment disorder', the jury cleared him of murder. The judge noted that while 'a human life has been lost', the marriage had been 'happy' and the defendant 'a good, placid and kind husband' who had been greatly distressed by changes in his life. He imposed a four-year sentence reminiscent of the risibly short sentences that had helped precipitate the reform movement.[37]

In a classic throwback to the taunting cases of old, Paula Clinton's husband said he killed her because she goaded him about his small penis and alcohol-induced bed-wetting and then tried to kill himself. She had wanted to leave him because of his excessive drinking. Tellingly, blood at the scene was daubed over papers marked 'ending a marriage'.[38] Hearing he had a depressive illness, the jury took less than three hours to find him not guilty of murder, testament to compassion's longevity in some quarters for men distressed by a departing, verbose wife. He received a 14-year sentence for manslaughter, the judge saying that while he could not rule he was dangerous to the public, he still bore 'a heavy responsibility' for the death of his wife despite his diminished responsibility.[39] In the third case, Sonita Nijhawan's Barclays banker husband felt he had 'no option' but to kill her when she asked for a divorce. With his 'battle with depression' spiralling out of control, he searched online how to commit suicide then knifed her 124 times, replacing the rings she had taken off on her body. He was found not guilty of murder by majority verdict. The judge was less sympathetic. Handing down an unusual life sentence for manslaughter for the 'brutal and sustained attack', he said there was 'a significant risk of causing serious harm to the public and in particular to any future intimate partner'.[40]

The only other man found not guilty of murder after pleading diminished responsibility was ordered to be detained in a secure hospital. He had killed his 23-year-old partner Natasha Wild after forming the paranoid belief she was having an affair with fashion guru Jimmy Choo. The judge said it was important not to 'lose sight of the fact a young woman died' but a psychiatrist had testified

37 Leicester Mercury (2013). See also Graham (2013).
38 Stewart (2013).
39 Stewart (2014).
40 Allen and Bishop (2016).

the killer was suffering with paranoid schizophrenia and so the emphasis had to be on treatment, not punishment.[41] Losing sight of victims is an occupational hazard for juries and judges in cases where the key issue is determining whether the fatal attack is symptomatic of an underlying illness. But the cases reveal that most juries and some judges are recognising that her right to leave trumps his right to a conviction for manslaughter. Law's authoritative discourse is starting to register a new truth about the twenty-first century English wife-killer and his victim. While exculpatory judgments about good, placid and kind husbands who just 'snap' when hurt are sometimes handed down today, the impassioned wife-killer of old is transforming into a dangerous offender, a pathetic and needy one at that, his credibility finally starting to falter in the face of the feminist challenge to law's long-standing truth that killing 'your' woman is a lesser form of homicide than murder.

As for the lawyer likening a departure case to a 'crime of passion', it needs emphasising that this was one of only four diminished responsibility pleas accepted by a jury out of the 34 submitted. Furthermore, as far as can be ascertained from media reports of the 400 post-reform cases that form the basis of my five-year study of English and Welsh intimate partner femicide cases, this was the only bid to resuscitate 'passion' as a defence. It is as if defence lawyers and juries alike have heeded the new legal status quo captured in the 2003 newspaper headline, '"Crime of passion" is no defence', heralding the planned shake up of the law of murder.[42] As Carol Smart acknowledges, sometimes law reform can be useful.[43] The feminist-inspired reforms revolutionising partial defences to murder is one of those times.

Othello on Trial

What though of Othello, Shakespeare's notoriously paranoid wife-killer? Plagued by unfounded suspicions about his wife, he fell into a jealous rage, killed her and then, on learning his suspicions were baseless, himself. *Othello on Trial*, the first play in my Theatre in Education public engagement project dramatising high levels of violence against women, puts him on trial for murder. Sub-titled *Or the Tragedy of Desdemona, the Wife* to signify the feminist inscription of victims (and not their killers) as the tragic figures of fictional and non-fictional intimate partner femicide, the play asks audiences acting as juries to deliver the verdict: murder or manslaughter? In this way, the play tests whether the age-old notion of a 'crime of passion' replete with its traditional cast of distraught killers, provocative victims and excusatory legal narratives has had its day in the court of public opinion. More broadly, *Act 3: The Jury* doubles as an open forum to discuss the key issues. Should extreme emotions – 'being wrought/Perplexed in the extreme' as

41 Halle-Richards (2017). A statement read on behalf of Natasha's mother said: 'She does not accept the diagnosis or the recommended order'.

42 Hinsliff (2003).

43 Smart (1989: 2).

Othello puts it, 'seeing red' as modern-day wife-killers put it – mitigate murder? Is it past time to question culturally based excuses for men's violence?

But first, why *Othello* and, by extension, why Shakespeare? Why recruit him for a feminist cause today? First, there's his unsurpassed cultural capital from which it follows, as one Shakespeare scholar suggests, that 'feminist revisions of his work, if accepted, could have real cultural – and therefore political – consequences'.[44] Second, politicised readings of the Shakespeare text that emerged in the late twentieth century and that are so reminiscent of Smart's reading of law featured Foucauldian readings of his work as discursive sites for contesting and denaturalising dominant truths. His plays in particular have been read as dramatisations of 'a world in which truth is discursively produced and authorised' by 'a set of practices, including theatre practices, which secure one understanding of the world at the expense of another'.[45] For the Shakespeare text and theatre practices substitute law and legal method and the parallels with Carol Smart's analytical approach in *Feminism and the Power of Law* becomes clear. As for *Othello*, it has been rated not only as 'a case study' for tracing the course of late twentieth century critical thinking about Shakespeare that registers all the concerns of newly emergent readings of gender, power, sexuality, race and empire; more, it was 'a key text in the works that introduced poststructuralist theory' to the interpretation of early modern English literature, thus underlining even more directly the link with Smart's work.[46]

Why though pick a play featuring a black protagonist, thereby running straight into a host of massively complex, intensely researched questions about Othello's identity and casting? After all, if – as has been suggested – *Hamlet* has 'ceded its place of favour and prominence' in the canon to *Othello*, it has done so because it speaks to contemporary racial questions.[47] However, it needs saying that *Othello*'s pivotal race question can over-determine readings of the play, blinding scholars and audiences alike to that fact that while it is absolutely essential to register – as *Othello on Trial* does – that Othello is not just a jealous husband but a Moor who is 'blackened' by racist language, it is also – as another Shakespearean scholar notes – 'equally important' to 'remain mindful' of what she calls 'women's issues'.[48] For *Othello* is at once a stunningly prescient challenge to the profoundly gendered or, as I prefer to say, sexed construction of 'crimes of passion' *and* 'a great test case for racial thinking'.[49] This makes Shakespeare's play an extraordinarily rich site for feminist appropriation – for exploring not only the discursive construction of the impassioned wife-killer and his time-honoured excuses for murder; but also for registering what the English law reformer Harriet Harman meant by calling provocation by sexual infidelity femicide 'our own version of honour killing'.[50]

44 Rackin (2016: 9–11).
45 Howard (1987: 173).
46 Orlin (2004: 1).
47 Smith (2016a: 107).
48 Rackin (2016: 9, 13).
49 Howard (2016: 112) and Howe (2008, 2014, 2015).
50 Quoted in Hinsliff (2008).

But crucially, it can become so only by transforming Othello into a white man, thereby targeting the very same dominant culture that law reformers named as a 'culture of excuses' for wife-killing.[51] Moreover, the overrepresentation of white men amongst suiciding wife-killers serves to reinforce the need to colour him white. As has been recognised in other murder-suicide studies, the man who annihilates his wife, sometimes his children and then himself is 'usually a middle-aged white man'.[52] And so it was with the suiciding men who killed their women partners in my study of femicide-suicides in England and Wales.

A fuller explication of the reasons for the shift from black protagonist in *Othello* to white defendant in *Othello on Trial* falls outside the scope of this chapter. Here I want to highlight what gets left out when the focus is exclusively on the question of Othello's blackness. In a paper titled 'Speaking of Race', Ian Smith analyses Othello's famous final speech, 'Speak of me as I am', reading it as expressing Othello's 'racial self-awareness' and concern about who will represent him fairly:

> among his white, Christian auditors, whom can he trust to tell his story or speak of him in a fair, balanced way? Who amongst them is sufficiently free of racial bias, stemming from stereotyping, that will allow for just representation?

In this reading, Othello is 'in effect, sensitive not just to the fact of murder' – (Smith assumes his crime is murder) – that 'casts him in the recognisable role of reckless black killer'. He is also sensitive to 'the perception that the black, racial stereotype of being "easily jealous" was the precipitating factor in his behaviour'.[53] In contrast, I read Shakespeare as gifting us a racialised protagonist who can, indeed must, be racialised as white when put on trial for murder today not only to avoid racist stereotyping of minority ethnic men but also to reflect the profile of today's femicide-suicides. Casting Othello as a white man makes whiteness 'visible and an object for critical interrogation' precisely as Smith deems necessary, registering whiteness as 'a fully realised racial category', thereby challenging the 'normative invisibility of whiteness'.[54]

But casting Othello as a white defendant in a murder trial does more. It queries what his crime is in English law while showing how Smith's analysis sells short the significance of Othello's final speech. In that masterpiece of dissembling self-justification, Othello dismisses his unfounded suspicions, jealous rage and fatal assault on his wife as 'Unlucky deeds', pleading with us to see him as 'one that loved not wisely but too well' and was 'perplexed in the extreme' when he killed her. 'Speak of me as I am', he begs, 'Nothing extenuate'. But in a court of law it is the job of the defence lawyer to do just that – to argue extenuating circumstances

51 Quoted in Scoop Independent News (2008).

52 Jack Levin, director or the Brudnick Centre on Conflict and Violence at Northeastern University in Boston, cited in Toolis (2002).

53 Smith (2016b: 119).

54 Smith (2016b: 119–122) and Smith (2016a: 107).

for homicidal men 'eaten up with passion'.[55] Accordingly, in my play, Othello pleads not guilty to murder on the grounds of loss of control and diminished responsibility, his lawyer drawing on extraordinarily prescient passages in *Othello* that foreshadow the legal defences to murder that would be deployed by wife-killers over the next 400 years.

Referencing the post-reform trials discussed in this chapter and in Chapter 1, his defence lawyer suspects it may be an uphill battle to argue loss of control given that provocation by sexual infidelity has been abolished as excuse for murder and today's juries are for the most part rejecting the new loss of control defence. Besides, Desdemona was 'innocent', so no blame to be apportioned there. On the other hand, there is evidence on which the defence might rely to argue that Othello suffered from an abnormality of mental functioning that arose from a recognised medical condition and that substantially reduced his responsibility for his actions as the new diminished responsibility plea requires. Shortly before killing his wife he had fits, falling to the ground in a trance and his greeting to Lodovici – 'You are welcome, sir, to Cyprus. Goats and monkeys!' – suggested a frail, deteriorating mental state, possibly a depressive illness. Has his mind been turned by the vision of Desdemona and Cassio copulating 'as prime as goats, as hot as monkeys?' Certainly, Lodovici found him unrecognisable from the man he knew in Venice. The once 'noble Moor' whom 'passion could not shake' was 'much changed' from the man he knew in Venice – 'Are his wits safe? Is he not light of brain?'[56]

Might this evidence lead Othello's defence to raise the 'Othello Syndrome?' As we have seen, the syndrome was revived at the 2013 *Mercati* coronial inquest, but the only time it was tried in an English court – in the 1979 wife-killing case of *Vinagre* – it did not fare well. The court felt the appellant was 'undoubtedly guilty of homicide of some kind', but what? Following the logic of the medical evidence about the syndrome, it seemed to be necessary to determine whether there was evidence that his wife had been unfaithful. If so, it was a 'straightforward case of a jealous husband'. If not, 'Othello Syndrome' might be raised because his jealousy had no basis. The concept did not appeal to the appellant judges. It was all too complicated.[57]

There is little indication that English courts are more receptive to syndrome evidence today. In 2015 a court of appeal described *Vinagre* as a case in which a lower court's acceptance of a plea on the basis of diminished responsibility was 'understandably thought to have been inappropriate on the facts'. The court also declared that if in the past courts felt that the question of diminished responsibility

55 Shakespeare (2008): *Othello* 3.3.396.

56 Shakespeare (2008): *Othello* 4.1.260–266 and 3.3.408. See further Howe (2014). See Howe (2014) and (2016).

57 *R v Vinagre* (1979) 69 Cr App R 106–7. But as the trial judge had accepted the plea, they decided that whatever the appellant 'may have been suffering from when he killed his wife, he was not likely to have a reoccurrence and so reduced his sentence from life to seven years' imprisonment. See further Howe (2013).

ought to be determined by a jury, it was now 'plainly of public benefit for pleas of guilty of manslaughter to be accepted' by prosecutors if the defendant's mental responsibility for the killing was substantially impaired. There may though be 'the very occasional case which is of such public profile or concern that it has to be the subject of full trial'.[58] Othello's is such a case. A greater test case for racial *and* feminist thinking about 'our' legal and cultural reception of intimate partner femicide is difficult to imagine.

Conclusion

For Shakespeare scholars, no other writer goes beyond his ability 'to challenge, to interrogate, to illuminate and to insist we rethink ourselves and our cultural heritage'.[59] That heritage includes provocation by infidelity femicide – 'our own version of honour killing' – one of many pressing social issues Shakespeare was content to dramatise and 'leave the rest to his audience'.[60] Having read femicide-suicides, diminished responsibility cases and *Othello* as Carol Smart counselled, as discursive sites for contesting law and 'our' culture's truths about intimate partner femicide, I too am content to leave the rest to *Othello on Trial's* audiences.

References

Bates, J. 2009 *Soul of the Age: A Biography of the Mind of William Shakespeare* London: Penguin Books.

Bevington, D. 2016 'The Classroom' in D. Callaghan and S. Gossett (eds.) *Shakespeare in Our Time* London: Bloomsbury.

Howard, J.E. 1987 'Renaissance Antitheatricality in the Politics of Gender and Rank in *Much Ado about Nothing*' in J.E. Howard and M.F. O'Connor (eds.) *Shakespeare Reproduced: The Text in History and Ideology* London: Routledge.

——— 2016 'Is Black So Base a Hue?' in D. Callaghan and S. Gossett (eds.) *Shakespeare in Our Time* London: Bloomsbury.

Howard, J.E. and O'Connor, M.F. (eds.) 1987 *Shakespeare Reproduced: The Text in History and Ideology* London: Routledge.

Howe, A. 2008 *Sex, Violence and Crime: Foucault and the 'Man' Question* Abingdon, Oxon: Routledge.

——— 2013 '"Red Mist" Homicide: Sexual Infidelity and the English Law of Murder (Glossing *Titus Andronicus*)' 3 *Legal Studies* 407.

——— 2014 'Dramatising Intimate Femicide: Petitions, Plays, Public Engagement (with a Shakespearean Gloss)' 26 *Canadian Journal of Women and the Law* 276.

——— 2015 '*Othello on Trial*: Engaging with the "Extra-Academic Outside World"' 2(1) *Queen Mary Human Rights Law Review* 133.

——— 2016 '*Othello on Trial*: The Politics of Performance' 42(2) *Australian Feminist Law Journal* 197.

58 *Robinson v Trinidad and Tobago* [2015] UKPC 34, paras 28–29.
59 Bevington (2016: 42).
60 Bates (2009: 116).

Ingala Smith, K. 2012–2016 'Counting Dead Women' https://kareningalasmith.com/counting-dead-women

Orlin, L.C. (ed.) 2004 *Othello, New Casebooks: Contemporary Critical Essays* New York: Palgrave MacMillan.

Parker, P. 1987 *Literary Fat Ladies: Rhetoric, Gender, Property* London: Methuen.

Rackin, P. 2016 'Why Feminism Still Matters' in D. Callaghan and S. Gossett (eds.) *Shakespeare in Our Time* London: Bloomsbury.

Reed, A. and Bohlander, M. (eds.) 2011 *Loss of Control and Diminished Responsibility* Farnham, Surrey: Ashgate.

Shakespeare, W. 2008 'Othello' in S. Greenblatt et al. (eds.) *The Norton Shakespeare* New York: W.W. Norton and Company.

Smart, C. 1989 *Feminism and the Power of Law* London: Routledge.

Smith, I. 2016a 'We Are Othello: Speaking of Race in Early Modern Studies' 67(1) *Shakespeare Quarterly* 104.

——— 2016b 'Speaking of Race' in D. Callaghan and S. Gossett (eds.) *Shakespeare in Our Time* London: Bloomsbury.

Newspapers (all accessed March 18 2018)

Allen, D. and Bishop, R. 2016 'Banker Who Beat Wife to Death after She Demanded Divorce Was Found Stabbing Himself in Pool of Blood' *Mirror* www.mirror.co.uk/news/uk-news/banker-who-beat-wife-death-9374879

BBC News 2013 'Ty Medland Guilty of Murdering Wife in Brighton Street' www.bbc.com/news/uk-england-sussex-23467176

——— 2014a 'Jonathan and Derisa Trenchard Inquest: Husband "Paranoid" about Relationship' www.bbc.com/news/uk-england-cornwall-28677760

——— 2014b 'Christopher Parry Shot Wife Caroline Dead "Because She Left"' www.bbc.com/news/uk-wales-south-east-wales-28020746

——— 2014c 'Christopher Parry Jailed over Murder of Caroline Parry' www.bbc.com/news/uk-wales-south-east-wales-28261224

——— 2015 'Stacey Henderson Had "Started Divorce" before Death Stabbing' www.bbc.com/news/uk-wales-south-east-wales-34790974

——— 2016 'Retired Soldier "Stabbed Wife before Gassing Them Both"' www.bbc.com/news/uk-england-devon-38053374

——— 2017 'Man Killed Fiancée in Christmas Present Row' www.bbc.com/news/uk-england-devon-38747452

Derbyshire Times 2016 '"Bully" Gary Tyson Jailed for Life for Killing Gemma Stevens' www.derbyshiretimes.co.uk/news/murder-trial-guilty-bully-gary-tyson-jailed-for-life-for-killing-gemma-stevens-1-8182586

For Our Daughters 2013a 'Julie Connaughton' https://forourdaughters.co.uk/index.php/julie-connaughton/

——— 2013b 'Josephine Gilliard' https://forourdaughters.co.uk/index.php/josephine-gilliard/

Graham, S. 2013 'Are These Domestic Violence Sentences Fair' sarah-graham.co.uk/2013/12/18/are-these-domestic-violence-sentences-fair/

Halle-Richards, S. 2017 'Student Natasha Wild Was Stabbed to Death by Paranoid Boyfriend Who Believed She Was Having Affair' *Manchester Evening News* www.manchestereveningnews.co.uk/news/greater-manchester-news/student-stabbed-death-paranoid-boyfriend-13827864

Hinsliff, G. 2003 'Harman and Law Lord Clash over Wife Killers' *The Guardian* www.theguardian.com/politics/2008/nov/09/harriet-harman-defence-of-provocation

Hodgson, B. 2016 'Family of Melissa Liddle Say Killer's Sentence Is the Best They Could Hope for' *ChronicleLive* www.chroniclelive.co.uk/news/north-east-news/family-melissa-liddle-say-killers-10939482

Isle of Wight County Press 2013 'Coroner's Tribute after Family's Devastating Loss' www.iwcp.co.uk/news/news/coroners-tribute-after-familys-devastating-loss-49879.aspx

Leicester Mercury 2013 'Leicester Man Jailed for Killing Wife' https://ssristories.org/leicester-man-jailed-for-killing-wife-leicester-mercury/

McCarthy, N. 2014 'Jilted Solihull Man Murdered Partner after She Told Him Relationship Was over' *Birmingham Mail* www.birminghammail.co.uk/news/midlands-news/jilted-solihull-man-murdered-partner-7715373

McQueeney, K. 2012 'I Just Wanted to Hurt Her Because She'd Hurt Me' *Daily Mail* www.dailymail.co.uk/news/article-2192118/Samantha-Laney-killing-Thomas-Dalton-tells-court-did-mean-kill-ex-girlfriend-stabbed-her.html

Mulligan, S. 2016 'Inquest Hears "Extremely Sad Case" of Pensioner Who Strangled His Wife and Then Took His Own Life at Carr Mill Dam' *Bolton News* www.theboltonnews.co.uk/news/14328510.Inquest_hears__extremely_sad_case__of_pensioner_who_strangled_his_wife_and_then_took_his_own_life_at_Carr_Mill_Dam/

Murdermap 2015a 'Case: Murder and Suicide in Bloomsbury: Margaret Mercasti' www.murdermap.co.uk/pages/cases/case.asp?CID=514709944&VID=944&Case=Murder-and-suicide-in-Bloomsbury:-Margaret-Mercati

——— 2015b 'Case Killed by Jealous Boyfriend: Denisa Silmen' www.murdermap.co.uk/pages/cases/case.asp?CID=281428934&VID=1196&Case=Killed-by-jealous-boyfriend:-Denisa-Silmen

——— 2015c 'Case: Killed by her Partner: Ravinder Jutla' www.murdermap.co.uk/pages/cases/case.asp?CID=853971458&VID=1248&Case=Killed-by-her-partner:-Ravinder-Jutla

Osuh, C. 2017 'Mum Stabbed in the Heart by Husband after Affair Told Him "I Still Love You" Moments before She Died' *Manchester Evening News* www.manchestereveningnews.co.uk/news/greater-manchester-news/mum-stabbed-heart-husband-after-12845679

Patient, D. 2017 'Soldier Knifed Lover to Death "Just to Shut Her Up" and Told Kids Blood Was "Ketchup"' *Daily Star* www.dailystar.co.uk/news/latest-news/603371/Soldier-knifed-to-lover-death-kids-blood-ketchup-Bournemouth-Dorset

Rkaina, S. 2014 'Pensioner Killed Fifth Wife Then Hanged Himself Because He Couldn't Face Another Divorce' *Mirror* www.mirror.co.uk/news/uk-news/pensioner-killed-fifth-wife-hanged-4117980

Scheerhout, J. 2015 'Yvonne Davies: Jealous Husband "Hanged Himself after Stabbing PR Boss Wife to Death in Rage over Her Affair"' *Mirror* www.mirror.co.uk/news/uk-news/yvonne-davies-jealous-husband-hanged-5942554

Scoop Independent News 2008 'UK Murder Law Reforms: Provocation Not an Excuse' www.scoop.co.nz/stories/WO0807/S00844/uk-murder-law-reforms-provocation-not-an-excuse.htm

Silverman, R. 2013 'Diamond Thief Who Killed Himself and Wife Had "Othello Syndrome"' *Telegraph* www.telegraph.co.uk/news/uknews/law-and-order/10273979/Diamond-thief-who-killed-himself-and-wife-had-Othello-syndrome.html

Smith, L. 2013 'Canal Boat Horror: Murderer Strangled His Partner Then Kept Victim's Daughter on Board for Six Days' *Mirror* www.mirror.co.uk/news/uk-news/norfolk-broads-murder-john-didier-1561791

Stewart, G. 2013 'Man Stabbed His Wife to Death after Manhood Jibe' *Liverpool Echo* www.liverpoolecho.co.uk/news/liverpool-news/liverpool-man-stabbed-wife-death-6185608

——— 2014 'Businessman Who Stabbed His Wife to Death Jailed for 14 Years' *Liverpool Echo* www.liverpoolecho.co.uk/news/liverpool-news/john-clinton-jailed-14-years-6684880

Stretch, W. 2012 '"Tick Tock, Tick Tock . . . You Are Just a Walking Dead Woman": Ex-Cop's Threat to His Wife' *Mirror* www.mirror.co.uk/news/uk-news/ex-policeman-ivan-esack-stabbed-estranged-1485304

Toolis, K. 2002 'When Fathers Murder Their Families' *The Times* 19 September.

Walsh, P. 2013 'Cromer Double Death Inquest Verdict' *Eastern Daily Press* www.edp24.co.uk/news/cromer-double-death-inquest-verdict-hearing-hears-how-cromer-council-leader-keith-johnson-made-deliberate-decision-to-kill-his-wife-andrea-and-then-himself-1-2800469

Ward, V. 2017 'Killer Who Shot His Wife and Daughter Was "Controlling, Vitriolic Bully" Say Sons' *Telegraph* www.telegraph.co.uk/news/2017/06/01/killer-shot-wife-daughter-controlling-vitriolic-bully-say-sons/

Willgress, L. 2016 'Retired Vet Killed His Wife, 89, Because He Did Not Want Her to Become a "Decrepit Old Hag"' *Telegraph* www.telegraph.co.uk/news/2016/08/04/retired-vet-killed-his-wife-89-because-he-did-not-want-her-to-be/

5 Fighting femicide in Turkey – feminist legal challenges

Daniela Alaattinoğlu and Cemre Baytok

Introduction

This chapter provides an account of feminist femicide watching and litigation in Turkey to illustrate the kind of feminist engagement with law in practice that Carol Smart's *Feminism and the Power of Law* inspires. Our analysis is particularly indebted to Smart's view of law constituting 'a discursive field'.[1] Rejecting the idea of law as a simple tool of oppression, looking instead at how it 'constitutes a kind of institutionalised and formalised site of power struggles'– always already discursive struggles – Smart acknowledges that law 'remains an important strategic element in political confrontations'.[2] Embracing this approach, we shall analyse femicide cases that illustrate the challenges facing Turkish feminists engaging with law today. The case analysis provides yet another site on which to continue the kind of feminist work that Smart advocated, challenging law's discursive construction of the 'truth' about femicide. Informed by observations made through participation in feminist femicide watching, the chapter provides insider insights into the operation of feminist challenges to law's received truths.[3]

Feminist struggle in the field of law

Since the publication of *Feminism and the Power of Law* feminists have developed and expanded femicide litigation practices.[4] In Turkey, feminists now go beyond the role of observers to take an active role in the legal process, including that of acting as representatives for the families of femicide victims. The establishment of feminist court watches in Turkey and elsewhere provide a space for feminists to monitor

1 Smart (1989: 49). See also Bourdieu's account of the juridical field, Bourdieu (1987).
2 Smart (1989: 138).
3 The chapter builds on Cemre Baytok's observations as a feminist activist in Turkey. Baytok (2012). The term 'femicide' is generally not used by feminists in Turkey who usually refer to these killings as 'women's killings', with the aim of highlighting their systematic nature. All translations from Turkish are ours.
4 Colker (1990); Burns (1990); Cahn (1991); Bottomley and Conaghan (1993); and Vojdik (1998).

and report on femicide cases. These watches have gone from being a relatively marginalised phenomenon, to becoming practiced at a global level, with the United Nations Special Rapporteur on Violence against Women, Dubravka Šimonović, recently recommending that a femicide watch be established in every country.[5]

Feminist activists in Turkey have been analysing the link between men's violence against women and law for the last thirty years. In the late 1980s, they organised protests and campaigns challenging different forms of violence against women. One important example was the demonstrations in May 1987, when women rallied in protest at a judge's use of the Turkish proverb 'a woman should always have a stick on her back and a child in her belly' to ground his rejection of a woman's request for a divorce from her husband based on his violence.[6] Such campaigns were pivotal to the development of Turkish feminist movements.[7] Over time, law gradually became a part of the feminist struggle with the growing recognition of how profoundly gendered legal regulations and court decisions are.

In the 2000s, feminists started to challenge law in practice in a more organised manner, engaging in litigation and monitoring cases both as lawyers and non-lawyers in recognition that collective organisation was essential. Law and courts became compelling spaces, providing multiple stages of encounter, not restricted to contesting perpetrator-friendly court decisions in cases of violence against women. Feminists challenged the judicial process at every stage of the complaint, trial and decision process as experienced by women taking action to escape men's violence. Importantly, their engagement in femicide trials as lawyers and spectators has exposed gendered power dynamics of both the family and the courtroom.

The same decade brought with it legislative change. Challenging the Turkish Penal Code in 2004 was a galvanising moment. Feminists formed a platform to intervene in the reform process, insisting on changing critical articles on child abuse, sexual harassment and the notion of provocation. When the Penal Code was amended the same year, it took into consideration much of the feminist criticism. It did not however, take up feminism criticism of the mitigation clause 'unjust provocation' in the Turkish Penal Code. The clause allows for a substantial sentence reduction for 'any person who commits an offence in a state of anger or severe distress caused by an unjust act'.[8] Given its open formulation, judges may implement it to partially excuse defendants in intimate partner femicide cases if they have been 'provoked' by their victims, an implementation which feminists have criticised for years as being gender-biased.[9]

How the clause operates is illustrated in the following judgments handed down by the Turkish Court of Cassation *(Yargıtay)*. In the first, the defendant had killed his sister. The judge was concerned with the behaviour of the victim, focusing on rumours that she was cheating on her husband, leading to the relationship

5 ACUNS (2017: 1).
6 Örer (2007) and Armutçu (2007).
7 Sirman (1989).
8 Türk Ceza Kanunu [Turkish Penal Code] No. 25611 (2004), Section 29.
9 See Koğacıoğlu (2004); Eyüboğlu (2009); and Alaattinoğlu (2016).

between the families being 'completely cut'. In the judge's view, this 'caused the family of the victim to blame her for the lowering of family honour and dignity', later leading to her brother killing her.[10] In another case, a wife-killing, the judge noted that even though the defendant's mother 'bears witness that the victim was a clean and honourable bride', the victim might have caused her own death. After all, the defendant claimed his wife 'had extramarital relations twice, which made him angry on the night of the events'.[11] In the end, the court did not apply the 'unjust provocation' clause in these cases. Nevertheless, the cases demonstrate that when the court considers the application of the clause, it leads to a discourse that scrutinises the behaviour of the victim, thereby diverting attention away from the defendant and his actions. As in other jurisdictions, the victim-blaming provocation narrative is critical to the success of the defence strategy of minimising the seriousness intimate partner femicide as a crime.[12] Accordingly, the 'unjust provocation' clause remains an important site of feminist engagement with law in Turkey.

In another significant development, Turkey has also come under the spotlight of international human rights during the last decade. *Opuz v. Turkey*, litigated by a feminist lawyer before the European Court of Human Rights, was a landmark femicide case.[13] Nahide Opuz's ex-husband had physically, mentally and emotionally terrorised her and her mother for years. Finally, he killed her mother. Handing down its judgment in 2009, the court decided that the failure of the Turkish state to protect victims and adequately prosecute and sentence perpetrators of domestic violence was a violation of the European Convention on Human Rights. More precisely, the court concluded that Turkey had violated the victims' right to life, the prohibition of torture and ill treatment and the prohibition of discrimination.[14] Importantly, the European Court of Human Rights highlighted the responsibility of the state authorities to actively prevent domestic violence and femicide:

> the Court notes that despite the deceased's complaint that H.O. had been harassing her, invading her privacy by wandering around her property and carrying knives and guns . . . the police and prosecuting authorities failed either to place H.O. in detention or to take other appropriate action in respect of the allegation that he had a shotgun and had made violent threats with it . . . the Court observes that it is not in fact apparent that the authorities assessed the threat posed by H.O. and concluded that his detention was

10 The Turkish Court of Cassation, Decision no. 2009/293, File no. 2008/10901 (2009). Åkers (2014: 62–63).

11 The Turkish Court of Cassation, Decision no. 2012/1724, File no. 2010/3234 (2012). Åkers (2014: 63).

12 For critiques of the discursive construction of 'provocation' in Australian and Engish courts, see Howe (2012, 2013, 2014). See also Alaattinoğlu (2016) and Åkers (2014).

13 European Court of Human Rights, *Opuz v. Turkey*. Application no. 33401/02 (2009).

14 As protected in ECHR Articles 2, 3 and 14 in conjunction with 2 and 3. European Court of Human Rights, *Opuz v. Turkey*. Application no. 33401/02 (2009).

> a disproportionate step in the circumstances; rather the authorities failed to address the issues at all.[15]

The court also highlighted that as a member state of the Council of Europe, Turkey must prioritise victims' right to life when addressing cases of domestic violence:

> In any event, the Court would underline that in domestic violence cases perpetrators' rights cannot supersede victims' human rights to life and to physical and mental integrity.[16]

The case, a crucial reference point for Turkish and European feminist legal criticism, was a stepping stone for the establishment of the 2011 Council of Europe Convention on Preventing and Combating Violence against Women and Domestic Violence, the so-called Istanbul Convention. Through the treaty, state failure to actively prevent violence against women according to the principle of due diligence – taking reasonable steps to avoid violation of the convention – has become subject to further legal scrutiny, both regionally and domestically.[17]

Femicide has also been subject to scrutiny in the Turkish media. According to official numbers reported by the newspaper *Bianet*, the femicide rate in Turkey had increased by 1,400 per cent between 2002 when 66 women were reported to be killed and 2009 when an alarming number of 953 women were killed.[18] Importantly, misogynist court decisions in femicide cases were also reported on the news. A headline in the newspaper *BirGün* in 2008 read: 'Out of 59 "honour" murders, 46 benefited from "provocation"'.[19] Under the headline 'The Injustice of Unjust Provocation', another newspaper also reported on the problematic use of the unjust provocation clause that has been long criticised by feminists. Among other cases, it referred to the murder of Sevgi Aguş by her husband in front of their two children. In court, her husband benefited from the 'unjust provocation' clause based on the fact that his wife had worn jeans and asked another man what time it was in what he said was 'a flirtatious way'.[20] As a result of this heightened media attention, feminists have been galvanised to once again prioritise violence against women, femicide included, via collective litigation and engagement with the judicial process.

15 European Court of Human Rights, *Opuz v. Turkey*. Application no. 33401/02 (2009) para 147.
16 European Court of Human Rights, *Opuz v. Turkey*. Application no. 33401/02 (2009) para 147.
17 See Bianet (2009). On the principle of due diligence, see Hasselbacher (2010) and Edwards (2011). Internationally, the Inter-American Court case 'Cotton Field' from 2009 is important for due diligence and violence against women. Inter-American Court of Human Rights, 16 November 2009, *Gonzalez et al ('Cotton Field') v. Mexico, Preliminary Objection, Merits, Reparations and Costs*. Series C No. 205. See also Chapter 3 in this volume.
18 Bianet (2011). Most of the cases are intimate partner femicides.
19 BirGün (2007).
20 Savaş (2008).

When Turkish feminist activist Sevim Zarif was killed in 2007 by her ex-husband on the street eleven years after their divorce, feminists and feminist lawyers intensified their engagement with the law. They publicised and took on her case, legally representing the relatives of the victim whom the Turkish judicial system recognises as indirect victims. A press release by the Socialist Feminist Collective provided a Smart-inspired 'alternative reality to the version which is manifested in legal discourse'.[21] Addressing themselves as a party in his trial, they insisted her killing was 'not just any murder' as 'every single one of us is under the threat of being victimised in this kind of murder'. Accordingly:

> We are a party in the trial, as it is in our interest that these types of crimes are tried and punished. We are a party in the trial, as we oppose the patriarchal system that lets men violate women's rights to their own bodies and lives in the name of honour.[22]

Collectivising the trial – 'we are a party' – to express the feminist interest at stake was central to the feminist counter-discourse. Sevim Zarif's case was picked up by Turkish media.[23] This type of feminist challenge, aiming at affecting the awareness of the judiciary through press releases and feminist litigation, is an excellent example of feminist resistance to law in practice as advocated by Smart.[24] The judge considered Sevim's killing to be an aggravated homicide, without extenuating circumstances. Not approving the claim of unjust provocation, the judge sentenced the ex-husband to life in prison.[25]

For Turkish feminists involved in court watches and litigation, femicide is a systematic political problem that is irreducible to individual acts.[26] This is so regardless of the alleged 'cause', whether it be honour, custom, divorce, cheating, wearing a skirt or not passing the salt at the dinner table; and whoever the perpetrator, Turkish, Kurdish, unemployed, worker or teacher and whatever their political persuasion. When engaging with femicide trials, feminists politicise not only killings *per se*, but previous violent episodes such as routine degradation, threats or insults at home and sexual violence. Crucially, by using the slogan 'man hits, state protects', they have highlighted how law operates as what Smart referred to as a 'gendering strategy' which constructs people's bodies and lives differently depending on their gender.[27] In short, men who are violent against their partners and ultimately kill them are often protected by law in practice.[28]

21 Smart (1989: 160).
22 Sosyalist Feminist Kolektif (2007).
23 Bianet (2008a, 2008b).
24 Smart (1989).
25 Bianet (2008a).
26 On politicising trials of violence against women see Ulmschneider (1995).
27 Smart (1989: 90–98) and Smart (1992: 34–39).
28 Hacıvelioğlu (2010) and Eyüboğlu (2010). See also European Court of Human Rights, *Opuz v. Turkey*. Application no. 33401/02 (2009).

Şefika Etik, a case study

Şefika Etik was killed by her husband in October 2011. The case, like many other Turkish femicides, was reported in the leading newspaper *Habertürk*. What separated the Şefika case from the others was that the newspaper published a photo of her naked body lying in a pool of blood with a knife in her back on its first page. Public reaction was divided. Some supported the newspaper's 'courage'. Others condemned the photo as pornographic. *Habertürk* insisted that printing such photos were a strategy to make femicide more publicly visible.[29] Feminists staged a protest outside of the newspaper's premises in Istanbul, arguing that focusing on nudity and violence obscured the role of the perpetrators and the state's failure to protect women.

Şefika had been married to İbrahim Etik for 19 years. They had two children. He battered her throughout their marriage. In September 2011 she moved to a women's shelter, a place that should be safe – in practice, confidential – according to the Istanbul Convention, which Turkey has ratified.[30] But he knew its location and went there to bring his wife back home. On the evening of her return, he stabbed her while she was showering. Only hours later, her naked and blood-splattered picture appeared on the newspaper. Months after Şefika's death, two young and inexperienced lawyers hired by Şefika's family – recognised as indirect victims by the Turkish judicial system – to represent them sent out a group email, asking for help. The email mobilised feminists all over the country and requested support from feminist lawyers to intervene in Şefika's killer's trial. Feminist lawyers did get involved – providing the lawyers hired by Şefika's relatives with legal analysis and feminist argumentation – perceiving the case as a valuable opportunity to highlight the broader problem of men's violence against women.

During the first oral hearing of the trial in the first-instance Manisa Criminal Court, three hours of testimonies addressing the question of whether Şefika had cheated on her husband, were full of attacks on her personal life. The accused testified that he had forgiven his wife but she continued to cheat on him. In a blind rage, he lost his self-control and killed her, though he only remembered having stabbed her once. Focusing on her inappropriate behaviour, his violence appeared less significant than her performance as a spouse and mother. This gave the impression that the final fatal attack – his lost control – was the logical consequence of her actions:

> When he talked about the events with his wife in the bathroom and she repeatedly said 'I talk to other men because you neglect me', he suddenly lost his temper and first stabbed his wife in her belly with the knife he had got from the kitchen, and then he did not remember.[31]

29 For a critical analysis of the media reporting of Şefika Etik's murder, see Toker and Altun (2015).

30 Council of Europe Convention on Preventing and Combating Violence against Women and Domestic Violence, 11 May 2011. CETS No. 210, Article 23.

31 Manisa Criminal Court, File No. 2011/246, Decision No.2012/153 (2012).

Şefika's family's lawyers challenged the defence's account, repeatedly telling the court that even if she had cheated on her husband that could not be an excuse for murder. They argued that 'adultery' in marriage is a matter of the Civil Code, not the Penal Code. As such it may be grounds for divorce, but never murder.[32] They also challenged the defendant's claim of 'unjust provocation', a challenge taken up and reported by the feminist watch present in the courtroom.[33] But tellingly, the prosecution disagreed with the feminist legal argumentation presented by the lawyers hired by Şefika's family. Underscoring just how difficult it is to contest the hegemonic notion that women provoke their own demise, he insisted that it was appropriate to apply the clause of 'unjust provocation' to her actions, specifically pointing to her phone conversations with other men overheard by the defendant.[34]

In all testimonies in the first hearing, the focus shifted from her husband's violence to Şefika's actions. Her life became constructed as provocation, justifying her untimely violent death through the words of the witnesses in the courtroom, most tellingly in her son's testimony which was uncritically reproduced in the judgment:

> There were times when he caught his mother Şefika talking to the landlord Ahmet Yavaş. To make sure that she had talked to Yavaş, he had immediately called the last dialled number from her telephone. He understood from the voice that responded that it was the landlord Ahmet Yavaş . . . when his mother had asked 'what will we do when your father comes', he had said 'I will tell my father what you have done'.[35]

In policing his mother's sexuality, her son becomes complicit in his father's fatal attack. But this was of no consequence to the court which was focused solely on the woman's contribution to her own death.

On the last day of the hearings, feminist activists gathered in front of the courthouse, shouting familiar slogans such as 'true justice, not male justice'. The defence asked for the unjust provocation clause to be applied, pointing to Şefika's phone calls to other men. The presiding judge rejected this application, deciding instead to apply the section on aggravated homicide in the Turkish Penal Code.[36] Şefika's murder was deemed as aggravated on three grounds – the killing was premeditated, committed with brutality or through torment and had a customary motive, namely family honour.[37] The perpetrator was given life imprisonment without any reductions.

32 On the criticism of adultery as provocation in criminal law, see Howe (2012).

33 See Sosyalist Feminist Kolektif (2012).

34 Manisa Criminal Court, File No. 2011/246, Decision No.2012/153 (2012).

35 Manisa Criminal Court, File No. 2011/246, Decision No.2012/153 (2012).

36 Türk Ceza Kanunu [Turkish Penal Code] No. 25611 (2004), Section 82/1-a-d-k.

37 This was justified through the testimonies of the perpetrator and the family members. It was also based on the geographical origin of the family (eastern Turkey). The latter ground can be criticised as a form of alterity. More on this criticism, see Koğacıoğlu (2004) and Åkers (2014).

This was the court's reasoning. While the Turkish Civil Code obliges married couples to be loyal to their spouse, this obligation does not mean that

> individuals cannot talk on the phone with people other than their family, cannot have friends they socialise with, talk with others on the Internet, go outside alone, or go to places like cafes and cinemas.[38]

Importantly, the court pointed out that 'these actions cannot be discussed in this context' – referring to the murder trial – 'since they are within the framework of an individual's rights and freedoms'. Unjust provocation should *not* be applied to Şefika's murder or any case where

> some families and men believe that women's bodies and emotions are theirs to determine and govern, committing murder on the grounds that their reputation and honour have been tainted due to the actions of a female family member, sister, wife or close relative, the perpetrators finding these actions contrary to dominant traditions and conventions of the social environment they live in, that is, when a murderer considers these reasons as factors that render the murder partially justified and excusable.[39]

Thus did the court signal its aversion to applying provocation clauses in cases where controlling 'families and men' kill women. Moreover, this aversion was not limited to Şefika's case. Similar tendencies – with judges rejecting provocation clauses – have been seen in the trials of the men who murdered Ayşe Yılbaş, Sevim Zarif, Nejla Yıldız, Ayşe Paşalı, Demet Eygi, Tuğçe Anlaş – all cases of femicide that feminists in Turkey have litigated and watched during the last decade.

Conclusion

For Carol Smart 'law should remain an important focus for feminist work, not in order to achieve law reforms (although some may be useful) but to challenge such an important signifier of masculine power'.[40] Through feminist litigation, and femicide watches, Turkish feminists have been doing just that, openly challenging the assumed anonymity and objectivity of the legal process; rendering victims' narratives visible and problematising judgments based on misogynist assumptions. The Şefika Etik case demonstrates that law's received truth about violence against women, including intimate partner femicide, can be successfully challenged. Most importantly, judges are generally not applying the clause of unjust provocation in cases that are monitored by feminists today.[41]

38 Manisa Criminal Court, File No. 2011/246, Decision No. 2012/153 (2012).
39 Manisa Criminal Court, File No. 2011/246, Decision No. 2012/153 (2012) – our emphasis.
40 Smart (1989: 2).
41 Sosyalist Feminist Kolektif (2011).

As in other jurisdictions discussed elsewhere in this book, Turkish feminists are transforming femicide cases into 'ideal sites' for discursive feminist engagement, converting them into what Adrian Howe calls 'a critical, pedagogical means of mobilising consciousness about emotional excuses for violence against women'.[42] Thanks to feminist campaigns such as 'We are revolting against women killings' and 'We will stop the femicides', there is a growing awareness of femicides in Turkey today. But we have a long way to go. Seen against the geo-political instability of the region and the state of emergency under an increasingly authoritarian regime, the prevention, prosecution and punishment of femicides in Turkey have not been given political priority. Apart from anecdotal references to the seriousness of the problem by individual politicians, there has been little reaction from the Turkish Government and authorities to feminist criticism and activism around femicides. Existing legal measures such as protection orders provided by the 2012 Act to Protect the Family and Prevent Violence against Women are reportedly not used to their full extent. Nor are they backed up by law enforcement which often turns a blind eye to violence against women in favour of 'family reconciliation'.[43]

This said, as Smart suggested 30 years ago, feminist legal engagement focusing on law as a discursive field challenges legal practices, provides alternative interpretation of laws and can lead to important changes in how law is practised. During times of global political populism and anti-feminism, such grass-root feminist initiatives and feminist awareness-raising efforts and struggles offer grains of hope.

References

Academic Council on the United Nations System (ACUNS) 2017 *Femicide: Establishing a Femicide Watch in Every Country* Vienna: Academic Council on the United Nations System (ACUNS) Publications.

Åkers, D. 2014 *Killed by Hatred or Killed by Love? An Intersectional Challenge to Legal Constructions of Gendered Violence in Finland and Turkey* Saarbrücken: Lambert Academic Publishing.

Alaattinoğlu, D. 2016 'Hedersvåld? Rättsliga konstruktioner av *den andra* i Finland och Turkiet [Honour Killing? Legal Constructions of *the Other* in Finland and Turkey]' 152(1–2) *Tidskrift utgiven av Juridiska föreningen i Finland* 93.

Al-Monitor 2017 *Turkey's Deepening Tragedy of Murdered Women* www.al-monitor.com/pulse/afp/2017/07/turkey-rights-women-murder.html

Armutçu, E. 2007 'Türkiye'de feminist hareket [The Feminist Movement in Turkey]' *Hürriyet* www.hurriyet.com.tr/kelebek/turkiyede-feminist-hareket-6505867

Baytok, C. 2012 *Political Vigilance in Court Rooms: Feminist Interventions in the Field of Law* Istanbul: Boğaziçi University, unpublished MA thesis:

Bianet 2008a 'Sevim Zarif'I Öldüren Eski Eşi İki Kez Müebbet Hapis Cezası [Two Life Sentences for the Ex-Husband Who Killed Sevim Zarif]' bianet.org/bianet/

42 Howe (2013: 143).

43 Ailenin Korunması ve Kadına Karşı Şiddetin Önlenmesine dair Kanun [Turkish Act to Protect the Family and Prevent Violence against Women] No. 6284 (2012); Al-Monitor 2017.

insan-haklari/110269-sevim-zarifi-olduren-eski-esine-iki-kez-muebbet-hapis-cezasi
——— 2008b 'Sevim Zarif'i Öldüren Eski Eşi "Haksız Tahrik İndirimi" Almaya Çalışyor [The Ex-Husband Who Killed Sevim Zarif Tries to Benefit from "Unjust Provocation"]' bianet.org/kadin/toplumsal-cinsiyet/104366-sevim-zarif-i-olduren-eski-esi-haksiz-tahrik-indirimi-almaya-calisiyor
——— 2009 'Türkiye, AİHM'de Kadını Korumadığı İçin Mahkum Olan İlk Ülke [Turkey Was the First Country to Be Convicted by the ECtHR for Not Protecting a Woman]' m.bianet.org/bianet/dunya/115094-turkiye-aihm-de-kadini-koruma digi-icin-mahkum-olan-ilk-ulke
——— 2011 'Number of Women Murders Increased by 1400 Per Cent' bianet.org/english/gender/132753-number-of-women-murders-increased-by-1400-percent
BirGün 2007 '59 "Namus" Cinayetinin 46'sına "Tahrik" İndirimi [Out of 59 "Honour" Murders, 46 Benefited from "Provocation"]' www.birgun.net/haber-detay/59-namus-cinayetinin-46-sina-tahrik-indirimi-37631.html
Bottomley, A. and Conaghan, J. 1993 'Feminist Theory and Legal Strategy' 20(1) *Journal of Law and Society* 1.
Bourdieu, P. 1987 'The Force of Law: Toward a Sociology of the Juridical Field' 38 *Hastings Law Journal* 805.
Burns, S. 1990 'Notes From the Field: A Reply to Professor Colker' 13 *Harvard Women's Law Journal* 189.
Cahn, N. 1991 'Defining Feminist Litigation' 14 *Harvard Women's Law Journal* 1.
Colker, R. 1990 'Feminist Litigation: An Oxymoron? A Study of the Briefs Filed in *William L. Webster v. Reproductive Health Services*' 13 *Harvard Women's Law Journal* 137.
Edwards, A. 2011 *Violence against Women under International Human Rights Law* Cambridge: Cambridge University Press.
Eyüboğlu, O.M. 2009 'Erkek Vuruyor, Devlet "Haksız Tahrik" Diyor . . . [Man Hits, State Says "Unjust Provocation" . . .]' (1) *Feminist Politika* 10.
——— 2010 'Şiddet Değil, Erkek Şiddeti [Not Violence, Male Violence]' (4) *Feminist Politika* 24.
Hacıvelioğlu, F. 2010 'Kadın Katillerini Kim Koruyor? [Who Protects Women's Murderers?]' (5) *Feminist Politika* 26.
Hasselbacher, L. 2010 'State Obligations Regarding Domestic Violence: The European Court of Human Rights, Due Diligence, and International Legal Minimums of Protection' 8 *Northwestern University Journal of International Human Rights* 190.
Howe, A. 2012 'Enduring Fictions of Possession: Sexual Infidelity and Homicidal Rage in Shakespeare and Late Modernity (Glossing *Othello*)' 21(3) *Griffith Law Review* 772.
——— 2013 'Mastering Emotions or Still Losing Control? Seeking Public Engagement with "Sexual Infidelity" Homicide' 21 *Feminist Legal Studies* 141.
——— 2014 'Fatal Love' 2(1) *Griffith Journal of Law and Human Dignity* 4.
Koğacıoğlu, D. 2004 'The Tradition Effect: Framing Honour Crimes in Turkey' 15(2) *Differences: A Journal of Feminist Cultural Studies* 119.
Örer, A. 2007 'Turkish Women Celebrate Feminist Anniversary' *Bianet* bianet.org/english/politics/96403-turkish-women-celebrate-feminist-anniversary
Savaş, M. 2008 'Haksız Tahrik'in Yarattığı Haksızlık [The Injustice of Unjust Provocation]' *Haber Vesaire* habervesaire.com/haksiz-tahrik-in-yarattigi-haksizlik/
Sirman, N. 1989 'Feminism in Turkey: A Short History' 3 *New Perspectives on Turkey* 1.

Smart, C. 1989 *Feminism and the Power of Law* London: Routledge.
——— 1992 'The Woman of Legal Discourse' 1(1) *Social and Legal Studies* 29.
Sosyalist Feminist Kolektif 2007 'Sevim Zarif' www.sosyalistfeministkolektif.org/kampanyalar/parcas-olduklar-m-z/kadn-cinayetlerine-isyandayz/sevim-zarif/
——— 2011 'Takip Ettiğimiz Davalarda Haksız Tahrik Indirimi Yok! [There Has Been No Reduction for Unjust Provocation in the Trials We Have Followed]' www.sosyalistfeministkolektif.org/kampanyalar/parcas-olduklar-m-z/kadn-cinayetlerine-isyandayz/takip-ettiimiz-davalarda-haksz-tahrik-indirimi-yok/
——— 2012 'Şefika Etik Davasında Yine Erkek Yalanlar [More Male Lies in the Şefika Etik Case]' www.sosyalistfeministkolektif.org/kampanyalar/parcas-olduklar-m-z/kadn-cinayetlerine-isyandayz/efika-etik-davasnda-yine-erkek-yalanlar/
Toker, H. and Altun, D. 2015 'Toplumsal Şiddetin Aktarım Yoluyla Yeniden Üretilmesi: Basının Televisiyonlaşması Bağlamında Şefika Etik Cinayeti [Reproducing the Violence via Media Transmission: The Murder of Şefika Etik, the Process of the Press to become Similar to Television]' 9(1) *Selçuk İletişim* 115.
Ulmschneider, G.W. 1995 'Rape and Battered Women's Self-Defense Trials as "Political Trials": New Perspectives on Feminists' Legal Reform Efforts and Traditional "Political Trials" Concepts' 29(1) *Suffolk University Law Review* 115.
Vojdik, V. 1998 'Afterword: A Thought about Feminist Litigation Strategies' 20(1) *Western New England Law Review* 139.

6 The Canadian Femicide Observatory for Justice and Accountability

Myrna Dawson

Introduction

This chapter discusses the evolution of a long-standing research endeavour in Canada that culminated in the Canadian Femicide Observatory for Justice and Accountability, a national initiative launched in 2017. Its overarching mandate is to establish a visible and national focus on social and state responses to femicide. Highlighting the value of Carol Smart's call to focus on understanding 'law in practice' almost 30 years ago, the Observatory and its activities underscore the recognised legitimacy of Smart's argument that feminism has the power 'to expose how law operates in all its most detailed mechanisms'.[1] The early inception of this feminist-inspired research sought to document intimate femicide in one province and to examine the role of intimacy in law. In the following, this research is described and its path traced to the establishment of the Observatory (hereafter referred to as the CFOJA) and its objectives.

The underlying premise of this chapter is that, despite the introduction of various legislative and policy initiatives in recent decades to prevent femicide and violence against women, feminists must continue to interrogate what is meant by intimacy in the legal process in Canada and internationally. The meaning of intimacy and other concepts that perpetuate and maintain damaging stereotypes related to gender and violence must be problematised and challenged given their use in law to capture what is ***known*** about violence against women by men. While this research may come with many challenges, there remains a crucial need for feminist researchers to continue to decentre law as argued by Smart nearly three decades ago.

Background context

The role of intimacy in law's response to violence is arguably one of the most ignored relationships while, at the same time, one of the most contested among social science and legal researchers. Historically, intimacy served to mitigate the seriousness of men's violence against women in the eyes of the law. If a man victimised a female partner, the legal response was typically more lenient than if there

1 Smart (1989: 25).

had been no prior relationship and this remained true, albeit less lenient, if the man and woman were former partners.[2]

Today, given social and legal transformations of the past four decades, the role of intimacy in law is less clear and it continues to garner little attention in research compared to other factors such as race and gender. When considered, intimacy is often conflated with gender – what it means to be a woman – both when law is responding to violence and by researchers. Is it intimacy that matters or is it gender? Can the two be separated when examining violence against women? Despite crucial contributions, particularly by feminist theorists and researchers, about gender and law, it is time to turn our attention more fully to the role of intimacy and what this means for women's access to justice.[3]

Femicide is most often perpetrated in Canada, and globally, by current or former male partners – referred to as intimate femicide.[4] Responding to a series of these killings in Canada's most populous province, a group of eight Ontario women working in shelters for abused women met in 1989 – the same year that *Feminism and the Power of Law* was published – to share experiences and provide emotional support. They had worked with or had been friends of women who were killed by male partners. The group named themselves the Women We Honour Action Committee and set out to learn more about women killed by male partners by launching a study with three goals: first, to document the incidence of these killings; second, to describe the characteristics of those involved and the circumstances; and third, to present the stories of some of the women killed. Occurring in two stages focusing on the period 1974–1994,[5] the study documented 1,206 femicides involving women aged 15 and older from official records (e.g. coroner's files, police and court records). Of 1,120 cases with identified killers, 705 or 63 per cent of the killers were current or former male partners.[6]

The results of the first stage of the study were released in 1992 when I was an undergraduate immersed in a course on women and the criminal justice system. The report came to my attention at the same time as a Canadian law journal article suggested that there appeared to be a move away from viewing intimacy as a mitigating rather than an aggravating factor. It stated that: 'The recognition of the horrific brutality implicit in the killing of someone in a relationship of trust is a significant step both in understanding and addressing crimes of violence against women'.[7] The fact that the courts would see intimacy as a mitigating factor was unexpected because I was still naïve about law in practice. Embarking on a review of the literature, I realised there was a paucity of systematic research despite the

2 Black (1976, 1993) and Rapaport (1994).
3 Walklate (2008).
4 It is also referred to as *intimate partner femicide*; however, intimate femicide is the term most commonly used in the Canadian context given that the first study to focus on this phenomenon in Canada described here used this term.
5 Crawford et al. (1992) and Crawford et al. (1997).
6 Gartner et al. (1999).
7 Scassa (1993: 282).

common assumption that intimacy would lead to criminal justice leniency. Therefore, when I became involved in the second phase of the study, my goal was to begin to contribute to this gap in the Canadian context by documenting patterns in legal responses to femicide. Two key questions became central to my larger and now longitudinal examination of criminal justice responses to homicide and femicide – does intimacy matter and, if so, why?

My ongoing research continues to document the incidence of and patterns in homicide and femicide in Ontario with specific emphasis on court responses. Until now, there have been legislative and policy changes which have transformed social and legal environments. For example, wife abuse, broadly referred to as family or domestic violence, was historically perceived as private violence, not appropriate for legal intervention. There was no mention of the relationship between a victim and a defendant and its meaning in the criminal process.[8] Over time, though, this type of violence became labelled as deviant, and then criminal. In 1996, Canadian sentencing principles were amended to stipulate that relationships offenders have or had with their victims may act as an aggravating factor in determining punishments.[9] Therefore, it would be expected that significant changes have occurred in law's response to violence, including intimate femicide, but systematic research addressing this and other important questions remains scarce.

The Canadian study described below is unique internationally given the length of time covered, the number of variables examined, and the emphasis on documenting legal responses. While primarily quantitative, the research was influenced by Daly's *Gender, Crime and Punishment* which emphasised the integral and complementary nature of qualitative and quantitative methods when examining criminal justice.[10] The challenge of accessing sentencing transcripts served too great an obstacle in the early research to pursue the qualitative focus systematically which is less an issue today given the rise of online legal databases. However, early reliance on quantitative data shows these methods have much to offer in understanding patterns in how law operates which are now being complemented by qualitative analyses using more readily available court judgments.

Law's response to femicide in Ontario

Recognising the limitations of the intimate/non-intimate dichotomy relied upon by many researchers, my early research conceptualised intimacy as a continuum, identifying five victim-defendant relationship categories – intimate partners, family members (not including spouses), friends, acquaintances and strangers.[11] The main hypothesis was that cases involving intimate partners – those conceptualised as having the highest degree of intimacy – would be treated most leniently by the courts. Given social and legal transformations, it was further

8 Grant et al. (1998).
9 Grant (2010).
10 Daly (1994).
11 Dawson (2004).

hypothesised that any documented leniency should diminish over time. To test these hypotheses, the study focused on the city of Toronto and the 1,003 of 1,533 documented homicides that were handled through the adult criminal justice system during a 23-year period (1974–1996). Controlling for various legal and extra-legal factors, results showed that intimacy did affect criminal justice responses to violence, but its impact was contingent upon the decision-making stage and the relationship type. Specifically, those who killed intimate partners were less likely to be charged with first-degree murder and to have their cases resolved at trial. Furthermore, those who killed intimate partners or other family members received shorter sentences than other killers. As such, when leniency was evident, defendants who shared the closest relationship to their victims – intimate partners – were most often recipients of such treatment, but effects did diminish somewhat over time.

Recognising that intimacy between intimate partners can also vary along with case characteristics, I examined whether the *state* of a relationship played a role in determining law's response to violence, comparing cases involving intimate partners who were attempting to leave the relationship, or had already left, to cases involving current partners.[12] Almost exclusively perpetrated by males, results showed that relationship state was associated with punishment severity at sentencing: male offenders who killed female partners from whom they were, or about to be, separated, received sentences that were about two years longer than sentences imposed on defendants who killed current partners.[13]

Expanding the years examined, subsequent research examined the 1996 introduction of intimacy as an aggravating factor.[14] Focusing on 1974–2002, criminal justice outcomes for cases involving intimate partners were compared to all other relationships. Differential treatment of intimate partner and non-intimate partner killers was again evident at some, but not all, stages and not always in the expected direction. Those who killed intimate partners continued to be more likely to have their cases resolved by plea than other killers. When cases went to trial, however, intimate partner killers were more likely to be found guilty than those who killed other victims, but intimacy did not lead to differential sentences. These findings might be explained by the effects of time and the introduction of intimacy as an aggravating factor. For example, comparing 1974–1983 to 1984–2002, results show that intimate partner killers were more likely to be found guilty at trial compared to those who killed non-intimate partners in the more recent, but not in the earlier, period. In addition, when examining the severity of conviction, intimate partner homicides resolved in early years were less likely to result in murder convictions than non-intimate partner homicides. In the latter period, there was no evidence of differential treatment.[15]

12 Dawson and Gartner (1998) and Dawson (2003).

13 Given the small sample size and the focus on a single urban jurisdiction, this question is currently being reexamined using data from the longer study period for the province of Ontario.

14 Dawson (2012, 2016b).

15 Dawson (2012).

Moving to a broader focus on how femicides are treated in law compared to homicides, the analysis focused on all killings in Ontario in 1974–2012 to examine gender and punishment.[16] Results demonstrated a 'female victim effect': cases involving femicide victims were treated more punitively than those with male victims at all stages of the process. But does this differential treatment stem from the gender of the victim – is it a 'female victim' effect? Femicide often involves sexual violence which is an aggravating factor in some jurisdictions and research has shown that sexual violence conditions the association between victim gender and punishment.[17] The question becomes, then, when sexual violence is considered, does the victim's gender remain a significant determinant of punishment? Are there other circumstances in femicide that are distinct from homicide that can explain what has been interpreted as the 'female victim' effect? Some of these questions are currently being examined in the Canadian context where murder is first-degree if the killing occurred during the commission of various sexual assault offences, underscoring the presence of statutory aggravation when sexual violence is involved. Therefore, sexual violence and excessive violence – referred to as 'overkill' and common in femicides – may explain what appears to be more punitive responses to femicides. How gender and intimacy intersect in determinations of punishment is also not well understood.

Why does intimacy matter?

Referred to here as the 'intimacy discount', defendants who killed women with whom they shared closer relationships continue to be subject to lighter punishments than those who shared more distant relationships although legislative and policy changes may be contributing to improved social and legal responses. The question remains, however, why does intimacy continue to matter? I argue that intimacy matters in law because of entrenched stereotypes that continue to resonate in the legal and public domain.[18] These stereotypes are so common in our everyday world, and everyday court interactions, they are part of conventional and sociological wisdom, like Hagan and O'Donnel's argument about gender over three decades ago.[19] There is no solid base of empirical evidence that supports their validity or contributes to an understanding of their role in law.[20] Furthermore, the way in which intimacy and gender are intricately linked is so ingrained that their combined influence on law has largely been ignored, precluding the recognition that most stereotypes are really about men's violence against female partners. One illustrative example is provided to underscore the importance of problematising and challenging stereotypes as an important site of feminist contestation and a key focus of the CFOJA.

16 Dawson (2016a).
17 Gillespie et al. (2013) and Williams et al. (2007).
18 Dawson (2006, 2016b).
19 Hagan and O'Donnel (1978).
20 For a detailed discussion of these stereotypes, see Dawson (2006).

One explanation for the role of intimacy in law distinguishes between 'cold-blooded' and 'hot-blooded' crimes. Cold-blooded violence, often referred to as instrumental violence, is most often associated with offenders motivated by rational calculation, risk minimisation, or some type of gain such as robbery. In contrast, hot-blooded, expressive violence typically lacks rational consideration, stemming instead from a desire to retaliate. Thus, killing out of anger or strong emotion may decrease defendant culpability because it undermines the capacity to deliberate and plan or reduces agency and self-restraint. Intimate partner homicide, and particularly intimate femicide, has traditionally been viewed as the archetype of expressive, hot-blooded acts because of the intensity of such relationships.[21] Killings by strangers, in contrast, are more often instrumental, primarily committed for gain. While the validity of these typologies is challenged, expressive violence continues to be linked with intimacy and instrumental violence with strangers.[22]

If intimate partner homicides more often involve mitigating emotions, evidence of premeditation/intent should be less evident. However, using various indicators for premeditation and intent, an exploratory study showed that evidence of premeditation/intent was more frequent among cases involving intimate partners (41 per cent) than other cases (31 per cent).[23] This finding challenges the stereotype that intimate partner homicides are primarily spontaneous involving mitigating emotions. It was also demonstrated that, despite greater evidence of premeditation/intent and similar case characteristics, intimate partner killers received shorter sentences overall. This example calls into question the validity of 'common sense' stereotypes, highlighting the need to systematically interrogate them and their role in law.[24] This is one of several key objectives of the Canadian Femicide Observatory for Justice and Accountability discussed next.

The Canadian Femicide Observatory for Justice and Accountability

A call for action from the United Nations Human Rights Office of the High Commissioner Special Rapporteur on violence against women, its causes and consequences parallels, in part, what Smart called for three decades ago in relation to law.[25] In 2015, and several times since, the Special Rapporteur has called on countries to establish a femicide watch or observatory to collect, analyse and review data on femicide. This call, along with Smart's earlier call to document and challenge 'law in practice' served as the impetus for the

21 See for example Messner and Tardiff (1985); Sampson (1987); Parker and Smith (1979); Smith and Parker (1980); Loftin (1986); Maxfield (1989); and Rojek and Williams (1993).

22 See for example Dawson (2006); Polk and Ranson (1991); Felson and Messner (1996); Miethe and Drass (1998); and Miethe and Regoeczi (2004).

23 Wallace (1986) and Dawson (2006).

24 Dawson and Sutton (2017).

25 Smart (1989). See also Laurent et al. (2013) and Nowak (2012).

Canadian Femicide Observatory for Justice and Accountability. Established by the Centre for the Study of Social and Legal Responses to Violence at the University of Guelph, the CFOJA and its website was officially launched on 6 December 2017, Canada's National Day of Remembrance and Action on Violence against Women.

The goals of the feminist-led CFOJA are multi-faceted but focus specifically on documenting social and state responses to femicide in Canada to bring visible and national attention to the phenomenon of femicide. A key prevention goal is to highlight the ways in which stereotypes about intimacy, gender and violence perpetuate and maintain violence against women in its varying forms, including femicide. However, the CFOJA recognises the importance of other social identities that impact the treatment of female victims by society such as indigeneity, racial/ethnic identity, sexuality, disability, age and so on. As such, its expert advisory panel brings multiple expertise that captures feminist, and more importantly, multiple and intersecting perspectives to highlighting social and state responses to femicide with the goal of prevention.

Focusing on responses to femicide *after* it occurs, and recognising how broader societal contexts facilitate femicide, the CFOJA is undertaking several initial activities. First, to capture the larger context, it will identify legislation, policies and practices in social and state responses to femicide with two goals in mind: 1) To examine whether different parts of the country are more or less 'resourced' to respond to violence against women; and 2) To assess how these higher-level resources may perpetuate and maintain social structures and gender inequalities conducive to the perpetration of femicide. The ways in which legislations, policies and programmes address (or not) vulnerable and marginalised groups of women and girls will also be examined including, but not exclusively, indigenous women, immigrant and refugee women, older women and disabled women.

Second, the CFOJA will identify stereotypes and biases that underpin social and state responses. Focusing on the media as one type of social response and the courts as representative of the legal response, the way in which varying social identities, including that of intimate partners, are constructed by state actors when responding to femicides when they occur will be interrogated. In addition, recognising that justice often varies by geography, how social and state responses may vary across the country will also be examined (e.g. regions, urban/rural locations).

Finally, the CFOJA will facilitate the exchange of information, reliable data, and current knowledge to advance legislative, policy and programme change to enhance the prevention of femicide in Canada. To do so, it will monitor emerging issues and trends related to femicide and violence against women more generally; provide user-friendly, reliable information, resources and research on femicide and act as a knowledge broker for researchers, professionals, policy-makers, media and the public. In short, it will serve as a web-based research and information centre which aims to conduct, mobilise, exchange and promote research and knowledge to prevent femicide and other forms of gender-based killings in Canada. The CFOJA represents the first time there has been a single location to mobilise knowledge and action for femicide victims in Canada.[26] Its current efforts to facilitate research on the courts (and the media) responds to Smart's call to feminists 'to sustain its challenge to the power of law to define women in law's terms'.[27]

Two clear priorities pose significant challenges to moving forward, however. The first is the need to develop more innovative ways to identify and collect systematic and detailed data. This requires that we acknowledge the limitations of current data sources such as sentencing transcripts which come with limitations (e.g. not all cases are reported, what is reported may not capture all relevant information). The second priority is the need to better operationalise reliable and valid indicators of key factors in law's response to violence, particularly those that capture stereotypes about intimacy and violence (e.g. premeditation, victim provocation). In doing so, we need to remember that the goals of researchers and the courts are not the same – and may be at odds. Addressing these challenges requires increased collaborations among feminists, social scientists, legal scholars, court and state actors. Legislation represents symbolic efforts to address perceived problems but, as Smart argues, it is 'law in practice' that requires our attention if we are to ensure equitable access to justice for girls and women.[28]

During the past several decades, the social construction of intimacy in law has undergone fundamental changes. National and international debates continue, however, over the degree to which this type of violence should be treated as criminal and, if so, what punishments are most appropriate. Much discussion has focused on the appropriate legal responses to intimate partner homicide.[29] Historically and still today, the provocation defence has been the subject of much controversy internationally. As discussed elsewhere in this book, some jurisdictions have abolished or reformed the partial defence of provocation. Others have sought to make punishments more appropriate through sentencing reforms, but little is known about the impact of such moves.[30] Many share Carol Smart's scepticism about the willingness of criminal justice actors to seriously address the problem of intimate partner violence and homicide despite these transformations, given the recognition that 'law in practice' is often much different than what is or has been legislated.[31] Traditional ideologies or stereotypes may continue to downplay the seriousness of some violence. Further, what might be considered improvements in the court's response to femicide may be explained in part due to increasing punitiveness in Canadian sentencing overall.[32] Alternatively, some of this improvement may be due to increased legislative and policy attention

26 For more information, see Canadian Femicide Observatory for Justice and Accountability (2018).
27 Smart (1989: 25).
28 Smart (1989: 25).
29 See for example Johnson and Dawson (2011).
30 Dawson (2012).
31 See for example Fineman (1994) and Sheehy (2014).
32 Doob and Webster (2006).

to femicide, particularly intimate femicide, and other forms of violence against women more generally.

Much more nuanced and systematic research is required, however, before we can answer the preceding questions and recent contributions of the intersectionality framework underscore the need to understand what groups of women have been affected by these changes and in what way.[33] In Canada, the disproportionately higher risks faced by indigenous women highlight the need to prioritise examining responses to killings of this group of women and girls.[34] Collecting information on indigenous status and other racial/ethnic groups from court records is a challenge and missing information is a common problem, not unique to Canada. Regardless, understanding how the law's symbolic – and real – response might be contributing to risk for these and other groups of vulnerable and/or marginalised women and girls is paramount and requires more innovative and collaborative efforts. Increased collaboration and prioritisation of community mobilisation are core goals of the CFOJA aimed at developing a better understanding of social and state responses to femicide. Building on and complementing progress to date, the CFOJA will continue to identify and develop methods which can more adequately capture the detail required to more fully understand and expose the complexities of law 'in all its most detailed mechanisms' just as Carol Smart wisely counselled all those year ago.[35]

References

Black, D. 1976 *The Behavior of Law* New York: Academic Press.

——— 1993 *The Social Structure of Right and Wrong* San Diego: Academic Press.

Canadian Femicide Observatory for Justice and Accountability 2018 *Femicide is Preventable* www.femicideincanada.ca

Crawford, M. et al. 1992 *Woman Killing: Intimate Femicide in Ontario, 1974–1990* Toronto: Women We Honour Action Committee.

——— 1997 *Woman Killing: Intimate Femicide in Ontario, 1991–1994* Toronto: Women We Honour Action Committee.

Crenshaw, K. 1991 'Mapping the Margins: Intersectionality, Identity Politics, and Violence against Women of Colour' 43(6) *Stanford Law Review* 1241.

Daly, K. 1994 *Gender, Crime and Punishment* London: Yale University Press.

Dawson, M. 2003 'The Cost of 'Lost' Intimacy: The Effect of Relationship State on Criminal Justice Decision-Making' 43(4) *The British Journal of Criminology* 689.

——— 2004 'Rethinking the Boundaries of Intimacy at the End of the Century: The Role of Victim-Defendant Relationship in Criminal Justice Decision-Making over Time' 38(1) *Law & Society Review* 105.

——— 2006 'Intimacy, Violence and the Law: Exploring Stereotypes about Victim-Defendant Relationship and Violent Crime' 96(4) *Journal of Criminal Law and Criminology* 1417.

33 Crenshaw (1991).

34 Native Women's Association of Canada (2010).

35 Smart (1989: 25).

——— 2012 'Intimacy, Homicide, and Punishment: Examining Court Outcomes over Three Decades' 45(3) *Australian and New Zealand Journal of Criminology* 400.

——— 2016a 'Punishing Femicide: Criminal Justice Responses to the Killing of Women over Four Decades' 64(7) *Current Sociology* 996.

——— 2016b 'Intimacy, Gender and Homicide: The Validity and Utility of Common Stereotypes in Law' in K. Fitz-Gibbons and S. Walklate (eds.) *Gender, Murder and Responsibility: An International Perspective* Abingdon, Oxon: Routledge.

Dawson, M. and Gartner, R. 1998 'Differences in the Characteristics of Intimate Femicide: The Role of Relationship State and Relationship Status' 2 *Homicide Studies* 378.

Dawson, M. and Sutton, D. 2017 'Similar Sentences, Similar Crimes? Using Deep Sample Analysis to Examine the Comparability of Crimes and Punishments by Victim-Defendant Relationship' 49 *International Journal of Crime, Law and Justice* 58.

Doob, A.N. and Webster, C.M. 2006 'Countering Punitiveness: Understanding Stability in Canada's Imprisonment Rate' 40(2) *Law and Society Review* 325.

Felson, R.B. and Messner, S.F. 1996 'To Kill or Not to Kill? Lethal Outcomes in Injurious Attacks' 34(4) *Criminology* 519.

Fineman, M.A. 1994 'Preface' in M.A. Fineman and R. Mykitiuk (eds.) *The Public Nature of Private Violence* New York: Routledge xi.

Gartner, R. et al. 1999 'Woman Killing: Intimate Femicide in Ontario, 1974–1994' 26 *Resources for Feminist Research* 151.

Gillespie, L.K. et al. 2013 'Exploring the Role of Victim Sex, Victim Conduct, and Victim-Defendant Relationship in Capital Punishment Sentencing' 18(2) *Homicide Studies* 175.

Grant, I. 2010 'Intimate Femicide: A Study of Sentencing Trends for Men Who Kill Their Intimate Partners' 47 *Alberta Law Review* 779.

Grant, I. et al. 1998 *The Law of Homicide* Scarborough, Ontario: Carswell.

Hagan, J. and O'Donnel, N. 1978 'Sexual Stereotyping and Judicial Sentencing: A Legal Test of the Sociological Wisdom' 3(3) *The Canadian Journal of Sociology* 309.

Johnson, H. and Dawson, M. 2011 *Violence against Women in Canada: Research and Policy Perspectives* Toronto: Oxford University Press.

Laurent, C. et al. 2013 *Femicide: A Global Issue That Demands Action* Vienna: Academic Council on the United Nations System (ACUNS) Publications.

Loftin, C. 1986 'Assaultive Violence as a Contagious Social Process' 62 *Bulletin of the New York Academy of Medicine* 550.

Maxfield, M. 1989 'Circumstances in Supplementary Homicide Reports: Variety and Validity' 27 *Criminology* 671.

Messner, S.F. and Tardiff, K. 1985 'The Social Ecology of Urban Homicide: An Application of the Routine Activities Approach' 23 *Criminology* 241.

Miethe, T.D. and Drass, K.A. 1998 'Exploring the Social Context of Instrumental and Expressive Homicides: An Application of Qualitative Comparative Analysis' 15(1) *Journal of Quantitative Criminology* 1.

Miethe, T.D. and Regoeczi, W.C. 2004 *Rethinking Homicide: Exploring the Structure and Process Underlying Deadly Situations* New York: Cambridge University Press.

Native Women's Association of Canada 2010 *What Their Stories Tell Us: Research Findings from the Sisters in Spirit Initiative* Ottawa: NWAC.

Nowak, M. 2012 *Femicide: A Global Problem* Geneva: Small Arms Survey.

Parker, R.N. and Smith, D.W. 1979 'Deterrence, Poverty and Type of Homicide' 85(3) *American Journal of Sociology* 614.

Polk, K. and Ranson, D. 1991 'Patterns of Homicide in Victoria' in D. Chappell and H. Strang (eds.) *Australian Violence: Contemporary Perspectives* Canberra: Australian Institute of Criminology 53.

Rapaport, E. 1994 'The Death Penalty and the Domestic Discount' in M.A. Fineman and R. Mykitiuk (eds.) *The Public Nature of Private Violence* New York: Routledge 224.

Rojek, D. and Williams, J. 1993 'Interracial vs. Intraracial Offences in Terms of the Victim/Offender Relationship' in A.V. Wilson (ed.) *Homicide: The Victim/Offender Connection* Cincinnati: Anderson 249.

Sampson, R.J. 1987 'Personal Violence by Strangers: An Extension and Test of the Opportunity Model of Predatory Victimization' 78(2) *Journal of Criminal Law and Criminology* 327.

Scassa, T. 1993 'Sentencing Intimate Femicide: A Comment on *R. v. Doyle*' 16 *Dalhousie Law Journal* 270.

Sheehy, E. 2014 *Defending Battered Women on Trial: Lessons from Transcripts* Vancouver: UBC Press.

Smart, C. 1989 *Feminism and the Power of Law* London: Routledge.

Smith, M.D. and Parker, R.N. 1980 'Type of Homicide and Variation in Regional Rates' 59(1) *Social Forces* 136.

Walklate, S. 2008 'What Is to Be Done about Violence against Women? Gender, Violence, Cosmopolitanism, and the Law' 48 *The British Journal of Criminology* 39.

Wallace, A. 1986 *Homicide: The Social Reality* Sydney: New South Wales Bureau of Crime Statistics and Research.

Williams, M.R. et al. 2007 'Understanding the Influence of Victim Gender in Death Penalty Cases: The Importance of Victim Race, Sex-Related Victimization, and Jury Decision-Making' 45 *Criminology* 865.

7 Judicial discourse versus domestic violence death review

An Australian case study

Emma Buxton-Namisnyk and Anna Butler

Introduction

One of Carol Smart's central contentions in *Feminism and the Power of Law* is that law is a powerful discourse that claims to establish the truth and seriousness of any sequence of events through its internal rigour and logic. Analysing law as a form of power, she highlights the insidious ways in which law can extend its influence beyond legal issues into issues of everyday life, lending legitimacy to judges' perspectives on distinctly non-legal issues.[1] Following Smart's call for an ongoing analysis of the discursive power of law's truth, this chapter examines judicial sentencing remarks in intimate partner femicide cases in New South Wales, Australia between 2000 and 2014, comparing them to in-depth qualitative and homicide census review information uncovered through domestic violence death review investigation processes. To what extent do judicial narratives operate to reinforce stereotypes of 'provocative' victims and excusable perpetrators of intimate partner femicides? Do they still excuse, mutualise or normalise violence against women? Do judges still make claims about domestic violence that disqualify feminist narratives, ignoring the central issue of gender inequality in intimate partner homicides? By contrast, do the narratives told in domestic violence death reviews offer the prospect of a promising feminist-inflected alternative discourse?

Judicial discourse

The research for this chapter has been undertaken in our capacity as the secretariat of the New South Wales Domestic Violence Death Review Team (DVDRT).[2] The DVDRT is a committee comprised of government and non-government members whose legislative mandate is to conduct in-depth review of domestic violence related deaths with a view to recommending improvements to domes-

1 Smart (1989: 10–13).

2 The research is produced under s101M(1)(b) of the *Coroners Act 2009* (NSW) and pursuant to the research function of the team's secretariat and is the authors' own work. It does not necessarily reflect the views of individual team members of the Domestic Violence Death Review Team.

tic violence systems and services. In supporting the work of the DVDRT, the secretariat maintains continuous whole of population homicide census data and collate and report on comparative data on all homicides that occur within the state, including domestic violence related intimate partner homicides perpetrated by men and women.[3] The dataset for this study comprises 103 intimate partner femicide cases; all were preceded by an identifiable history of violence.[4]

A common feature in sentencing was that judges would regularly make an assessment of the relationship between the defendant and victim, including adjudicating the question of 'how serious' the domestic violence was prior to the fatal episode. Such assessments often mutualised the violence between the parties, disqualifying the victim's narratives about the seriousness of physical and non-physical manifestations of violence, including coercive and controlling behaviours on the part of their eventual killers.[5] Judges often deployed discursive manoeuvres that had the effect of minimising the killer's abusive behaviour and erasing his agency, locating the problem instead in a 'volatile' relationship.[6] It was common for judges to describe the victim's relationship with her killer prior to her death as having been 'stormy', 'tumultuous', 'turbulent', 'difficult', 'unsettled', 'troubled', 'not tranquil', as characterised by 'domestic disputes' and being 'far from happy'.[7]

While some judges mutualised histories of violence by suggesting both parties were responsible for a 'volatile' relationship that resulted in the woman's death, others minimised histories of violence altogether, by describing the relationships as positive, using terms such as 'normal', 'ordinary' or 'by all accounts . . . happy' prior to the fatal episode of violence.[8] Relationships were also frequently described as being 'good' prior to some seminal event occurring – an event that judges took to signify the beginning of the violence and the dissolution of the relationship and one typically attributed to the victim's alleged actions. Commonly, this event was the abuser's suspicion that the victim had entered into another relationship, usually referred to as an 'affair' or being 'unfaithful'.[9] An

3 See DVDRT (2017).

4 This number excludes cases that were not finalised by way of criminal conviction (such as murder-suicides during the reporting period) and several cases where sentencing remarks were unavailable.

5 See Stark (2007).

6 *R v Stephenson* [2007] NSWSC 672; *R v Sean Lee King* [2013] NSWSC 801; *R v Neave* [2012] NSWSC 229; *R v Robert Theo Sievers* [2002] NSWSC 1257. On the operation of discursive manoeuvres in non-feminist accounts of men's violence, see Howe (2008), Chapter 2.

7 *R v Benjamin Walkington* [2003] NSWSC 517; *R v Gittany* (No 5) [2014] NSWSC 49. *R v Hogan* [2004] NSWSC 959; *Regina v Joseph* [2003] NSWSC 1080; *R v Laures* [2003] NSWSC 785; *R v Kenning* [2003] NSWSC 84; *R v Williams* [2004] NSWSC 189; *R v Andrew Terrance Whiting* [2002] NSWSC 827; *Regina v Joiner* [2001] NSWSC 11 63; *R v Mencarious* [2006] NSWSC 719.

8 *R v Biddle* [2011] NSWSC 1262; *R v KJS* [2011] NSWSC 1690; *R v Simon Taouk* [2004] NSWSC 981.

9 See for instance, *R v Connolly* [2001] NSWSC 787 para 11; *R v Kenning* [2003] NSWSC 84 para 5.

alternative seminal event considered to spark the abuser's violence against the woman was the birth of a child.[10] Moreover, although a history of violence featured in all these cases, some histories did not meet the threshold to be brought into evidence at trial such that the homicide was viewed as something anomalous or unexpected, rather than occurring against a pattern of behaviour.

The overall effect of this process is the creation of a fictional narrative of violence that obscures women's histories of victimisation, a narrative that is far removed from that uncovered by the DVDRT investigation. This was particularly evident in one case where an older man killed his partner and their grandchildren. In the sentencing remarks for this case, the judge apparently disregarded evidence of a long history of violence by the man towards his wife and children, giving the impression that the final fatal attack was an isolated event attributable to some kind of abnormality in the perpetrator's state of mind, albeit one that resisted definitive diagnosis. The judge commented that a 'disturbing feature of this case is the absence of any explanation for the offences'.[11] In contrast, the DVDRT investigation revealed that the homicide was the culmination of decades of possessiveness, control and abuse.

In these discursive moments where judges provide their understanding of what constitutes a healthy or unhealthy relationship, they simultaneously demonstrate their lack of understanding of the nature and impact of domestic. When these kinds of judicial assessments are reproduced in the media they tacitly or expressly rely on law's truth to determine what can and cannot be said to constitute violence against women. Such adjudications of the significance of histories of violence in relationships are often invoked during discussions of the 'agreed facts' between the crown and the defence, meaning that judges do not always access the complete history when they adjudicate histories of violence at trial or on sentence. However, where evidence of violence is brought into trial, judges often fail to appreciate that domestic violence constitutes a pattern of behaviour, instead adjudicating the seriousness of individual episodes of violence. This was evident in the case of *R v Edward David Zammit*, a manslaughter case in which the judge said:

> there is nothing to suggest that this was an incident occurring in an abusive relationship. There were two separate assaults but the background was the same and on each occasion the offender was intoxicated. The assaults were hard pushes rather than kicks, punches or the use of a weapon and, therefore, they were of a less serious nature than is often found in this type of offence.[12]

Sometimes such commentary is made in the course of a 'properly legal' function such as determining whether a prisoner has 'good' prospects of rehabilitation

10 See for instance, *R v Lechmana* [2010] NSWSC 849 para 5; *R v Gerry Osman Mehmet* [2002] NSWSC 1154 para 6.
11 *R v John Walsh* [2009] NSWSC 764 para 22.
12 *R v Edward David Zammit* [2008] NSWSC 317 para 21.

or when assessing whether a case is analogous to a precedent.[13] However, at other times judges proffer generalisations evaluating the nature of the relationship between perpetrator and victim or the circumstances surrounding the death in ways that shift blame to the victim.

In *R v Wang*, for example, the victim attempted to end her relationship with the perpetrator before he travelled from China to Australia to live with her, telling him she had formed a new relationship. He decided to travel to Australia anyway, a decision the judge described in terms of his preparedness

> to maintain his commitment to the plan that they would build a life together in this country. In the meantime, he had obtained another professional position, but was prepared to forego it and start his career afresh in Australia with the deceased.[14]

The day he arrived in Australia, he murdered her. This relates to another common feature of sentencing in intimate partner femicides, namely the conflation of domestic violence with serious physical harm. For instance, in the case of *R v Stephenson*, a case involving significant coercive and controlling behaviours by the defendant towards the victim, the judge found it 'sufficient' to say that it was a relationship

> characterised by jealousy, with each party tending to suspect the other of infidelity. There was an obsessive quality to the relationship, particularly on his part, and there were many arguments. However, he had never struck her before, although he acknowledged . . . that on a few occasions he may have pushed her.[15]

An emphasis on physical assault as the most serious form of abuse reinforces narrow legal understandings of domestic violence and demotes other forms of abuse that women find extremely damaging to the status of a lesser wrong. Consider, for example, a case where a woman had tried to end a relationship that a man wanted to continue. As the judge saw it, 'things became awkward'.[16] In fact, the victim had taken out two apprehended violence orders against the offender which he had breached. Uninformed about the impact of coercive and controlling behaviours on women trapped in violent relationships, judges routinely failed to see reproductive coercion as a form of violence or abuse. For instance, the defendant in *R v Stephenson* did not want his partner to keep their baby. The judge noted that although she wanted to continue with the pregnancy, she 'eventually had an abortion, it being agreed that she should work for a period of years before they had a child'.[17] While he noted that the victim had been 'affected

13 *R v Stephenson* [2007] NSWSC 672 para 19.
14 *R v Wang* [2015] NSWSC 433 para 10.
15 *R v Stephenson* [2007] NSWSC 672 para 6.
16 *R v Brian Andrew Kaiser*; *Regina v Jeremy Michael Hunt* [2007] NSWSC 1362 para 2.
17 *R v Stephenson* [2007] NSWSC 672 para 7.

badly' by the abortion, he did not register that this behaviour was a manifestation of what has long been recognised as 'coercive control' in the critical literature.[18]

While judicial discourse harnesses law's power to shape domestic violence narratives that sideline the victim's experience while excusing the abuser's controlling behaviours, it also becomes clear that the process of sentencing itself continues to be dominated by a methodology that is antithetical in many ways to the complex and gendered nature of intimate partner femicide. As Smart argues, drawing on Mary-Jane Mossman's analysis, the traditional legal method has three main elements: 'boundary definition' through which the law conveys its own neutrality; 'determining relevance' and 'case analysis' which involves drawing on prior cases post-hoc to justify a particular conclusion.[19] This is particularly noticeable when it comes to judicial assessments of an offender's 'good character' as a mitigating factor in sentencing. Judges continue to understand domestic violence in archaic ways, failing to recognise the different behaviours that may constitute domestic abuse. For example, in one case where the offender had previously been found guilty of damaging the victim's vehicle, the judge determined that despite 'occasional acts of aggression' in his 'volatile relationship' with his victim, he was 'generally of good character'.[20] Moreover, he had

> accepted the first separation and made no attempt to molest or interfere with his ex partner over a period of almost seven years. There was some previous threat that he would kill her and the daughter, but I doubt that it was seriously meant or seriously taken by KAO. The extent of the violence displayed on this occasion and the use of a weapon are uncharacteristic of him.[21]

In another case in which the defendant had killed his partner after a long history of violence against her, the judge noted that he was prepared to treat the defendant as a person of good character and that any violence involving his wife 'was not serious and can be disregarded'. Moreover, he appeared to be a 'loving and caring father' despite the fact that he had killed the child's mother.[22] These kinds of references to defendants being 'good fathers' also appeared in other cases.[23] In *R v Eaglesham*, where a woman was murdered by her estranged husband while she was holding their child, the judge noted that

> The offender was very fond of the child and by all accounts a good father. He pursued the deceased, partly to do what he could to save the marriage and partly because he wanted to continue to see and care for the child. Things

18 Stark (2007).
19 Smart (1989: 21–22) citing Mossman (1986).
20 *R v DWC* [2006] NSWSC 1335 para 28.
21 *R v DWC* [2006] NSWSC 1335 para 28.
22 *R v Goodwin* [2004] NSWSC 757 para 26.
23 See for instance, *R v Lutu* [2014] NSWSC 413; *R v Eaglesham* [2004] NSWSC 747; *R v Raju* [2007] NSWSC 1418.

> reached the stage when the deceased told her colleagues at the bank not to put through to her calls that the offender was making.[24]

The concept of 'prior good character' also worked in favour of defendants who, while having no previous convictions for domestic violence offences, had anecdotal histories of abuse towards victims.[25] In assessing the likelihood that offenders would reoffend, some judges were of the opinion that this was unlikely, despite histories of violence against women. For instance, in *R v Elie Zeilaa* the judge thought it unlikely that the offender would have

> the ability to carry out significant acts of violence, either because his physical condition will deteriorate or because of the absence of any personal relationship that is likely to bring him into conflict with any person. It is clear that the killing of his wife was a symptom of his domineering relationship toward her and an example of his history of the use or threat of violence against her to make her compliant. It erupted into actual violence of a most serious kind on this occasion because his ability to control his behaviour or exercise judgment was substantially impaired by reason of his mental condition.[26]

Other judges made their assessments without a clearly articulated set of reasons, thereby missing an opportunity to address the seriousness of previous domestic violence.[27] For instance, in *R v Raju* the judge said that the defendant was unlikely to reoffend and taking his age into account, he considered that 'his prospects of rehabilitation are satisfactory'.[28] Given the abuser's long history of violence towards the woman he killed, it is difficult to ascertain why his rehabilitation prospects would be satisfactory without a comprehensive assessment.

In some cases judges did recognise that the killer was not of good character, notably when they had killed previous partners and in one case when the abuser had a history of violence towards his wife over many years.[29] In *R v Gierczynski*, the judge did not consider the offender's lack of criminal record in Australia to be a mitigating factor 'of any weight in the circumstances of the present case'. Indeed, the evidence at trial was 'replete with examples of his violent conduct' towards his wife over many years which did not result in prosecution

> because on each occasion he persuaded Danuta, either by intimidating her or manipulating her love for him, not to give evidence against him, to lie to

24 *R v Eaglesham* [2004] NSWSC 747 para 2.

25 See for instance, *R v Hassan* [2014] NSWSC 280, *R v Borg* [2010] NSWSC 951; *R v Do* (No 4) [2015] NSWSC 512; *R v KJS* [2011] NSWSC 1690.

26 *R v Elie Zeilaa* [2009] NSWSC 532 para 12.

27 See for instance, *R v Raju* [2007] NSWSC 1418; *R v Flanjak* [2003] NSWSC 779; *R v KJS* [2011] NSWSC 1690; *R v Do* (No 4) [2015] NSWSC 512.

28 *R v Raju* [2007] NSWSC 1418 para 53.

29 For example, *R v Robert Theo Sievers* [2002] NSWSC 1257.

> the police about what happened or not to report his assaults to the police at all. His conduct towards Danuta for 28 years and his interference with the reporting by her and his children of his assaults deprive him of the benefit of the suggestion that, but for the murder, he was otherwise of good character.[30]

This case aside, the notion that killers with a history of violence against women may – *notwithstanding* that history – be of good character or that they may be good fathers despite being abusive intimate partners minimises the seriousness of violence against women. This approach also fails to locate domestic violence within a culture that reinforces men's sense of entitlement over women.

It is notable that some judges in New South Wales appear to have been influenced by 'feminist concerns' in relation to sentencing in intimate partner femicides, particularly in recent years. For instance, in *R v Mahon* the judge noted that

> Typically, the male partner will inflict physical violence upon his weaker and more vulnerable female partner. Such physical violence is often, but not always, accompanied by verbal abuse and other forms of abuse including controlling behaviour, bullying, verbal and physical threats and any conduct which denies or in any way prevents the female partner exercising her freedom to go about her ordinary life in the way she chooses. Domestic violence is antithetical to a democratic society where individual freedom is cherished it undermines the principle of gender equality.[31]

Similarly, in *R v Gierczynski*, the judge noted that

> The offender's violence towards Danuta throughout their marriage and in the final minutes of her life was, in my view, an expression of his desire to exert his power over her because she was his wife. When she complied with his demands he was happy; when she did not meet his unreasonable standards or accede to his every wish, he retaliated, at times violently.[32]

The judge also rejected the suggestion that the victim 'was responsible for the conflict, rather than an unwilling victim of it'. He went further, acknowledging that he considered the offender not to have good prospects of rehabilitation. Notwithstanding his lack of a criminal record, he believed him to be a danger to 'any, and perhaps every, woman with whom he is in an intimate relationship'.[33]

On the evidence of this brief analysis of judicial discourse in New South Wales, many judges are still routinely diluting the gendered harm of domestic violence, mutualising or side-lining victim's histories and narratives of abuse when

30 *R v Gierczynski* [2013] NSWSC 1870 paras 75–76.
31 *R v Mahon* [2015] NSWSC 25 para 101.
32 *R v Gierczynski* [2013] NSWSC 1870 para 64.
33 *R v Gierczynski* [2013] NSWSC 1870 para 67.

sentencing defendants. Judges continue to underestimate the harm of domestic violence, thereby missing an opportunity to recognise femicide as a foreseeable fatal conclusion to a pattern of behaviour. However, these findings also highlight some episodes of promising judicial practice, and with the increasing prominence of feminism in Australia in recent years and a growing attention within academic discourse to the role of judges in respect of violence against women, there is also evidence to suggest that we may be witnessing a shift in power relations between law and feminism.[34]

Domestic violence death review

While judicial discourse still works to disqualify feminist and victim narratives, it is also a site where law's truths about violent interpersonal relationships can and should be challenged through alternative discourses. As Smart says, 'feminism must sustain its challenge to the power of law to define women in law's terms'.[35] In Australia today there are a number of initiatives that are doing just that. One is the process of domestic violence death review.

Domestic violence death reviews – also known as Domestic Violence Fatality Reviews, or Domestic and Family Violence Homicide Reviews – investigate homicides or suicides occurring in a domestic violence context. Such review teams operate in the United States, Canada, the United Kingdom, Australia and New Zealand. While they have different operational models, they are typically focused on contextualising and understanding domestic violence and domestic violence homicide.[36] In Australia the majority of death review processes are located in coronial jurisdictions.[37] These processes have been criticised for lacking a visible feminist praxis. For instance, Canadian legal academic Liz Sheehy has expressed concern that there is a real danger that death review processes may 'de-gender' domestic violence via neutralising language and methodologies.[38] These criticisms notwithstanding, such processes can offer – as the New South Wales DVDRT attempts to do – an alternative normative avenue for understanding and contextualising intimate partner homicides.

In contrast to criminal trial and sentencing processes, the DVDRT review process is not methodologically bound by rules of evidence. In preparing death reviews, investigators conduct a desktop review examining the complete pre-trial brief of evidence, trial transcripts, all unreported and reported histories of violence evident on the brief including police interviews with friends and family members, non-finalised police reports from domestic violence 'callouts' identified through

34 See Hunter (2012); Hunter (2015); Hunter and Tyson (2017); and Buxton-Namisnyk and Butler (2017).
35 See Smart (1989: 25).
36 For further information see Dawson (2017).
37 See Butler et al. (2017). It is noted that in Western Australia the domestic violence death review function is vested in the office of the Ombudsman.
38 See Sheehy (2017: 374–375).

police data systems and other records and materials called for pursuant to the DVDRT's extensive powers under the *Coroners Act 2009* (NSW). Qualitative data from this dataset consistently illustrate what has been found to be the case in numerous studies, namely that most intimate partner homicides are perpetrated by men.[39]

A key contribution of the DVDRT has been the public provision of case investigation summaries or in-depth case reviews that encompass women's narratives, including drawing on the knowledge and expertise of victims where their voices can be heard and of victims and abuser's friends and family. While this knowledge is ordinarily excluded in criminal trials as hearsay, the incisive and wide-ranging inquisitorial approach of the DVDRT investigation provides for recognition of the knowledge that women may impart. The circumstances in which that knowledge is received and processed may be of a different character to that which reaches the threshold for inclusion at trial or on sentence. Through the wide-ranging review process undertaken by the DVDRT, unreported histories are combined with critical analysis of the sentencing remarks, identifying limitations within the criminal justice process. The DVDRT makes these case summaries public, publishing shortened and de-identified versions of these reviews in its reports which are tabled in New South Wales Parliament.[40]

This kind of approach, one that privileges the femicide victim's story without the limitations associated with sentencing, can be seen clearly in one case review published in the DVDRT's 2015–2017 report, the murder of Suzy by Adam.[41] As there was no police reported history of violence in this case, much of the evidence relied upon in the DVDRT review was derived from the statements of family, friends and neighbours. The narrative developed through these statements highlight that the perpetrator Adam was abusive towards the victim Suzy throughout their relationship, including being emotionally, economically, socially and physically violent towards her. Suzy's experiences of violence are highlighted along with the barriers she faced in her attempts to leave Adam. We learn that they had resumed their relationship approximately six months before she was killed and that she made further disclosures of abuse after they reconciled, 'telling a neighbour that Adam had physically assaulted her and destroyed some of her belongings'. The neighbour told Suzy to contact police but she admitted that she was 'too ashamed and embarrassed to report Adam's abusive behaviour. Suzy also told the neighbour that she did not want her family to find out that Adam was continuing to abuse her'.[42]

Another aspect of feminist praxis identifiable in the work of the DVDRT is the centring of gender in the review process such that it becomes clear not only that domestic violence homicide is a gendered crime, but that non-fatal domestic violence behaviours are most often used by men against women.

39 See DVDRT (2017).
40 DVDRT (2011, 2012, 2015a, 2015b, 2017).
41 DVDRT (2017: 29–30).
42 DVDRT (2017: 30).

Our research shows that the death review process – at least as it operates in New South Wales – views the cases through a feminist lens. Furthermore, by working with a whole-of-population comparative dataset, the process situates and contextualises the phenomena within a framework of violence and homicide more broadly. This approach adds contextual weight to feminist concerns about men's violence against women, and provides a rich alternative to judicial discourse.[43]

A final contribution that death reviews can make is that such processes can decentre law by contributing to alternative discourses around the need for sustained and comprehensive responses to domestic violence beyond the narrow criminal law framework. The New South Wales DVDRT parliamentary reports consistently highlight the need for ongoing attention to the structural components of men's violence against women. While the death review process does not fulfil the same function as sentencing, which tends to be a comparatively narrow offender-focused exercise, it seeks to publically reframe understandings of men's lethal and non-lethal violence against women. In building this function, the DVDRT secretariat and the team's convenor regularly present the review work in public forums, academic journals and in the media. One particular aspect the secretariat has pursued is the importance of incrementally shifting the way the media and the judiciary use domestic violence narratives and language, including encouraging the rejection of mutualising terms and encouraging gendered analysis through these public discourses.[44]

Conclusion

As Carol Smart argued three decades ago, law remains a powerful discourse that disqualifies feminist knowledge. As it refracts through sentencing processes, law is still producing truths about intimate partner femicide that can have the effect of silencing feminist discourses and obscuring its profoundly gendered constitution. Law's ability to create its own harms – its juridogenic potential – is evident in the ways in which sentencing judges continue to disqualify women's narratives, de-politicising and de-gendering the perpetrators of domestic violence and the violence itself. However, there are signs of hope, notably incremental shifts in the way some judges approach these cases. Furthermore, domestic violence death review as it is undertaken in New South Wales is providing a rich site for challenging judicial narratives about intimate partner femicide and men's violence against women more broadly. Crucially, it is also offers a site for promoting feminist knowledge as an evidentiary-based alternate discourse to dominant forms of legal power. Death review is actively challenging the ways in which law constructs and denies women's experiences of violence just as Smart advocated all those years ago.

43 See for example Gilmore (2018).
44 See for example Buxton-Namisnyk and Butler (2017).

References

Butler, A. et al. 2007 'Australia' in M. Dawson (ed.) *Domestic Homicides and Death Reviews* London: Palgrave MacMillan.

Buxton-Namisnyk, E. and Butler, A. 2017 'What's Language Got to Do with It? Learning from Discourse, Language and Stereotyping in Domestic Violence Homicide Cases' 29(6) *Judicial Officers Bulletin* 49.

Dawson, M. 2017 *Domestic Homicides and Death Reviews* London: Palgrave MacMillan.

DVDRT 2011 *Domestic Violence Death Review Team Annual Report 2010–2011* Sydney: Domestic Violence Death Review Team.

——— 2012 *Domestic Violence Death Review Team Annual Report 2011–2012* Sydney: Domestic Violence Death Review Team.

——— 2015a *Domestic Violence Death Review Team Annual Report 2012–2013* Sydney: Domestic Violence Death Review Team.

——— 2015b *Domestic Violence Death Review Team Report 2013–2015* Sydney: Domestic Violence Death Review Team.

——— 2017 *Domestic Violence Death Review Team Report 2015–2017* Sydney: Domestic Violence Death Review Team.

Gilmore, J. 2018 'Fact or Fiction: Every Third Victim of Intimate Partner Violence Is a Male' *Sydney Morning Herald* 24 January accessed 26 February 2018. https://www.smh.com.au/lifestyle/fact-or-fiction-every-third-victim-of-intimate-partner-violence-is-a-male-20180124-h0nkwz.html

Howe, A. 2008 *Sex, Violence and Crime: Foucault and the 'Man' Question* Abingdon, Oxon: Routledge.

Hunter, R. 2012 'The Power of Feminist Judgments' 20 *Feminist Legal Studies* 135.

——— 2015 'More Than Just a Different Face? Judicial Diversity and Decision-Making' 68 *Current Legal Problems* 119.

Hunter, R. and Tyson, D. 2017 'Justice Betty King: A Study of Feminist Judging in Action' 40 *University of New South Wales Law Journal* 778.

Mossman, M.J. 1986 'Feminism and Legal Method: The Difference It Makes' 3 *Australian Journal of Law and Society* 30.

Sheehy, E. 2017 'A Feminist Reflection on Domestic Violence Death Reviews' in M. Dawson (ed.) *Domestic Homicides and Death Reviews* London: Palgrave MacMillan.

Smart, C. 1989 *Feminism and the Power of Law* London: Routledge.

Stark, E. 2007 *Coercive Control: How Men Entrap Women in Personal Life* New York: Oxford University Press.

8 Italian legal feminism – engaging with the power of law

Ilaria Boiano

Introduction

Carol Smart's *Feminism and the Power of Law* has been a key reference for Italian feminist critiques of law. Indeed, her critique of how law is gendered remains a pillar around which Italian feminism continues to question law. In this chapter I retrace the trajectories of Smart's influence with reference to differences of opinion within Italian legal feminism and feminist legal practice. Investigating how law plays an important role in reinforcing hegemonic understandings of intimate partner violence but also has potential as a tool of change, I explore judgments made in Italian criminal courts in femicide cases with a view to suggesting how feminist legal practice can contest and subvert the dominant legal culture.

Italian legal feminism

When Sylviane Colombo introduced the term 'legal feminism' to Italian feminists in 1992 she described it as a set of critical perspectives on law produced by feminist scholars in the context of Anglo-American academia. While she rated its critique of legal formalism, she was less sure about its benefits for Italian feminist scholars dealing with law, most of whom did not work in law schools.[1] But she appeared to be unaware that in *Feminism and the Power of Law* Carol Smart had already commenced a critique of the quest for a feminist jurisprudence, a critique introduced to Italian feminists by leading socio-legal scholar Tamar Pitch in the late 1990s.[2] Pitch began by noting significant differences between the common law system that Smart addressed and the Italian civil law system, pointing out how in common law systems, particularly in the United States, 'the language of rights' predominated.[3] The context of the debate was also different: Italian feminist criticism of law had developed outside academia because law schools were

1 Colombo (1992: 247). The translations from Italian are Ilaria Boiano's. The editors would also like to thank Chiara Florio for assistance with the translations.

2 Smart (1989). Smart's works have not been translated into Italian, except for Smart (1976) (Italian translation 1981).

3 Pitch (1998: 219).

largely resistant to feminist analysis.[4] Furthermore, Italian feminists preferred to distance themselves from traditional disciplinary boundaries in order to develop an analysis that they felt was closer to the real life needs and desires of women.[5] Nevertheless, what Pitch found useful in Smart's approach was her identification of three phases in the development of the idea that law was gendered. The first stage represents law as 'sexist'; the second, as 'male' add the third, Smart's preferred stage, as 'gendered', a stage where a critical question is posed: how does gender 'work in law and how does law work to produce gender?'[6]

To answer this question, Pitch investigated the results of Italian feminist engagement since the 1970s in reforms in family, abortion and sexual violence laws. She found that despite the value of legal reforms for achieving political changes in relation to women's position in Italy, reforms necessarily included women in a system that was originally conceived to exclude them as autonomous and free subjects. Following Smart, Pitch suggested an alternative strategy, one that decentered law, recognising that 'its autonomous and self-referential nature' rendered it 'impervious to the influence of other discourses such as feminism'.[7] Nevertheless, she insisted that this does not mean refraining from engaging with law. Rather, she proposed a form of legal feminism that queried law's conventional taken-for-granted categories such as 'subject of law', 'legal norm', 'rights', 'equality', 'difference' and 'justice'.[8]

Pitch also pointed out that while Italian feminist perspectives are often represented as polarised over whether law is or is not an effective political tool for women, this does not do justice to the complexities of the relationship between law, politics and legal practice in the Italian feminist experience.[9] Some, misunderstanding Smart's position, found in her framework a justification for denying any positive value to law and its regulation, seeing it instead as repressive of women's freedom.[10] Others formed groups and networks that continued to demand legal reforms, particularly in the area of equal opportunities.[11] A third strategy,

4 Feminist perspectives, especially on law, have been largely if not completely ignored in Italian academia, and confined within the narrow margins of cultural studies. See Cavarero and Restaino (2002: 24). It is in the last few years that feminist perspectives have entered law schools as a framework useful for encouraging a gender analysis of law and supporting the recognition of minorities' rights. See Scarponi (2014). In 2016, within the Italian section of the International Association of Women Philosophers (Iaph Italia) the Atelier for Legal Feminism was established: a group of scholars and lawyers working on proposing the framework of legal feminism as a field of research, aiming to spread feminist critiques of law among scholars, practitioners and policy makes.

5 Libreria delle donne di Milano (1987) (English translation 1990): 9 ff.

6 Pitch (1998: 213) and Smart (1992: 30, 34).

7 Pitch (1998: 214–215).

8 See Pitch (1989, 1993, 1998, 2004).

9 Pitch (1998: 230).

10 Bocchetti (1995); Pitch (1983); Cigarini (1995); and Tatafiore (1996).

11 Many measures have been adopted to enhance women's participation in political life, public administration and the labour market, including maternity support. A Ministry for Equal Opportunities has been established, and is today an internal department of the Presidency of the Council of Ministers.

one favoured by lawyers working for feminist women's shelters, is to practice law in court in a feminist way by representing women who have experienced men's violence.[12]

Lia Cigarini, a civil lawyer and founder of the *Libreria delle donne di Milano*, exemplifies the first approach by suggesting that women should position themselves 'above the law'. They should refuse the binary choice of an 'excluded/included-by-law model' or of an 'included/assimilated-by-law model' because 'women are not a social group but a political movement claiming their freedom'.[13] To better understand this kind of feminist critique, it might help to briefly mention the Italian debate on sexual offences reform. In 1979, the Movement for Women's Freedom, the Union of Italian Women and the Roman collective *Pompeo Magno* proposed a law on sexual violence to reform the criminal code which at the time punished sexual violence as a crime against public morality.[14] Some Italian feminists, including Cigarini, opposed this strategy to modify the pervasive rape culture with legal reforms. In their view, law is the result of compromises and as such contravenes the principle that 'each woman speaks for herself, there is no representation or delegation'.[15] Furthermore, they argued that reform of laws relating to sexual violence was inscribed within the punitive dimension of criminal law, constructing women as victims without agency. What was required was political action aiming at changing the symbolic relationship between women and men. Law and legal reform seen as 'male' was inadequate to this task. Rather, women should try to profit from law's gaps.[16]

Certainly, the difficulty of changing the symbolic relationship between men and women through legal reform was demonstrated in the mid-1990s process of enacting new criminal provisions punishing sexual violence as a 'crime against the person' rather than an offence to public morality. Despite these changes however, women were still not recognised in law as sovereigns of their own bodies. Stereotypes and prejudices still prevailed in the first application of the new provisions. In 1998, one court, for example, considered rape impossible if the alleged victim was wearing jeans.[17] Furthermore, women who lodged rape complaints have been exposed to secondary victimisation in the courts.[18] They have also been left to organise their own support groups and shelters as no support services and programmes have been provided by the state.[19]

12 See Creazzo (2008).
13 Cigarini (1995: 85).
14 On the debate, see Pitch (1995).
15 Cigarini (1995: 85); Tatafiore (1996); and Pitch (1998: 153).
16 Libreria delle donne di Milano (1987: 110).
17 Court of Cassation, judgment no 1636 (1998). The Court considered that rape was impossible in these circumstances as jeans cannot be removed without the cooperation of the victim.
18 Manente (2009).
19 The first National Action Plan, adopted in 2013, nationally systematised the funding of women's shelters.

These problems have confirmed feminist suspicions about the efficacy of legal reforms to assist victims of sexual violence, leading some activists to turn instead to promoting the establishment of independent women's shelters and refuges.[20] Here law becomes a multidimensional strategy with feminist activists responding to the concrete needs of women escaping from violence, simultaneously tackling the sexist paradigms that hinder women's access to justice while building a narrative of violence against women which corresponds to their experience. The primary goal in such feminist activism is to ensure that each woman is recognised as the sole person entitled to pronounce a credible account of her experience of violence. This has been pursued by means of the 'practice of entrustment' (*affidamento*) of each woman to her lawyer who is not disinterested or detached as traditionally required for legal practitioners, but driven to oppose the spread of sexist stereotypes, including that of law's 'ideal victim'.

Italian legal reforms

In the last twenty years, Italy has witnessed a continuous process of legal reforms relating to intimate partner violence. However, as the Court of Cassation recently pointed out, when it comes to dealing with violence against women, Italian jurists are confronted with an unsystematic and confusing 'archipelago of normative provisions'.[21] Here is a sample. Since its enactment in 1930, the Italian Penal Code has criminalised acts of violence committed within the family. Domestic violence was then conceived as a violation of the family's integrity and a line was drawn between the 'legitimate power of correction' belonging to the father or the husband (Article 571) and the abuse of this power (Article 572). Other provisions in the 1930 Penal Code punished beatings, threats and injuries. However, these crimes were punished very lightly if committed by the head of household as a reaction to the violation of family honour – the so-called 'honour crimes', abolished in 1981.[22] After a long debate about sexual violence reforms a set of criminal provisions were adopted in 1996 with sexual violence punished as a crime against the person instead of against morality. In the same year, new provisions were introduced regarding cross-examination to protect victims during the trial. According to these provisions, the victim must be protected from intrusive questions and investigation concerning her morality and sexual habits.[23] This was an important rupture with the 'honour era', a strong challenge to a victim-blaming judicial culture which was accustomed to treating victims as if they were defendants.[24]

20 On the critics of law produced by feminist legal experts of women's shelters see Manente (2018: 75–89); Boiano (2015: 217 ff); and Creazzo (2008: 15–42).
21 Court of Cassation, judgment no 101959 (2016).
22 Act 442/ 1981 on the repeal of the criminal relevance of the cause of honour.
23 Act 66/1996, Article 15.
24 For a critique of the persistence until 1981 of criminal relevance of 'honour' in the Italian legal system as exemplifying cultural justifications of male violence supported by law, see United Nations General Assembly Human Rights Council (2009).

Criminal reforms concerning violence against women continued in the 2000s. In 2001, protection orders were enacted both as civil and penal measures, an important reform that saw the beginning of joint cooperation between legislators and lawyers working for women's shelters.[25] In 2009 stalking was criminalised and a specific protection measure introduced.[26] But feminists criticised the new law because it was introduced by an emergency decree and contained provisions concerning general issues of public order and security. Violence against women, they pointed out, was not a 'law and security' issue but rather a wider cultural and social problem deriving from the historical imbalance of power between men and women.

In 2013, following Italy's ratification of the Istanbul Convention, a set of provisions was integrated into the Penal Code and the Criminal Procedure Code. The media referred to this reform as the 'law against femicide', although this term did not appear in its provisions.[27] Disappointingly, the integration process meant that once again, violence against women was placed in the context of public order and security, ignoring the reiterated demands of feminist lawyers, activists and scholars for a comprehensive and multidimensional strategy against gender-based violence.[28] The law was amended in response to feminist criticism, its final provisions extending police powers to adopt temporary protection measures. It also introduced the concept of 'aggravating circumstances' in the context of intimate partner violence such as the very fact that the victim was an intimate partner, was pregnant or was attacked in the presence of minors.[29] The state was also obliged to provide victims with information, including information about women's shelters and legal assistance and aid was extended in cases of battery, stalking or sexual violence.[30]

The new laws are constantly monitored by women's shelters' lawyers who report on their effectiveness to the domestic Supreme Council of Magistrates and to the international Committee on the Elimination of Discrimination against Women. Unfortunately, there are worrying signs that the laws are ineffective, with a recent special parliamentary commission of inquiry on femicide finding that in Italy 40 per cent of cases of gender-based violence reported to judicial authorities are dismissed.[31]

Finally, EU directives have brought about changes for crime victims in general and for victims of intimate partner violence in particular.[32] Now victims recognised as vulnerable can testify without having to see the defendant.[33] In 2014 and

25 Act 154/2001 on measures against family violence.
26 Act 39/2009.
27 Act 119/2013.
28 See Platform 30 Years CEDAW (2011).
29 Act 119/2013 and Decree 93/2013.
30 Articles 101 and 384 of the Criminal Procedure Code as amended by Act 119/2013.
31 Commissione di inchiesta parlamentare sul femminicidio 2018.
32 See Lupária (2015).
33 See PICUM (2012) on the access to justice of irregular migrant women victims of gender-based violence and the campaign designed and launched in 2016 by the Platform for International

2015, feminist lawyers once again stressed the need for a gender-based approach when the European directives on the rights of victims of trafficking and on the rights of victims of crime were implemented in Italy.[34] These legislative initiatives notwithstanding, it is vital that feminists continue to monitor their implementation. For example, the concept of vulnerability is already raising the spectre of medicalising victims, some judges interpreting vulnerability as a pathological status to be ascertained by a medical expert.[35]

Case studies – non-fatal attacks

The transformative potential of legal feminism as it has been practiced by feminist lawyers working in women's shelters can be illustrated with cases litigated by the legal office of the NGO *Differenza Donna*, a feminist organisation that has evolved around the idea of a women's shelter as a political space of and for women. It has been active in Rome since 1989. The cases highlight how courts condone violence against women via inadequate and ineffective interventions.[36]

Until the 1960s, courts refused to 'see' domestic violence unless they recognised it as serious and recurring, thereby compromising the personal integrity of a family member. While the crime punished by Article 572 of the Penal Code is currently conceptualised by courts as a violation of individual integrity, including psychological violence, judges still look for tangible and visible signs of physical violence. In most of the cases litigated by *Differenza Donna*, criminal protection orders are not adopted during the investigation unless there are medical reports of physical injuries.[37] Furthermore, prosecutors and judges underestimate the impact of acts of denigration and humiliation, urging the woman to speak instead about the physical violence she suffered during her cross-examination.[38] Moreover, it is still commonly believed that intimate partner violence is difficult to demonstrate in court as it takes place in the 'private' sphere. Accordingly, feminist lawyers have had to work hard to get courts to recognise the value of the victim's testimony and to ensure her felt sense of safety as a witness.

Thanks to this feminist work, courts are starting to acknowledge the complexity of domestic violence which frequently involves coercive control and psychological violence. This is illustrated in a case litigated by *Differenza Donna* before the Rome Court of Appeal in 2008. This was a case in which

---

Cooperation (PICUM) together with Women Against Violence Europe (WAVE), a feminist platform of feminist women's shelters.

34 Directives 2011/36/EU and 2012/29/EU.

35 See Platform 30 Years CEDAW (2011).

36 As was recently stressed in ECtHR, *Talpis v Italy*, 412317/14 (2017).

37 Differenza Donna (2014).

38 Manente (2018).

the judge clearly appreciated the seriousness of denigrating acts committed by the accused:

> The fact that the violence has occurred in the presence of other people has certainly wounded the victim's dignity, causing feelings of overwhelming fear and a state of intense uneasiness and extraordinary emotional distress.[39]

To ensure the disclosure during the cross-examination of all the forms of violence suffered by the victim, the woman's lawyer usually follows the scheme of the 'spiral of violence' developed by the women's shelter to increase awareness about the different forms of violence to which women are exposed. In this way, the survivor can offer a more complete and detailed statement not only about physical assault, but also the different elements of coercion imposed on her life by the accused, leaving her with psychological, rather than visible and physical scars. For example, in a 2009 case before the same court it was said that:

> The evidence has shown not only episodes of physical violence but also and predominantly, repeated episodes of psychological violence, including insults, threats, humiliations and an utter display of contempt for the wife's dignity. This occurred in the presence of relatives who testified about the accused's behaviour, including his comments about the woman's appearance. The fact that such behaviours were infrequent and left no trace on the woman's body is not relevant.[40]

Here we see a court accepting the testimonies of relatives, friends, employers and colleagues to reinforce the credibility of the victim's statement. In cases litigated by *Differenza Donna*, shelter workers also participate in the trials as expert witnesses, informing the court about the woman's situation and providing a feminist analysis of violence against women.

In *Differenza Donna's* litigation, it has also become clear that women who report violence in intimate relationships are often accused of falsely accusing their partner in order to benefit from, for example, full child custody.[41] Moreover, they are viewed as inadequate mothers, both because they report the father of their children to the authorities and because they stayed in the abusive relationship for a long time. Many women are also not believed if they appear to have professional or economic agency or if they are 'too vocal', revealing anger towards the perpetrator. Another common remark is that the woman provoked her partner's violence. For example, in a 2007 case the judge said that:

> The high level of conflict between the spouses does not demonstrate that in the facts of the case there was unilateral conduct on the part of the accused

39 Rome District Court, judgment no 9598 (2008).
40 Rome District Court, judgment no 5 (2009).
41 CEDAW Committee (2017).

> aimed at inflicting continuous moral and physical violence on the victim responding to the crime punished by Article 572 of the Penal Code. At most, it demonstrates a degeneration of the familiar relationship, within which episodes of physical and verbal violence could be reactions to a state of tension provoked by the woman.[42]

The 'episodes of physical violence' were certified by three medical reports, attesting to the fact that the woman was found with serious injuries which were all ignored by the judge.

One final case demonstrates the negative impact of gender biases on women's access to justice. A young woman was subjected to her husband's psychological, physical and sexual violence for five years, commencing when she was a minor. He also forced her into prostitution. She was subjected to violence but the police and medical staff who attended her underestimated the degree of violence she experienced, instead criticising her for failing to comply with the image of the 'ideal victim'. She eventually escaped from her husband once she realised that her life was at risk. On reporting the sexual violence, sexual exploitation and a coerced abortion she had endured, the prosecutor accused him of slavery, sexual exploitation and sexual violence. During her ten hours of cross-examination in the court, she testified about her five years of torture. However, the judge found her declarations to be characterised by incoherence and inconsistency. It was considered suspicious that during her three periods of apparent freedom, she did not feel the need to report her abuser even though she had the opportunity to do so. Moreover, the judge criticised her lack of compassion for her abuser.[43]

Accordingly, the accused was acquitted of all charges. The victim appealed, knowing she would have to be cross-examined again. Her lawyer pointed out the sexist prejudices that had informed the legal interpretation and appraisal of facts in the lower court, demanding a revised judgment. The Rome Court of Appeal found the first-instance judgment to be 'very misleading', the judge having ignored 'the rawness of the victim's story', instead siding with the accused 'against all logic'.[44] However, although the appellate court sentenced the accused for the crime of abuse of his wife, it did not find that he had put her into slavery. The case is currently pending before the Court of Cassation, the appellant claiming she was deprived of her freedom and that the Court of Appeal did not correctly apply the provision punishing such deprivation under Article 600 of the Penal Code.

The case is important for demonstrating how feminist litigation can expose how stereotypes influence judges to discredit survivors, sometimes blaming them for the violence because they do not fit the 'ideal victim' archetype, while forming a favourable view of the accused. Furthermore, though the survivor was subjected to secondary victimisation through cross-examination, she was motivated by the political aim of making clear that what she had suffered should not be legally

42 Rome District Court, judgment no 24510 (2007).
43 Rome District Court, judgment no 3302 (2016).
44 Rome Court of Appeal, judgment no 48 (2017).

interpreted as a merely conflictual conjugal relationship – it was a serious violation of her fundamental rights and as such should not be condoned by the courts.

Femicide in Italy

But what of intimate partner femicides? In Italy the terms 'femicide' and 'feminicide' were introduced only relatively recently. While 'femicide' refers to the killing of a woman because she is a woman, 'feminicide' refers to the general context of gender-based discrimination and violence against women, including practices of public authorities that contribute to a culture of domination by allowing men to commit violent acts with impunity. The *Unione donne italiane* first used the term 'feminicide' (*femminicidio* in Italian) in 2006. Then in 2009 the lawyer and activist Barbara Spinelli introduced the theoretical framework underlying the terms as theorised by the Mexican feminist Marcela Lagarde.[45] Since then, Italian women's organisations and activists have advocated that 'feminicide' be used to refer to the killing of women in the context of a sexist culture that facilitates men's violence against women by excusing it.

It should be emphasised that the term 'feminicide' is preferred by feminist activists and organisations because of its larger inclusive provenance encompassing the multiplicity of social, historical and cultural factors legitimising violence against women. However, for Italian public authorities the term is restricted to the killing of a woman. But given that most femicides occur after women have lodged criminal complaints against their partners and expressed their fear of being killed, it becomes apparent why 'feminicide', rather than 'femicide' is the preferred term, the former emphasising the phenomenon in all its complexity, including the state's omissions in protecting women. Not that Italian feminists want 'femicide' or 'feminicide' designated as specific crimes. Taking into account feminist criticism of such crimes when they have been introduced in other legal systems, for example in South America, they prefer that the terms be used only to define the phenomenon socially and culturally.[46] After pressure from feminist movements, the national institute for statistics has started to include feminicide in its research on violence against women in Italy. In 2017 the Italian Senate established a special investigative commission on feminicide and all forms of violence against women.[47]

But how serious is the problem of femicide in Italy? In the last five years, 774 women were killed, an average of 150 women per year, more than 100 of whom were killed by partners and former partners.[48] But in the face of the statistics, the media continues to concoct a narrative of feminicide connected to sudden mental illness or to a desperate extreme reaction to women's requests for separation, thereby holding fast to the traditional story of justification and commiseration for men who kill 'their' women.

45 Lagarde (2005).
46 See Chapter 3 in this book.
47 Commissione parlamentare di inchiesta sul femminicidio 2018.
48 Torlone (2017) and Commissione parlamentare di inchiesta sul femminicidio 2018.

Femicide cases

Two cases decided in 2017 provide some insights into legal responses to fatal and near fatal violence against women in Italy. In one, an attempted murder case, a woman had a relationship with a married man who repeatedly promised that he would leave his wife for her. After years of broken promises, she decided to reveal their relationship to the man's wife and then to leave him. Regarding this plan as outrageous, he set a trap for her in an isolated place of the city where he attacked her, causing serious injuries. The Rome District Court convicted him of attempted murder, basing its decision on the victim's statement, photographs of her condition immediately after the assault and the medical report.[49] The Rome Court of Appeal however, acquitted him of this crime. It its view, the accused only intended to injure her. While the 'core of the action' was retaliation 'against an antagonist whom he perceived as his enemy', his aim was to cause her suffering but not to kill her.[50]

Compare a femicide case in which a young woman had decided to leave her boyfriend because of his continuous attempts to control all aspects of her life, including her attendance at her university lectures. After she left him, he continued stalk her. She did not report him. One night he followed her home after she had spent an evening out with friends, killed her and set her body on fire. *Differenza Donna* intervened in the criminal trial as a civil party in order to present the court with a feminist analysis. Importantly, it managed to convince the judge that the stalking which preceded the murder was the result not of the killer's psychopathology as the media suggested but rather a consequence of the typically controlling behaviour of a man who believed a woman did not have the right to withdrawal from a relationship, seeing her instead as his 'absolute property'. The judge determined that the killing took place in the context of a 'very sexist culture' that degraded love to a desire to control. Within such a culture, there was an 'inadmissible and socially unacceptable' belief in the right to dominate a woman and punish her for her 'rebellion and affirmation of her dignity and value as human person'. Yet while the court recognised that the victim had been punished in this way, it felt that in order to emphasise the seriousness of the crime, it needed to recall the central role of the family in the Italian Constitution and 'the priority that women have within the family'. In the final analysis, that seemed to be more important than the violation of the victim's individual fundamental rights.[51]

Concluding remarks

As Smart observed, law's truth is often in conflict with women's experience.[52] The Italian legal system still has a long way to go in its handling of intimate

49 Rome District Court, judgment no 5115 (2016).
50 Rome Court of Appeal, judgment no 4708 (2017).
51 Rome District Court, judgment no 807 (2017).
52 Smart (1990: 1).

partner violence. But while feminist legal practice has not yet made many inroads into law's truth, it has at least dented it. Moreover, by providing women with access to justice, feminist lawyering has helped to identify problematic laws and court practices, thereby promoting what Peter Goodrich called a 'minor jurisprudence', one that 'neither aspires nor pretends to be the only law or universal jurisprudence' but nevertheless challenges law, threatening its 'monopoly of legal knowledge'.[53] Smart herself is persuaded by the idea of such a minor jurisprudence, agreeing with Karen Van Marle that it is no longer necessary to see the search for a feminist jurisprudence as 'a quest for a new grand theory' as she did in *Feminism and the Power of Law*. A 'more modern version' will do, one that takes the form of 'a complex, tentative, questioning engagement with law'. This seems to her to be 'entirely plausible and captivating'.[54] With this in mind, Italian feminists like others elsewhere are determined to keep challenging the power of law, just as Smart always advocated.

References

Bocchetti, A. 1995 *Cosa vuole una donna: Storia, politica, teoria. Scritti 1981/1995* Milan: La Tartaruga.

Boiano, I. 2015 *Femminismo e processo penale* Rome: Ediesse.

Cavarero, A. and Restaino, S. 2002 *Filosofie femministe* Milan: Bruno Mondadori.

Committee on the Elimination of Discrimination against Women (CEDAW Committee) 2017 *Concluding Observations on the Seventh Periodic Report of Italy* UN Doc. CEDAW/C/ITA/CO/7.

Cigarini, L. 1995 *La politica del desiderio* Parma: Pratiche Edizioni.

Colombo, S. 1992 'Femminismo giuridico' 8 *Discipline privatistiche* 247.

Commissione di inchiesta parlamentare sul femminicidio 2018 *Relazione Finale* Doc XXII-bis 9 Rome: Senato della Repubblica.

Creazzo, G. 2008 'La costruzione sociale della violenza contro le donne in Italia' 2 *Studi sulla questione criminale* 15.

Differenza Donna 2014 *Report sull'attuazione della legge n. 119/2013* Rome: Differenza Donna.

Goodrich, P. 1996 *Law in the Courts of Love: Literature and Other Minor Jurisprudence* New York: Routledge.

Lagarde, M. 2005 'El feminicidio, delito contra la humanidad' in Camara de Diputados del H. Congreso de la Unión – LIX Legislatura *Feminicidio, justicia y derecho* Mexico City: Congreso de la Unión 151.

Libreria delle donne di Milano 1987 *Non credere di avere dei diritti* Turin: Rosenberg & Sellier.

Lupária, L. (ed.) 2015 *Victims and Criminal Justice: European Standards and National Good Practices* Rome: Wolters Kluwer.

Manente, T. 2009 *Dossier sull'applicazione delle norme in materia di violenza domestica* Rome: CSM.

53 Goodrich (1996: 2).

54 Smart (2012: 164) citing Van Marle (2012).

——— 2018 'La pratica femminista del processo penale come strategia di difesa dei diritti delle donne vittime di violenza maschile' in A. Simone and I. Boiano (eds.) *Femminismo ed esperienza giuridica* Roma: Edizioni Efesto.

PICUM 2012 *Strategies to End Double Violence against Undocumented Women Protecting Rights and Ensuring Justice* Brussles: Beëlzepub.

Pitch, T. 1983 'Tra diritti sociali e cittadinanza. Il movimento delle donne e la legge sulla violenza sessuale' 27–28 *Problemi del socialismo* 192

——— 1989 *Responsabilità limitate. Attori, conflitti, giustizia penale* Milan: Feltrinelli.

——— 1993 'Diritto e diritti: un percorso nel dibattito femminista' 2 *Democrazia e Diritto* 4.

——— 1995 *Limited Responsibilities: Social Movements and Criminal Justice* London: Routledge.

——— 1998 *Un diritto per due* Milan: Il Saggiatore.

——— 2004 *I diritti fondamentali: differenze culturali, disuguaglianze sociali, differenza sessuale* Turin: Giappichelli.

Platform 30 Years CEDAW: Work in Progress 2011 *Shadow Report* tbinternet.ohchr.org/Treaties/CEDAW/Shared%20Documents/ITA/INT_CEDAW_NGO_ITA_49_9220_E.pdf

Scarponi, S. 2014 *Diritto e genere* Padua: Cedam.

Smart, C. 1976 *Women, Crime and Criminology: A Feminist Critique* London: Routledge and Kegan Paul.

——— 1989 *Feminism and the Power of Law* London: Routledge.

——— 1990 'Law's Truth/Women's Experience' in R. Graycar (ed.) *Dissenting Opinions: Feminist Explorations in Law and Society* Sydney: Allen & Unwin.

——— 1992 'The Woman of Legal Discourse' 1 *Social & Legal Studies* 29.

——— 2012 'Reflection' 20 *Feminist Legal Studies* 65.

Tatafiore, R. 1996 *De bello fallico. Cronaca di una brutta legge sulla violenza sessuale* Milan: Stampa Alternativa.

Torlone, G. 2017 'Ogni due giorni una donna viene uccisa dal compagno. I numeri della violenza di genere' *L'Espresso* espresso.repubblica.it/attualita/2017/06/19/news/femminicidi-1.304466

United Nations General Assembly Human Rights Council 2009 *Report of the Special Rapporteur on Violence against Women, Its Causes and Consequences, Yakin Ertürk* UN Doc. A/HRC/11/6/Add.5.

Van Marle, K. 2012 '"We Exist, But Who Are We?" Feminism and the Power of Sociological Law' 20 *Feminist Legal Studies* 149.

9 Legal education – challenging the Finnish criminal law syllabus

Daniela Alaattinoğlu and Johanna Niemi

Introduction

> In Finland, like many other countries, it seems to be quite possible to be a respected male academic without paying any attention at all to feminist and critical gender scholarship, including that on men.[1]

So often is Finland pictured as a champion of gender equality that it could be said to have reached the position of a commercial brand. Reaching a zenith in 2017, the centenary of its independence, Finland became the first country in the world to establish an 'International Gender Equality Prize'. Yet, recent studies on domestic violence and violence against women – including intimate partner femicide – highlight a high level of violence in Finland compared to other European countries.[2] This violent reality and its consequent gender inequality is typically disavowed, ascribed no legal relevance in Finnish law schools. Intimate partner femicide is yet to be registered as a first-order political problem. This chapter asks how far, if at all, Finnish feminist critiques of law's handling of these cases has translated into mainstream legal education. We shall focus on the literature used in Finnish law faculties' mandatory criminal law courses, analysing it as a site of legal knowledge production. In doing so we draw on Carol Smart's assessment in *Feminism and the Power of Law* of feminist approaches to the law question that were being developed in the 1980s, noting her preference for the emphasis placed on 'law in practice' as advocated by the Norwegian feminist scholar Tove Stang Dahl. While agreeing with her that Dahl's approach is preferable to pushing 'fruitlessly' against the 'immovable object' of legal method, we shall explore the legal method deployed in Finnish criminal law texts, reading them as Smart advocated, as discursive sites on which to explore and challenge gendered constructions of intimate partner femicide.[3]

1 Hearn (2015: 41).
2 European Union Agency for Fundamental Rights (2014) and European Institute for Gender Equality (2015: 123–136).
3 Smart (1989: 25). All translations are ours.

Finnish feminist legal critique

Feminist and gender studies in law have developed in Finland largely since the 1990s, establishing a presence at Finnish law faculties, even though this presence is far from taken for granted. In their bid to establish a new discipline, Finnish feminist legal scholars were inspired by the successful push – much admired by Carol Smart – for the institutionalisation of 'Women's Law' at Oslo University by Norwegian feminists, preeminently Tove Stang Dahl. Today there is national funding for feminist legal research as well as courses taught in gender and law.[4] Moreover, introductory mandatory first year law courses in Helsinki and Turku – two of four law faculties in the country – have come to include at least a snapshot of gender and law research. Student feedback indicates that there has been a clear change from open resistance in the early 1990s to interest in and recognition of gender issues today. General awareness of gender has increased with the shift from 'Women's Law' to 'Law and Gender' and over the years, several optional courses have offered topics about gender and gender-based violence.[5]

Generally speaking, Finnish feminist research in law has been theoretically and critically oriented, analysing the legally 'taken for granted' such as the legal subject or the paradigm of rights. Foundational texts include the first feminist doctoral thesis, Liisa Nieminen's 'The Emancipatory Potential of Constitutional Rights?' published in 1990, which critically assesses the concept of rights, drawing on feminist theory.[6] In 'Trapped in Equality', her 2009 pioneering treatise on the history of women's rights and legal subjectivity, Anu Pylkkänen argued that the strong belief in equality as an already achieved state, the so-called 'equality myth', blinded Finnish society from existing inequalities.[7] The concept of the equality myth is today generally accepted among Finnish feminist legal scholars, including those working on criminal law.

Regulating interpersonal and gender-based violence, Finnish criminal law has been a central site of feminist scholarly engagement. Already by the 1990s, violence against women was brought up and discussed in short criminal law articles and opinions, which, however, remained sporadic and did not lead to major debate.[8] While there is no Finnish study on femicide *per se*, two studies from the 2000s opened up the question of the role of gender in criminal law's handling of homicide cases. First, Johanna Niemi-Kiesiläinen's 2004 book focuses on

4 Nationally, there have been three competitive five-year professorships dedicated to feminist legal research. While feminist legal research has been relatively well funded in Finland, these investments have not been followed by permanent teaching positions.

5 Closest to criminal law comes the optional, popular interdisciplinary course 'Gender, Violence and Law', organised at the University of Helsinki 2002–2013. The course touched upon femicide from a criminological and doctrinal view. One important outcome of the organisation of the course is the publication Niemi et al. (2017).

6 Nieminen (1990).

7 Pylkkänen (2009).Pylkkänen 2009.

8 Examples of interventions in the 1990s are Pohjonen (1992) and Nousiainen (1999).

criminal procedure and intimate partner violence.[9] Second, Minna Ruuskanen's 2005 doctoral thesis addresses self-defence in cases where women killed their partners.[10] Inasmuch as both were inspired by Smart's poststructuralist approach to law, their studies exemplify how her socio-legal methodology has had an influence on Finnish feminist critique of criminal law. As lawyers, they felt that conventional legal methodologies were unhelpful. With the intuition that gendered structures mattered for the procedural unfolding and outcomes of court cases, they were nevertheless unaware of how to render these structures visible. Joining with sociologists to create a socio-legal research group and study circle on discourse analysis, they gained insights from social science methodologies, such as discourse analysis.[11]

While Smart is often interpreted as a pessimist regarding law's potential to change the world, Niemi-Kiesiläinen and Ruuskanen found her critique of the prevalent forms of legal feminism refreshing. Her view of law as a discursive field that produces gender was especially useful, opening up a new way of investigating law, beyond traditional doctrinal analysis.[12] Ruuskanen in particular argued for the benefits of discourse analysis when approaching legal texts inasmuch as law and legal discourse 'construct and reconstruct our understanding of gender'.[13] Take self-defence, for example. Analysing appeal court cases from police investigation to verdict, she found that women's claims of self-defence were *never* successful. In fact, women's claim of self-defence were defeated at the investigation stage and consequently disappeared in the criminal justice process.[14] More broadly, courts constructed violence as a mutual fight or mutual loss of control, as a continuation of a quarrel between two partners equally prone to violence and assumed to be equal in power.[15]

As Niemi-Kiesiläinen explained, if the key question to be addressed was whether the criminal law was gendered, the answer was surely 'affirmative' – it was gendered in respect of 'the elements of the crime, general doctrines and case law'.[16] Challenging Finnish criminal and procedural law, particularly its gender blindness, she paid attention to statistics which showed that women in Finland were killed by their partners at an alarming rate. By comparing Finland's rates of female homicide victims to that of Sweden, a country often serving as a reference point for Finnish lawyers, she discovered that the number was roughly the same: about 30 victims annually at the time. This said, the striking difference was that the Swedish population, then nine million, was

9 Niemi-Kiesiläinen (2004).
10 Ruuskanen (2005).
11 The research group included Johanna Niemi(-Kiesiläinen), Minna Ruuskanen, Päivi Honkatukia, Sari Näre, Tanja Mansikka, Helena Jokila and Heini Kainulainen.
12 Smart (1992: 31). Another important bridging text was Naffine and Owens (1997).
13 Ruuskanen (2005: 83).
14 Ruuskanen (2001, 2005).
15 Ruuskanen (2005: 74) and Niemi-Kiesiläinen (2004: 66).
16 Niemi-Kiesiläinen (2004: 112).

almost double that of Finland, then 5.2 million, making Finnish femicide rates proportionately double.[17]

Through both doctrinal and discourse analysis, Niemi-Kiesiläinen showed that the victim's perspective was given little importance in Finnish criminal law and none in mainstream legal theory. It was not just that the 'subjective' experience of the victim, her felt sense of lethal danger, did not count. Even the victim's 'objective' experience – what is obvious to an 'outside observer', an evaluation normally central to Finnish criminal law – was considered irrelevant. She also found that intimate partner violence was not considered an aggravating circumstance by Finnish courts. On the contrary, the fact that violence occurred within an intimate relationship could be seen as a mitigating factor, leading to a reduced penalty. Consider for example two cases of intimate partner violence adjudicated by the Finnish Supreme Court where defendants were charged with attempted manslaughter. One had hit the victim with a hard object several times in the head, vocally threatening to kill her. The court decided that as his acts were unlikely to cause her death, the offence should be downgraded to aggravated assault, prompting Niemi-Kiesiläinen to comment: 'there seems to be no ambiguity about the intention of the perpetrator' who several times during the battery and later told police he had intended to kill her.[18] In the second case, the defendant had battered the victim by strangling her with his hands and his belt to the extent that she lost consciousness. The court came to a similar conclusion. Finding that as there was not enough proof to show that the defendant intended to kill the victim, the court regarded the violence as assault. Once again, Niemi-Kiesiläinen noted the court's disregard of the explicit 'threats to kill'.[19]

By the mid-2000s then, Finnish feminist researchers, some directly influenced by Smart's work, had started to explore the discursive construction of gender in Finnish criminal law, including its construction of domestic violence cases. The question now is whether this feminist critique has had any effect on the law school curriculum.

Criminal law texts

One of the problems Smart identified with legal method was the way it taught students how to code and divide situations into the legally 'relevant' and 'irrelevant'.[20] The relevant goes into legal analysis, constructed as the legal truth. What is seen as irrelevant, on the other hand, goes out. With this in mind, let us turn to criminal law textbooks, mandatory for law students at the University of Helsinki, the University of Turku, the University of Lapland and the University of Eastern Finland, to see how intentional killing is constructed and put into

17 Piispa and Heiskanen (1998) and Lundgren et al. (2001).

18 Finnish Supreme Court KKO:1993:5.Niemi-Kiesiläinen (2004: 106, 110).

19 Finnish Supreme Court KKO 1998:1; Niemi-Kiesiläinen (2004: 110).

20 Smart (1989: 22). Importantly, this hierarchy can be seen as an expression of law's 'ability to disqualify other knowledges and experiences': Smart (1989: 11).

discourse.[21] Our analysis is confined to two representative books. One, titled *Criminal Law*, is used at the University of Helsinki; the other is *Central Crimes*, used at the Universities of Turku, Lapland and Eastern Finland.[22]

How do the texts represent homicide? The focus is on the circumstances in which men are killed.[23] In *Criminal Law*, the typical case of lethal interpersonal violence in Finland is constructed as 'drunk manslaughter' *(humalatappo)*, perpetrated by a friend or acquaintance where both perpetrator and victim were extremely drunk.[24] By contrast, *Central Crimes* employs a more gender-sensitive account of a typical homicide in Finland, acknowledging that most women are killed by their partners.[25] Secondly, homicide is represented as 'an exceptional crime'. As *Criminal Law* explains:

> The ones guilty of such a crime often deviate in their criminal profile from the people sentenced by the courts every day. The ones sentenced for homicide are older than other criminals, often seriously alcoholised, and often have an exceptionally extensive criminal record. At the same time, they have complex social and psychological problems.[26]

Such a construction ignores the fact that women's victimisation by their intimate partners is far from exceptional.

Deploying gender-neutral discourse, Finnish criminal law texts construct different types of intentional manslaughter – sometimes imaginary, sometimes based on the case law of the Finnish Supreme Court – to exemplify the elements of the crimes. The killer and the victim are typically termed A and B. Finnish, a language which lacks genders, is well suited to this type of discourse. For example:

> A, incarcerated because of intoxication, had strangled B, who was in the same cell, to death. A had taken off their shirt and strangled B with it, as A got angry being incarcerated, with B pushing them. The killing was not considered particularly brutal or cruel, and A was convicted for manslaughter.[27]

As and Bs are used to demonstrate a doctrinal argument which is independent of personal details or power relationships. What is considered important is only what happened at the immediate moment when the homicide took place – the perpetrator's mental state and actions – everything else is deemed legally irrelevant.

21 Only legal educations that lead to a Master of Laws degree have been taken into consideration. The course literature analysed is for the academic year 2016–2017.
22 The University of Helsinki uses Lappi-Seppälä et al. (2013). The other law faculties use Frände et al. (2014).
23 In other words, corresponding to the statistics on men's victimisation. See Lehti (2017).
24 Lappi-Seppälä et al. (2013: 469–470).
25 Frände et al. (2014: 187).
26 Lappi-Seppälä et al. (2013: 470).
27 Lappi-Seppälä et al. (2013: 471); Finnish Supreme Court, KKO: 1973-II-68.

The term 'femicide' has no place in this gender-blind discourse. While some cases of intimate partner femicide and cases where a child is killed as revenge against their mother are included in the texts, the gendered power relations between perpetrators and victims are often mystified. The personal details of A and B are rendered irrelevant in the name of legal objectivity. One example of an intimate partner femicide, based on a case before the Finnish Supreme Court, depicted in *Central Crimes*, tells the reader how A had bought a 22 calibre gun, ammunition magazines and pellets, and invited his wife B, 'who had moved out a couple of days before', to his apartment. According to A, they had then started 'a heated argument', and B had 'tried to leave the apartment'. A had then 'fired at least eight shots', hitting B in the 'upper and lower body'. B then managed to leave the building, but fell on the ground outside. A 'returned to the apartment when the ammunition magazine was empty' and changed it with one that 'A had beforehand charged with at least four pellets and left under the sofa pillow'. After this, A 'came outside and shot at least four shots from a close distance, hitting B, who was lying on the ground, in the upper left back'. The example ends with noting that 'A was prosecuted for murder, with premeditation, particular brutality and cruelty as qualifying grounds'.[28]

Here the history and dynamics of A and B's relationship is erased. Why had B, the wife, moved out of the apartment? Was it because of previous violence? In this text, her story and experiences are rendered legally irrelevant and are thereby silenced.[29] Or consider another de-contextualised example from *Central Crimes.*

> A had decided to kill B on B's birthday . . . if B still rejected to continue their relationship. A had planned to kill B through wrapping B tightly into plastic bags, binding B with strings, leaving them for a month in the car, and then dumping B into a hole in the ice. When B's answers did not please A, A stabbed B 18 times on three different occasions. Even though A had committed his acts in a different manner and on a different day than planned, the killing was considered premeditated.[30]

Saying that personal details and relationships are considered legally irrelevant is not, however, to say that intimate partner femicides are viewed with leniency. On the contrary, many of the cases are constructed as 'murder' (*murha*), that is, the aggravated form of intentional homicide according to the Finnish Criminal Code.[31] However, this is based on the predefined legislated qualifying grounds for murder, such as premeditation, brutality or cruelty. Factors such as previous violence, relationship or power dynamics are *not* taken into account notwithstanding the fact that Finland is obliged to consider such factors as aggravating circumstances through its ratification in 2015 of the Istanbul Convention – the

28 Frände et al. (2014: 209); Finnish Supreme Court, KKO: 2004:80.
29 As also pointed out by Niemi-Kiesiläinen (2004: 106).
30 Frände et al. (2014: 205); Finnish Supreme Court, KKO: 1980-II-59.
31 Rikoslaki [Finnish Criminal Code] 39/1889, Chapter 21 Section 2.

Council of Europe Convention on Preventing and Combating Violence against Women and Domestic Violence.[32] It seems that Finnish criminal law is persistently rejecting – even in the face of international legal obligations – the notion that the whole context of intimate partner femicide matters. Rejecting the contexts in which men kill women includes disregarding histories of violence and so-called 'precipitating' factors such as the victim's desire to leave the relationship.

Finnish criminal law is reluctant to change its approach to interpersonal context as legally irrelevant. Analysing the textbooks, we can begin to trace the underlying reasons to its contextually deprived approach. Traditionally, as *Criminal Law* highlights, killing a close relative – parricide, for example – 'might be regarded as socially reprehensible, but it might not legally qualify as murder', that is, as the aggravated form of intentional homicide.[33] This constructs a 'traditional' attachment to family relations as old-fashioned, and through the example of killing one's father, paternal – even patriarchal. Modern criminal law, by contrast, is understood to treat individuals equally, regardless of their social or familiar position. It is 'neutral' and 'objective', just as in the discursive domains Smart described 30 years ago where bodies 'have become de-gendered, and the specific relevance of femaleness and maleness disappears'.[34] What is seen as legally relevant is what happened at the time of the offence, not who the victim and perpetrator are. And because women and men are seen as equal in modern Finland, there is no need to treat intimate partner femicide as a special case.

The image fades in the light of statistics showing a high prevalence of intimate partner femicide in Finland. According to the annual Finnish homicide study, 16 per cent or 255 of 1591 homicide victims from 2010 to 2016 were women killed by their partners, a rate of 36 women per year.[35] On average 29 women were killed each year from 2006 to 2015, down from an average of 35 during the previous years.[36] Statistics provided by the United Nations Office on Drugs and Crime indicate that the Finnish femicide rate is 0.74 per 100.000 which is comparatively high in the European Union, topped only by the Baltic countries.[37] Relative to other Nordic countries, the Finnish figures are very high, indeed as much as three times higher. For example, in Sweden, a country with a population twice the size of Finland's, on average 13 women were killed by their partners each year in the period 2008 to 2013.[38] In Germany in 2015 the relative intimate partner femicide rate was half that of Finland with 139 women killed.[39] While the femicide rates in the European Union countries and also in Finland are

32 Council of Europe Convention on Preventing and Combating Violence against Women and Domestic Violence (2011) CETS 210, Art. 46.
33 Lappi-Seppälä et al. (2013: 497).
34 Smart (1989: 92).
35 Lehti (2017).
36 Statistics Finland (2016).
37 United Nations Office on Drugs and Crime (UNODC) (2014).
38 Brottsförebyggande rådet (BRÅ) [The Swedish National Council for Crime Prevention] (2015: 8).
39 Burba and Bona (2017).

lower than in some other parts of the world, in the European context the Finnish femicide rate is alarmingly high.[40]

In the face of such staggeringly high rates of intimate partner femicide, attempts have been made to integrate the victimisation of women into criminal law texts, but sometimes in problematic ways. *Central Crimes*, for example, suggests that 'so-called honour killing, when a woman marries a man of her own choice' rather than one chosen by her family, 'is also likely to qualify as an aggravated homicide'.[41] This seems to suggest that 'honour killing' should receive a harsher punishment than other intimate partner femicides.[42] The statement also seems to indicate that the existing grounds in the Criminal Code suffice to cover typical situations where women are victimised. That said, there is no suggestion of a need to rethink the existing normative framework.

Some attempts have also been made to integrate feminist scholarship into mainstream legal texts. Under the heading of 'killing' (*surma*), the extenuated form of homicide in the Finnish Criminal Code, some attention is paid to 'exceptional and continuous' domestic violence.[43] *Criminal Law* refers to a situation where a killing which does not qualify as self-defence seems to be the only way to escape violence. But it does so without citing or engaging in feminist criminal law research. *Central Crimes* recounts a similar, though more gender-sensitive, example – with a passing reference to Ruuskanen in a footnote – of a 'wife who has suffered from her husband's violence, who does not dare to separate from her husband or ask for external help, kills him'. Here the books momentarily step out of their otherwise universalising, gender-neutral constructions, to imagine a battered woman's reality.[44] Nevertheless, this is done without engaging in any depth with feminist criticism. The result is superficial.

Both texts analysed hence deploy two main discourses. One, the 'A kills B' discourse, ignores gender and relationship context. The other – which can be seen more clearly in *Central Crimes* – acknowledges, albeit briefly, both gender and relationship inasmuch as it is a husband who kills his wife, not an A killing a B.[45] It pays attention to the victimisation of women, referring sporadically to feminist literature. But such an additive approach is nowhere near a satisfactory

40 UNODC (2014).

41 Frände et al. (2014: 225). The example is supported with a reference to the 2011 Istanbul Convention. Fascinatingly, this is the only reference to the Convention. Council of Europe Convention on Preventing and Combating Violence against Women and Domestic Violence (2011) CETS 210, Art. 12(5) and 42.

42 On the criticism of exoticising accounts of femicides in ethnic minorities, see for example Alaattinoğlu (2016); Åkers (2014); and Howe (2013: 158–159).

43 Lappi-Seppälä et al. (2013: 499). See also Frände et al. (2014: 227).

44 Frände et al. (2014: 227). It deserves to be mentioned that while *Central Crimes* refers both to Ruuskanen and Niemi-Kiesiläinen, *Criminal Law* does not even mention them in its very extensive list of criminal law literature.

45 The account of intimate partner violence is more explicitly developed by the author of the relevant text in *Central Crimes* in Matikkala (2017). However, this book is not used as mandatory course literature in Finnish law schools.

response to feminist challenges to law's handling of intimate partner femicides. The dominant discourse remains 'A kills B', the traditional discourse of modern Finnish criminal law. With defendants and victims reduced to alphabetic letters, Finnish law students would have difficulty even recognising that this is in fact an intimate partner femicide case, let alone understand the contextual dynamics of intimate partner relationships – unearthed by decades of feminist work – that characterise these cases. In short, teaching criminal law students how to 'objectively' conceptualise the legally relevant and irrelevant, reducing the parties to As and Bs, does not teach them how to think critically about the realities of intimate partner homicide.

Towards a consistently contextual approach

The pivotal importance of taking a contextual approach to intimate partner femicide cases, an approach notable for its absence from Finnish criminal law texts, is underscored by Finland's 2015 ratification of the Istanbul Convention. Through its focus on member states' obligation to prevent violence against women, the convention approaches violence in a gender-aware way. Ratifying states are obliged to ensure that measures taken to prevent violence are 'based on a gendered understanding of violence against women and domestic violence'.[46] The convention also orders states to safeguard that these measures are 'based on an integrated approach which takes into account the relationship between victims, perpetrators, children and their wider social environment'.[47] And crucially, it emphasises a contextual approach – one which is not gender-blind – to the problem of violence against women.

Feminists working in the criminal law field in Finland and elsewhere have long advocated taking context into consideration when analysing homicide cases.[48] But the way that Finnish criminal textbooks take account of context is definitely not what they mean. Here we find the assumption that context, culture and motive are only important in so-called 'honour killings' associated with ethnic minority communities, thereby overlooking the high number of femicides committed in majority communities.[49] This 'othering' practice narrating minority ethnic men as more violent and misogynist than majority men can also be observed in Finnish court cases. In one 2011 judgment from the Kouvola Court of Appeals, a woman had been murdered by her former husband. That he had cut her throat and was a Muslim were both viewed as significant, the prosecutor noting that the killing had 'traces of brutish, ritual slaughter'. The way the killing was carried out was considered 'rare in Finnish circumstances'.[50]

46 Council of Europe Convention on Preventing and Combating Violence against Women and Domestic Violence (2011) CETS 210, Art. 18(3).
47 Council of Europe Convention on Preventing and Combating Violence against Women and Domestic Violence (2011) CETS 210, Art. 18(3).
48 For example, Niemi-Kiesiläinen (2004).
49 Frände et al. (2014: 225) and Åkers (2014). See also Howe (2013: 158–159).
50 Kouvolan hovioikeus, R 10/1129 (2011).

By contrast, Finish courts do not describe throat-cutting by majority men as culturally inscribed. For example, in a case where a man killed his partner's child as an action of revenge against her mother, the Finnish Supreme Court did not feel the need to culturalise the act by referring to it as a 'ritual slaughter'. As it was a child who was killed, the court did consider the homicide aggravated.[51] But it is significant that when the case was before the first-instance court, one judge suggested in his dissenting opinion that the homicide was not aggravated as it was 'preceded by hours of nagging and acting up' by the victim.[52] That this standard nomalising victim-blaming narrative is just as culturally mandated as the racialised conception of 'ritualistic' femicides committed by minority ethnic men continues to pass Finnish courts by.

Conclusion

While Finnish feminist criminal legal analysis has won some scholarly ground over the last few years, it usually appears in an add-on capacity in the weighty handbooks of Finnish criminal law, the very 'women and' approach Carol Smart rejected as utterly inadequate in *Feminism and the Power of Law*.[53] She also targeted law's traditional differentiation of the legally relevant from the irrelevant as one of the central problems of legal method, a method she rejected back then as 'impervious' to feminist critique.[54] The marginalisation of feminist critique evident in Finnish criminal law educational material exemplifies this imperviousness once again. Rather than challenging the corner stones of criminal legal thinking, feminist insights have been translated as a 'subjective' alternative to the universalising, supposedly 'objective' narratives of mainstream criminal law. In a country where the myth of gender equality is strong and broadly marketed, it seems to be easier to ignore not only the high national prevalence of intimate partner femicides, but also the highly problematic ways in which law in textbooks and, crucially, in practice, construct law's truth about these cases.

References

Åkers, D. 2014 *Killed by Hatred or Killed by Love? An Intersectional Challenge to Legal Constructions of Gendered Violence in Finland and Turkey* Saarbrücken: Lambert Academic Publishing.

Alaattinoğlu, D. 2016 'Hedersvåld? Rättsliga Konstruktioner av den andra i Finland och Turkiet [Honour Killing? Legal Constructions of the Other in Finland and Turkey]' 152(1–2) *Tidskrift utgiven av Juridiska föreningen i Finland* 93.

Brottsförebyggande rådet (BRÅ) [The Swedish National Council for Crime Prevention] 2015 *Det dödliga våldet i Sverige 1990–2014 [The Lethal Violence in Sweden 1990–2014]* Stockholm: BRÅ Publications.

51 Finnish Supreme Court, KKO:2000:29. See also Åkers (2014).

52 Joensuun käräjäoikeus, R 97/963 (1998).

53 Smart (1989: 2).

54 Smart (1989: 22).

Burba, A. and Bona, M. 2017 'Femicide: The Numbers in Europe' *Observatorio balcani e caucaso* www.balcanicaucaso.org/eng/Areas/Europe/Femicide-the-numbers-in-Europe-184329

Council of Europe Convention on Preventing and Combating Violence against Women and Domestic Violence 2011 CETS 210. https://www.coe.int/en/web/conventions/full-list/-/conventions/treaty/210

European Institute for Gender Equality 2015 *Gender Equality Index 2015: Measuring Gender Equality in the European Union 2002–2015* Vilnius: European Institute for Gender Equality Publications.

European Union Agency for Fundamental Rights 2014 *Violence against Women: An EU-Wide Survey: Main Results* Luxembourg: Publications Office of the European Union.

Frände, D. et al. 2014 *Keskeiset rikokset [Central Crimes]* Helsinki: Edita Prima.

Hearn, J. 2015 *Men of the World: Genders, Globalisations, Transnational Times* London: Sage Publications.

Howe, A. 2013 'Mastering Emotions or Still Losing Control? Seeking Public Engagement with "Sexual Infidelity" Homicide' 21 *Feminist Legal Studies* 141.

Lappi-Seppälä, T. et al. 2013 *Rikosoikeus [Criminal Law]* Helsinki: Sanoma Pro.

Lehti, M. 2017 *Henkirikoskatsaus [Homicide Overview]* University of Helsinki, Institute of Criminology and Legal Policy Publications.

Lundgren, E. et al. 2001 *Slagen dam. Mäns våld mot kvinnor i jämställda Sverige – En omfångsundersökning [Beaten Lady: Men's Violence against Women in Gender Equal Sweden: A Prevalence Investigation]* Umeå: Fritzes.

Matikkala, J. 2017 'Parisuhdeväkivallasta [On Intimate Partner Violence]' in M. Lohiniva-Kerkelä (ed.) *Väkivalta. Seuraamukset ja haavoittuvuus – Terttu Utriaisen juhlakirja [Violence: Consequences and Vulnerability: Essays in the Honour of Terttu Utriainen]* Helsinki: Talentum 415.

Naffine, N. and Owens, R. (eds.) 1997 *Sexing the Subject of Law* North Ryde: LBC Information Services.

Niemi, J. et al. (eds.) 2017 *Sukupuolistunut väkivalta [Gender Violence]* Tampere: Vastapaino.

Niemi-Kiesiläinen, J. 2004 *Rikosprosessi ja parisuhdeväkivalta [The Criminal Process and Intimate Partner Violence]* Helsinki: Sanoma Pro.

Nieminen, L. 1990 *Perusoikeuksien emansipatoriset mahdollisuudet? Valtiosääntöoikeudellinen tutkimus legaalistrategioiden rajoista [The Emancipatory Potential of Fundamental Rights? Constitutional Research about the Limits of Legal Strategies]* Helsinki: Lakimiesliitto.

Nousiainen, K. 1999 'Equalizing Images? Gendered Imagery in Criminal Law' 24 *Suomen Antropologi* 7.

Piispa, M. and Heiskanen, M. 1998 *Usko, toivo, hakkaus [Faith, Hope, Battering]* Helsinki: StatFin.

Pohjonen, S. 1992 'Yksityinen perhe ja julkinen väkivalta [The Private Family and Public Violence]' 20 *Oikeus* 109.

Pylkkänen, A. 2009 *Trapped in Equality: Women as Legal Persons in the Modernisation of Finnish Law* Helsinki: Finnish Literature Society.

Ruuskanen, M. 2001 '"The Good Battered Woman": A Silenced Defendant' in K. Nousiainen et al. (eds.) *Responsible Selves: Women in the Nordic Legal Culture* Farnham, Surrey: Ashgate 311.

——— 2005 *Hätävarjelu ja parisuhdeväkivalta [Legitimate Self-Protection and Intimate Partner Violence]* Helsinki: Suomalainen Lakimiesyhdistys.
Smart, C. 1989 *Feminism and the Power of Law* London: Routledge.
——— 1992 'The Woman of Legal Discourse' 1(1) *Social & Legal Studies* 29.
Statistics Finland 2016 'Taulukot [Tables]' www.stat.fi/til/ksyyt/tau.html
United Nations Office on Drugs and Crime (UNODC) 2014 *Global Study on Homicide 2013* Vienna: United Nations Publications.

10 Finland on trial

Marjo Rantala

Introduction

Such is the power of the enduring myth that Finland is a land of gender equality that yet another intimate partner femicide always seems to come as a surprise to Finns. A man kills his partner, perhaps himself too. Sometimes there are children involved. The media speculates that the man had financial problems or that his partner wanted to leave him. Never have the neighbours, relatives or others close to them suspected that something like that could happen.[1] The killings are seen as entirely unexpected, Finnish feminist investigative research attempting to elevate intimate partner femicide into a first-order political problem passing most people by.[2]

This chapter tells the story of my involvement in a feminist human rights intervention in Finland, one born of frustration with the impoverished institutional space within which feminist legal scholars can challenge legal and public discourse about violence against women. Many of those who were present in academia during the 1990s when *women's law* was established in Finnish law schools remain active, but mainstream legal scholarship remains largely unmarked by feminist legal scholarship, leaving feminists to despair about the failure of criminal law to register violence against women as a serious social problem.[3] Embracing a 'neutral' and presumably equal approach while simultaneously dismantling the welfare state, current domestic legislation is failing to protect women.[4] Such is the level of frustration that in 2016, three feminist legal scholars, myself included, decided to bring a case of intimate partner femicide from Finland before a supranational

1 Nikupeteri et al. (2017: 301–302).

2 The Finnish Government has conducted two reports on 'family killings' and 'child killings' after few cases with minors were fiercely debated in the media; neither report included gender as an analytical aspect. Ministry of the Interior (2012 and 2014).

3 Nousiainen (1999); Niemi-Kiesiläinen (2004a); Piispa (2002); Ruuskanen (2005); Jokila (2010); Kotanen (2013); Kainulainen and Niemi (2017); and Nousiainen and Pentikäinen (2017). In the Faculty of Law of the University of Helsinki, the biggest of Finnish law schools, I am the only scholar in the field.

4 Pylkkänen (2007, 2009: 168, 232–233).

human rights body, the UN Committee on Elimination of Discrimination against Women (the CEDAW Committee).[5]

But why include a human rights intervention in a book honouring Carol Smart's *Feminism and the Power of Law* in which an entire chapter is devoted to 'The Problem of Rights?' There she catalogues all the problems with rights – they 'oversimplify complex power relations'; 'the resort to rights can be effectively countered by the resort to competing rights' and rights are 'often formulated to deal with a social wrong' yet they are always 'focused on the individual who must prove that her rights have been violated'. The final major problem with rights? – the way in which rights formulated to protect 'the individual against the state, or the weak against the strong', may be 'appropriated by the more powerful'. Sex discrimination laws, for example, might be used 'as much by men as by women'.[6] That was 1989. Might a rights-based approach to the problem of violence against women be more promising today? Might feminist engagement with supranational legal mechanisms today have the power to raise awareness and even force otherwise stubbornly resistant domestic legal systems to change? It is our hope that using an international instrument to hold Finland accountable for femicide will do just that.

Violence against women in Finland

Finland is often ranked among the best countries for women. Finnish women were the first women to gain the right to vote in Europe, they are highly educated and they participate actively in the labour market and politics. But when it comes to bodily integrity and the prospect of living a life free from violence, Finnish women are not doing so well. In the 'hegemonic discourse on gender equality' that dominates the country, statistics supporting the idea of emancipated Finnish women are embraced, while the prevalence of sexual violence and intimate partner violence are simply ignored.[7]

According to the Violence against Women Survey by the EU Fundamental Rights Agency in 2014, up to 55 per cent of Finnish women indicated that they knew someone in their circle of friends or family who had been a victim of domestic violence. The EU average was 39 per cent.[8] When Finnish women were asked if they had experienced physical and/or sexual violence since the age of 15, Finland's rate came out as the second highest with 47 per cent (EU average 33 per cent).[9] Interestingly, when women were asked how common they

5 As of January 2018, the case is pending as an individual communication, No 111/2017, against Finland.

6 Smart (1989: 144–145).

7 Holli (2012: 93, 2003). See United Nations Development Programme (UNDP) (2016: 5–6) and European Institute for Gender Equality (EIGE) (2017); OECD Gender Data Portal.

8 European Union Agency for Fundamental Rights (FRA) (2014: 16–17, 155–156).

9 FRA (2014: 28). Only 9 per cent replied 'fairly common', in contrast with the EU average of 27 per cent.

thought that violence against women was in their country, Finland had the lowest percentage.[10] In addition to this EU survey, a 2016 national report by the Institute of Criminology and Legal Policy reveals that intimate partner femicides constitute the second most common homicide type in the country.[11] The overall homicide rate has been in decline during the past twenty years but mostly due to changes in violence involving only men. Importantly, there is no decreasing tendency in intimate partner femicides.[12] Between 2009 and 2015, 65 per cent of adult female homicide victims were killed by their current or former male partners. In comparison, only 6 per cent of male homicide victims were killed by their female partner.[13]

In Finland, domestic violence and sexual violence within the family have long been accepted as ways to control women.[14] But the 1990s was a turning point. Marital rape and assault in private premises were criminalised and reforms to the Criminal Code introduced systematically gender-neutral language. All laws were now to be equally applicable to all within and without the family according to a liberal framework of freedom of choice and personal autonomy. But as feminists have pointed out, all that this gender-neutral language has done is to mask rather than eradicate the realities of domestic violence.[15] Moreover, while awareness on violence against women in Finland has increased since the 1990s, especially in the context of intimate partner violence, governments have not responded adequately to the problem.[16] There used to be national programmes to combat violence against women but the current government has not drawn one up. Prime Minister Sipilä's Government Programme simply remarks that 'Finland is also a land of gender equality'.[17] Unlike most other European countries, Finland has not established a national authority to coordinate policies and to set coherent minimum standards to tackle violence against women. Municipalities have the responsibility to secure adequate services, but do not have earmarked

10 FRA (2014: 152–154).

11 Lehti (2016: 25). The report does not refer to these homicides as femicides but discloses the sex of the perpetrator and the victim, and their relationship.

12 Lehti (2016: 8) and Piispa and Heiskanen (2017: 72).

13 Lehti (2016: 23). Nine per cent of female victims were killed by some other close relative. Of men, 1 per cent was killed by their same sex partner, and 7 per cent by some other close relative.

14 Lidman (2015) and Pylkkänen (2009).

15 Nousiainen (2004); Pylkkänen (2009: 185); Ruuskanen (2005); Niemi (2015); Niemi-Kiesiläinen (2004a); and Niemi-Kiesiläinen (2004b).

16 In the 1990s, the Subcommittee on Violence under the national Council for Gender Equality (TANE) was founded. The Subcommittee affirmed that domestic violence targets particularly women. Kuusinen (2012) and Kotanen (2013: 11). See also Törmä and Pentikäinen (2016); Kainulainen and Niemi (2017); Ronkainen (2017: 30–31); and Pylkkänen (2009: 184–185).

17 Finnish Government Programme (2015: 8). Former Finnish Government Programmes have addressed particular issues for gender equality, see Finnish Government Programme (2011: 66–67); Finnish Government Programme (2007: 55, 60–61).

resources for combatting violence against women.[18] Currently, the public debate revolves around social policy measures and the limited financial resources available to support them, ignoring the need for reform of criminal justice policies and legislation.

Disillusion and engagement

I first heard about the concept of femicide while on a visit to Chile in 2007. 'Watch your words, or you'll be this year's femicide number 42!' my Chilean friend teased his girlfriend. I was bewildered. Everyone seemed to know what a *femicidio* (femicide) was.[19] Not only did the national media count annual femicides, but it was generally agreed that *machismo mata*, machismo, was responsible for the killing.[20] During my stay, fellow law students and professors asked me to tell them more about Finland, the Nordic wonderland for women. The assumption was that there were no femicides in egalitarian Finland, that Finnish men respected women. At the time, I had not thought much about domestic violence, let alone femicide. I thought I *knew* that violence against women was not an issue in my country. This assumption, I now realise, comes from the general rejection in Finland that women who get killed by their partners would be killed because of their gender. Strikingly, however, the relative prevalence of femicide in Chile and Finland is roughly the same.

Had I not witnessed first hand the failure of the Finnish legal system to address violence against women, a Finnish intimate partner femicide case would not be currently pending before an international human rights body. The trigger to take action took place in 2013 when I was training on the bench in a local district court and was asked to be the secretary for a murder trial in which the defendant had killed his girlfriend and mother. Because the fatal attacks had been brutal and explicit evidence was to be presented, the judge wanted to ensure that I would remain professional during the trial. I assured him I would be, adding that given my previous experience with women's rights, it would provide an extraordinary opportunity to follow a domestic violence case. The judge dismissed my feminist viewpoint, saying: 'this has nothing to do with it' – 'the guy just went mad and thought they were UFOs or something and killed them'. Accordingly, gender did not play any role in the crimes. At the time, I did not know how to better address the case. 'Femicide' then – and still now – did not exist as an analytical let alone legal concept for lawyers in the Finnish legal system.

During the two-day oral hearing, medical experts gave evidence about the pain suffered by the victims. Should the offences be regarded as murder or manslaughter? The court speculated on the duration of the violence and the rapidness of the death. As is typical for Finnish criminal law proceedings, the personal history between the perpetrator and the victims was not addressed, the evidence

18 Lidman (2017: 37); Törmä and Pentikäinen (2016: 48); and Laine (2010: 195).

19 See Chapter 3 in this book and Toledo (2017) and Bueno-Hansen (2010).

20 Chilean Ministry of Women and Gender Equality (2017). See also Toledo in this book.

submitted restricted to the night of the killings.[21] A psychiatric examination of the defendant had been conducted and in the end, the court did not find him criminally liable. Instead of a criminal sanction, he was subjected to compulsory mental health treatment.

Neither the public prosecutor, the presiding judge or the three juror laymen discussed the issues stated in the pre-trial investigation report – how in the past the mother, fearful of her son, had called the emergency telephone number; how once, after a fight with the defendant, the girlfriend had needed surgery for a broken arm; how the defendant's neighbour had seen the girlfriend waiting in the stairwell outside of her boyfriend's flat because she was too afraid of going inside; how when she had left him he had gone to her parents' home, poured gasoline through the letter box and threatened to burn their house down. In my view, the case resembled a textbook example of violence against women, but nobody else could see this. I was appalled. It was not so much the verdict – two murders, aggravated by their brutality – that surprised me, but the court's abject failure to contextualise the killings.

During my year at the district court, I got acquainted with another domestic homicide case. A woman had gone to a shelter with her two daughters aged five and eight. While there, the public authorities had taken the girls into emergency custody. Their father was suspected of sexually abusing them and the mother was thought to be so under her husband's control and so afraid of him that she was deemed unfit to have sole custody. She then returned to her husband. During the police investigation into the alleged abuse and while the question of permanent custody was pending at the administrative court, the girls had a right to a monitored visit to see their parents. One day two child welfare officials escorted them to the parent's home, but left them alone for over an hour. In that time, the man killed his partner and the girls and was later found guilty of the murders committed under reduced criminal responsibility.

What is striking about the case is that the authorities were not held liable. The district court found that the 'child welfare notification and the consequential actions concerning the custody of children, taken by the public authorities' had 'initiated a series of events that resulted in a much unexpected outcome'.[22] The court saw the killings as unfortunate events, impossible to foresee by the authorities. Moreover, it constructed the murders as motivated by 'the family break-up', ignoring evidence of earlier abuse, including the 'alleged sexual abuse', the rationale being that as he had killed both the girls and their mother, that evidence was irrelevant.[23] This left me wondering about an alternative narrative, one that would include how the public authorities had been ignorant about the typical pattern of violence against women. I thought that if any case should be taken to a supranational human rights body it was this one. What was needed was a reconsideration of the case taking into account the asymmetrical gender relations

21 Kainulainen and Niemi (2017: 139–140, 154–155); Niemi-Kiesiläinen (2004a: 94, 97); Kotanen (2013: 170, 172); Ruuskanen (2005: 27, 30); and Hong (2017: 372).

22 Vantaa District Court, R 12/1628 (2012): 11.

23 Vantaa District Court, R 12/1628 (2012): 16.

resulting in the man's control over his partner and abuse of his children. Perhaps international human rights law could create a space for a feminist perspective on a violation of human rights? Might this in turn lead to reform of the law and could a reformed law help save lives?

As I had little knowledge of how to bring a case of alleged human rights violations before a supranational body, I set about finding how to do so with the help of two other feminist legal scholars. While getting acquainted with the case, I had invited Merja Pentikäinen to lecture about gender and human rights for my undergraduate students. She told them that she considered violence against women to be the most serious human rights violation in Finland. Hearing this, I realised she could be my ally. We were joined by friend and former colleague, Kevät Nousiainen. They had both researched, taught and advocated for years for a better legal understanding of violence against women and women's human rights.[24] We decided to work on the case together aware that no domestic legal aid is available in drafting an application and that Finnish attorney offices do not have *pro bono* systems for international human rights litigation. Reading the judgment and the pre-trial investigation report, we were convinced that taking the case to the CEDAW Committee seemed feasible.[25] The killer and his adult victim were both intellectually disabled. The younger child had spent her first year in hospital due to a serious illness. Since the family had received a great deal of public support, the public authorities had been recording the family history for years. Social welfare for the disabled, child welfare, public healthcare, day care, schools, family shelter personnel and the police all had extensive documentation of the family's difficulties. The child welfare authorities had been notified several times regarding the children.[26] Importantly, there were also records of the woman telling shelter personnel and police that she had been subjected to psychological abuse, that she was afraid of her husband and that he had threatened to kill himself and the children. Once the victims' family agreed to collaborate with us, we became convinced that this was a case that could be an eye-opener for Finland if it could be presented with an alternative normative interpretation of the family killings. We knew that external, supranational pressure had had a major impact on Finnish legislation in the past.[27] Perhaps we could now demonstrate how current laws fail women. At least we considered it worth trying.

The central argument in our appeal to the CEDAW Committee was as follows. The public authorities had prior knowledge of several factors that increase the risk of intimate partner femicide. Yet they did not foresee the fatal attacks and

24 Nousiainen and Pentikäinen (2017, 2013); Törmä and Pentikäinen (2016); Nousiainen and Chinkin (2016); and Nousiainen (1999).

25 All the facts regarding the case are drawn from the public parts of the pre-trial investigation report and of the judgment concerning the three murders. We have not had access to any confidential information.

26 Seven times concerning the eight-year-old and five concerning the five-year-old.

27 From, for example, international law and European non-discrimination law. Nousiainen (2005).

so did nothing. They never requested a restraining order, no police investigation was undertaken regarding menace and no support person was designated for the woman. Nor was she supported in her role as parent or given legal aid. Her personal safety was never assessed. According to the trial judgment, the husband had already started planning to kill his wife when she was at the shelter. After her death, public authorities never analysed the measures taken, if any, to protect the victims. Once again, it was assumed that the homicides were unfortunate though probably inevitable incidents that the authorities had no means of preventing.

Formulating femicide as discrimination and human rights violation

Violence targeting women or that affects women disproportionately is today defined as gender-based discrimination prohibited in international human rights law. The Council of Europe Convention on Preventing and Combatting Violence against Women and Domestic Violence (the Istanbul Convention) confirms this in its Article 3, and both the European Court of Human Rights (ECtHR) and the UN CEDAW Committee have substantiated the view.[28] When selecting the legal forum for our case, an individual communication to the CEDAW Committee seemed like the obvious choice. The CEDAW's contribution to women's rights is beyond comparison. Its admissibility criteria for individual communications are easier to fulfil than those of the ECtHR and the CEDAW Committee has had Finland under particular scrutiny concerning violence against women since the very first periodic review on Finland's compliance with the treaty obligations.[29]

As for framing violence against women as prohibited discrimination, two factors stand out in the international human rights system: due diligence and indirect discrimination. Firstly, the due diligence doctrine requires states to adopt measures concerning non-state actors.[30] Though the primary duty of states is to put in place effective national legislation, this must be backed up by effective implementation, including law enforcement machinery for prevention and punishment. The failure by the authorities to take measures which might have been expected to avoid a risk for the rights guaranteed in a convention gives rise to state responsibility based on due diligence.[31] The CEDAW Committee has specifically emphasised the obligation of state parties to act with due diligence in its jurisprudence regarding domestic violence, that is, when acts take place between

28 Council of Europe Convention on Preventing and Combating Violence against Women and Domestic Violence (2011) CETS 210; ECtHR, *Opuz v Turkey*, 33401/02 (2009); *MC v Bulgaria* 39272/98 (2003). CEDAW Committee (2017, 1992).

29 CEDAW Committee (1990: para 263); CEDAW Committee (2008: para 174); and CEDAW Committee (2014: paras 18–19).

30 CEDAW Article 2(e); Šimonovic (2014: 600).

31 More on due diligence and violence against women, see Bourke-Martignoni (2008); Ertürk (2008); Benninger-Budel (2008); and Merry (2006: 22).

intimate partners. The Committee has noted that for state responsibility to be actualised, it is sufficient that the authorities did not do all that could be reasonably expected of them to avoid real and immediate risks to human rights of which they had or ought to have had knowledge.[32]

With all this in mind, we submitted that the Government of Finland had not fulfilled its obligation of due diligence by failing to protect the victims' personal integrity, security, health and life. We argued that on the basis of the documentation on the family and the knowledge of the vulnerability of the family members accumulated over the years, the Finnish authorities knew, or they should have known, that there existed a real and immediate risk to the fundamental human rights of the victims. More specifically, we stated that the 'victims did not receive sufficient help even after they had sought help in the shelter'; that the authorities had 'failed to take measures within the scope of their powers which could have been expected to avoid the course of the events that eventually led to the death of the victims' and they 'failed to give due consideration to the particular vulnerability of the victims and the principle of the best interest of the child'.[33] Importantly, the authorities:

> failed to cooperate and coordinate their actions effectively and to resort to the measures available for them and prescribed by law (including requesting a restraining order and offering assistance for vulnerable persons). On the day of the killings of the victims, the protection by the authorities failed fatally. Without a number of omissions by the authorities on that very day, the victims could still be alive.[34]

Secondly, the CEDAW prohibits indirect discrimination, defined as 'any distinction, exclusion or restriction made on the basis of sex which has the *effect* . . . of impairing or nullifying the recognition, enjoyment or exercise by women . . . of human rights and fundamental freedoms'.[35] Thus, liability does not require intentional discriminatory action by public authorities. In human rights case law on discrimination the state is considered to have the burden of proof after the applicant has invoked discrimination.[36] Furthermore, the CEDAW Committee

32 CEDAW Committee *AT v Hungary* 2/2003 (2005); *Yildrim v Austria* 6/2005 (2007); *Goecke v Austria* 5/2005 (2007); *VK v Bulgaria* 20/2008 (2011); *Isatou Jallow v Bulgaria* 32/2011 (2012); and *González Carreño v Spain* 47/2012 (2014); CEDAW Committee (2017, 1992). See also Istanbul Convention, Article 5; ECtHR *Opuz v Turkey* 33401/02 (2009); *MC v Bulgaria* 39272/98 (2003).

33 CEDAW Committee, Individual communication 111/2017.

34 CEDAW Committee, Individual communication 111/2017.

35 Emphasis by the author. United Nations Convention on the Elimination of All Forms of Discrimination against Women. 1249 UNTS 13; 19 ILM 33 (1980), Art. 1.

36 According to the principle of presumption of discrimination. See EU directives on Equal Treatment between Women and Men (2006/54/EC, recast), Racial Equality (2000/43/EC), and Equal Treatment in Employment and Occupation (2000/78/EC). ECtHR *D.H. & Others v Czech Republic* 57325/00 (2007) is considered as a landmark case with this respect.

does not only assess the singular case and alleged violations against specified individual; it also revises the state party's overall policy framework and measures to protect women, requiring elimination of stereotyping, gender roles, and prejudices.[37] In our case, we argued that gender-segregated statistics on homicides demonstrating the prevalence of intimate partner femicides in Finland should constitute a presumption of prohibited discrimination. It was up to the Finnish Government to prove otherwise. Accordingly, we outlined the discrimination in the case as follows. We submitted that in addition to failing to fulfill its obligation of due diligence, the Government of Finland had failed to guarantee the equal rights and responsibilities in the family for the adult victim as protected under Article 16.1 of the Convention. The authorities had known that the defendant was controlling his family and making decisions for the whole family, and as a result the adult victim's rights under Article 16.1 were subjugated under her husband. They had made no efforts to enable her to enjoy her equal rights as a spouse and parent. Furthermore, we submitted that

> in cases of domestic violence and abuse of children by the father in Finland, the authorities tend to see the mother's role to protect children against the abusive father. If the mother is incapable of protecting her children against this abuse, her own parental rights are at risk and may be curtailed. This happened in the present case when the adult victim in practice lost her parental rights after she had sought protection in the shelter against violence by her husband and the father of her children.[38]

To put it simply, in this case as in other Finnish custody cases, the mother tends to lose custody of her children due to the father's violence.[39]

Conclusion

As we await the CEDAW Committee's findings, we keep in mind Carol Smart's warning to feminists not to be 'seduced' by law and to be wary of law-based strategies, especially rights-based ones.[40] Will she be proved right again? Will we regret our effort to bring this Finnish filicide and intimate partner femicide case before an international body? Will it go the way of the rights-based feminist strategies she critiqued in *Feminism and the Power of Law*, being countered by competing rights or appropriated by men? And even if our action succeeds, will it benefit other women? Only time will tell. But taking account of developments over the last three decades in international human rights law with regard to violence against women – particularly regarding its collective and transformative potential – it is just possible that Smart might be pleasantly surprised at what a rights-based approach

37 CEDAW Art. 5. Šimonovic (2014: 593–594); Cusack (2013); and Holtmaat (2013).
38 CEDAW Committee, Individual communication 111/2017.
39 Hiitola (2015: 106–158).
40 Smart (1989: 160).

can achieve. At any rate, we hope that by making Finnish femicides visible in an international forum, we have contributed to a process whereby violence against women becomes a political priority in Finland. Mainstream legal scholars might ignore feminist work but with feminists occupying the normative discursive space provided by international human rights law, it is becoming more difficult for the state to ignore femicide and violence against women.

References

Benninger-Budel, C. 2008 'Introduction' in C. Benninger-Budel (ed.) *Due Diligence and Its Application to Protect Women from Violence* Leiden and Boston: Martinus Nijhoff Publishers.

Bourke-Martignoni, J. 2008 'The History and Development of the Due Diligence Standard in International Law and Its Role in Protection of Women against Violence' in C. Benninger-Budel (ed.) *Due Diligence and Its Application to Protect Women from Violence* Leiden and Boston: Martinus Nijhoff Publishers.

Bueno-Hansen, P. 2010 'Feminicidio: Making the Most of an "Empowered Term"' in R.-L. Fregoso and C. Bejarano (eds.) *Terrorizing Women: Feminicide in the Americas* London and Durham: Duke University Press.

Committee on the Elimination of Discrimination against Women (CEDAW Committee) 1990 *Report of the Committee on the Elimination of Discrimination against Women 8th Session* (A/44/38).

——— 1992 *General Recommendation No. 19 on Violence against Women* UN Doc. A/47/38.

——— 2008 *Concluding Observations on Finland's 5th and 6th Periodic Reports* UN Doc. CEDAW/C/FIN/CO/6.

——— 2014 *Concluding Observations on Finland's 7th Periodic Report* UN Doc. CEDAW/C/FIN/CO/7.

——— 2017 *General Recommendation No. 35 on Gender-Based Violence against Women, Updating General Recommendation No 19* UN Doc. CEDAW/C/GC/35.

Chilean Ministry of Women and Gender Equality 2017 *Feminicidios* www.minmujeryeg.cl/sernameg/programas/violencia-contra-las-mujeres/femicidios/

Cusack, S. 2013 'The CEDAW as a Legal Framework for Transnational Discourses on Gender Stereotyping' in A. Hellum and H.S. Aasen (eds.) *Women's Human Rights: CEDAW in International, Regional and National Law* Cambridge: Cambridge University Press.

Ertürk, Y. 2008 'The Due Diligence Standard: What Does It Entail for Women's Rights?' in C. Benninger-Budel (ed.) *Due Diligence and Its Application to Protect Women from Violence* Leiden and Boston: Martinus Nijhoff Publishers.

European Institute for Gender Equality (EIGE) 2017 *Gender Equality Index 2017* eige.europa.eu/gender-equality-index

European Union Agency for Fundamental Rights (FRA) 2014 *Violence against Women: An EU-Wide Survey* Luxembourg: Publications Office of the European Union.

Finnish Government Programme 2007 *Pääministeri Matti Vanhasen II hallituksen ohjelma* [Prime Minister Matti Vanhanen's II Government Programme] Helsinki: Edita Prima.

——— 2011 *Pääministeri Jyrki Kataisen hallituksen ohjelma* [Prime Minister Jyrki Kataianen's Government Programme] Helsinki: Edita Prima.

——— 2015 *Finland, a Land of Solutions: Strategic Programme of Prime Minister Juha Sipilä's Government* Helsinki: Edita Prima.

Finnish Ministry of the Interior 2012 *Selvitys perhe-ja lapsensurmien taustoista vuosilta 2003–2012 [Report on the Circumstances of the Family and Child Killings 2003–2012]* Helsinki: Ministry of the Interior.

——— 2014 *Perhe-ja lapsisurmien ehkäisy ja estäminen ja viranomaisten välinen tiedonvaihto [Prevention of Family and Child Killings and the Cooperation between Public Authorities]* Helsinki: Ministry of the Interior.

Hiitola, J. 2015 *Hallittu vanhemmuus: Sukupuoli, luokka ja etnisyys huostaanottoasiakirjoissa [Governed Parenthood: Out-of-Home Placements and Gender, Class and Ethnicity]* Tampere: Tampere University Press.

Holli, A.M. 2003 *Discourse and Politics for Gender Equality in Late Twentieth Century Finland* Helsinki: University of Helsinki.

——— 2012 'Kriittisiä näkökulmia tasa-arvon tutkimukseen [Critical Perspectives on Gender Equality Resarch]' in J. Kantola et al. *Tasa-arvo toisin nähtynä [Equality from Another Point of View]* Helsinki: Gaudeamus.

Holtmaat, R. 2013 'The CEDAW: A Holistic Approach to Women's Equality and Freedom' in A. Hellum and H.S. Aasen (eds.) *Women's Human Rights: CEDAW in International, Regional and National Law* Cambridge: Cambridge University Press.

Hong, T. 2017 'Yhteisö, kontrolli ja oikeuden konteksti: suojaako rikoslaki yhteisöllisen väkivallan uhria? [Community, Control, and the Context of Justice: Does the Criminal Code Protect the Victim of Communal Violence?]' 115(3–4) *Lakimies* 362.

Jokila, H. 2010 *Tahdonvastainen suostumus ja liiallisen luottamuksen hinta: raiskauksen ja muiden seksuaalirikosten oikeudellisen tiedot konstruktiot [Consent against One's Will and the Price of Undue Trust: The Legal Constructions of Knowledge in Finnish Sexual Crimes]* Helsinki: Suomalainen Lakimiesyhdistys.

Kainulainen, H. and Niemi, J. 2017 'Parisuhdeväkivallan tunnistaminen rikosoikeudellisessa järjestelmässä [Recognition of Intimate Partner Violence in Criminal Legal System]' in J. Niemi et al. (eds.) *Sukupuolistunut väkivalta väkivalta [Gender Violence]* Tampere: Vastapaino.

Kotanen, R. 2013 *Näkymättömästä näkökulmaksi: parisuhdeväkivallan uhrit ja oikeudellisen sääntelyn muutos Suomessa [From Invisible to a Point of View: Victims of Intimate Partner Violence and Changes in Legal Regulation in Finland]* Helsinki: University of Helsinki.

Kuusinen, S. 2012 *Väkivaltajaosto: Naisiin kohdistuvan väkivallan vastustamistyötä 1990–1998 [Subcommittee on Violence: Lobbying against Violence against Women 1990–1998]* Sastamala: Tasa-arvoasiain neuvottelukunta.

Laine, T. 2010 'Turvakodit Suomessa [Family Shelters in Finland]' 75(2) *Yhteiskuntapolitiikka* 194.

Lehti, M. 2016 *Henkirikoskatsauksia 2016 [Homicide Review 2016]* Helsinki: Institute of Criminology and Legal Policy (Krimo).

Lidman, S. 2015 *Väkivaltakulttuurin perintö: Sukupuoli, asenteet ja historia [Legacy of a Culture of Violence: Gender, Attitudes, and History]* Helsinki: Gaudeamus.

——— 2017 *Kuka ottaa vastuun? Naisiin kohdistuva väkivalta ja ihmisoikeusvelvoitteiden toteutuminen [Who Takes the Responsibility? Violence against Women and the Realisation of Human Rights]* Helsinki: Amnesty International Finland.

Merry, S.E. 2006 *Human Rights and Gender Violence: Translating International Law into Local Justice* Chicago and London: University of Chicago Press.

Niemi, J. 2015 *Gender and Criminal Law Policy* Turku: University of Turku Press.

Niemi-Kiesiläinen, J. 2004a *Rikosprosessi ja parisuhdeväkivalta [Criminal Legal Procedure and Intimate Partner Violence]* Helsinki: Sanoma Pro.

——— 2004b 'The Reform of Sex Crime Law and the Gender-Neutral Subject' in E.-M. Svensson et al. (eds.) *Nordic Equality at a Crossroads: Feminist Legal Studies Coping with Difference* Aldershot and Burlington: Ashgate.

Nikupeteri, A. et al. 2017 'Potentiaalisesti tappava parisuhde? Erotilanteen uhkaavuus ja uhrien suojaamisen edellytykset sukupuolistuneen väkivallan viitekehyksessä [Potentially Fatal Partnership? The Threat of Death Related to Separation and Prerequisites for Protecting the Victims in the Frame of Gendered Violence]' 46(3) *Oikeus* 290.

Nousiainen, K. 1999 'Equalizing Images? Gendered Imagery in Criminal Law' 24(3) *Suomen Antropologi* 7.

——— 2004 'On the Limits of the Concept of Equality: Arguments for a Dynamic Reading' in E.-M. Svensson et al. (eds.) *Nordic Equality at a Crossroads: Feminist Legal Studies Coping with Difference* Aldershot and Burlington: Ashgate.

——— 2005 'Tasa-arvon monet kasvot. Kansainvälisistä vaikutuksista Suomen tasa-arvo-oikeudessa [Many Faces of Equality: On International Influences in Finnish Equality Law]' 103(7–8) *Lakimies* 1188.

Nousiainen, K. and Chinkin, C. 2016 *Legal Implications of EU Accession to the Istanbul Convention* Luxembourg: Publications Office of the European Union.

Nousiainen, K. and Pentikäinen, M. 2013 'Rise and Fall of the CEDAW in Finland: Time to Reclaim Its Impetus' in A. Hellum and H.S. Aasen (eds.) *Women's Human Rights: CEDAW in International, Regional and National Law* Cambridge: Cambridge University Press.

——— 2017 'Naisiin kohdistuva väkivalta ihmisoikeuskysymyksenä [Violence against Women as a Human Rights Issue]' in J. Niemi et al. (eds.) *Sukupuolistunut väkivalta [Gender Violence]* Tampere: Vastapaino.

OECD Gender Data Portal www.oecd.org/gender/data/

Piispa, M. 2002 'Complexity of Patterns of Violence against Women in Heterosexual Partnerships' 8(7) *Violence against Women* 873.

Piispa, M. and Heiskanen, M. 2017 'Sukupuoli ja väkivalta tilastoissa [Gender and Violence in Statistics]' in J. Niemi et al. (eds.) *Sukupuolistunut väkivalta [Gender Violence]* Tampere: Vastapaino.

Pylkkänen, A. 2007 'Onko oikeuden henkilöllä sukupuolta? [Does the Legal Subject Have a Gender?]' 36(2) *Oikeus* 147.

——— 2009 *Trapped in Equality: Women as Legal Persons in the Modernisation of Finnish Law* Helsinki: Suomalaisen Kirjallisuuden Seura.

Ronkainen, S. 2017 'Mitä väkivalta on? [What Counts as Violence?]' in J. Niemi et al. (eds.) *Sukupuolistunut väkivalta [Gender Violence]* Tampere: Vastapaino.

Ruuskanen, M. 2005 *Hätävarjelu ja parisuhdeväkivalta [Legitimate Self-Protection and Intimate Partner Violence]* Helsinki: Suomalainen Lakimiesyhdistys.

Šimonovic, D. 2014 'Global and Regional Standards on Violence against Women: The Evolution and Synergy of the CEDAW and Istanbul Conventions' 36(3) *Human Rights Quarterly* 590.

Smart, C. 1989 *Feminism and the Power of Law* London: Routledge.

Toledo, P. 2017 'Criminalisation of Femicide/Feminicide in Latin American Countries' 11(2) *Rivista di Criminologia, Vittimologia e Sicurezza* 44.

Törmä, S. and Pentikäinen, M. 2016 *Tavoitteena naisiin kohdistuvasta väkivallasta ja perheväkivallasta vapaa Suomi: Naisiin kohdistuvan väkivallan vähentämisen ohjelmasta Istanbulin sopimuksen toimeenpanoon [Striving for a Finland Free From Violence against Women and Domestic Violence: From the Programme of Reduction of Violence against Women to the Implementation of the Istanbul Convention]* Helsinki: Ministry of Social Affairs and Health.

United Nations Development Programme (UNDP) 2016 *Human Development Report: Finland* hdr.undp.org/en/countries/profiles/FIN

Epilogue

Adrian Howe and Daniela Alaattinoğlu

Adrian

Is it possible to speak of any form of violence against women today without someone diverting attention to the pressing contemporary issue of transgender? You have spoken about 'females', a woman said at a recent seminar discussion of my play *Othello on Trial*, she somehow overlooking the fact that I had definitely not referred to women as 'females' – and haven't since the 1980s when poststructuralists like Carol Smart displaced criminological positivism's preoccupation with 'male' and 'female' offenders with far more rigorous inquiries into the discursive production of 'men' and 'women'. 'Am I that name, Iago', Desdemona asked of Shakespeare's famous villain shortly before her husband killed her, showcasing the playwright's always already brilliantly prescient understanding of the discursive constitution of personhood. 'What name, fair lady?/Such as she said my lord did say I was'.[1] You spoke about 'females', my interlocutor said, but what about transgendered women? As far as the records show there was only one transwoman amongst the victims in my study of 317 femicides committed in England and Wales between 2012 and 2016. Vanessa Sentillan was killed in March 2015 by her husband who was convicted of murder and imprisoned for life.[2] There was also a transwoman defendant. Twenty-year old Bethany Hill was murdered in what was described in court as a 'sadistic killing' by a former boyfriend and his current transgender girlfriend.[3] Also, just for the record, six weeks into their marriage, Frances Cleary-Senior discovered that her husband was an alcoholic and a transvestite. He murdered her years later during a confrontation over his drinking, not his cross-dressing.

Of course, there may well be more transwomen as yet unidentified amongst the tens of thousands of victims in the killing field of intimate partner femicide that feminists across the globe are transforming into a first-order political problem. And if in the future transgendered women start to be killed by their partners at the rate of, say, the two a week that has been reported for women killed

1 Shakespeare (2008): *Othello* 4.2.121–122.
2 BBC (2015).
3 BBC (2017).

in the UK over the last several decades, feminists will be amongst the first to draw attention to this emergent social problem. In the meantime, I assured my questioner, if their number remains as negligible as the available records indicate to date, including transgendered women in the intimate partner femicide body count might be an option. After all, though it's a controversial issue for some, they identify as women.

In short, the transgender question is diversionary, the latest manifestation of that extraordinarily persistent and widespread disavowal of the sexed asymmetry of intimate partner homicide that is an occupational hazard for feminist researchers and activists confronting it. What about women who kill men or children? What about ethnic minority men and 'honour' crime? And now – what about transgender? What about anything at all except confronting the realities unearthed by feminist investigative research is the standard non-feminist response to feminist speech about femicide.

Daniela

Adrian is right to express concern about the impact of the trans question, at least with regards to the diversionary discussions that it tends to awaken. But a reviewer of our book proposal asked whether we would be including transwomen in our study and in my view, this raises an important question about how 'femicide' and more specifically, 'intimate partner femicide' should be defined.[4] While this book does not focus on intimate partner femicide of transwomen, it does not seek to exclude them. Nor is the book about the diversionary and divisive debate – often fraught with bio and identity politics – about who can be classified as a woman. Intimate partner femicide statistics may include transwomen as they are mainly based on victims' legally registered sex.[5] However, due to limited research on victimisation, we do not know whether transwomen are particularly vulnerable to intimate partner violence and femicide.

Facing a lack of trans specific statistics, we can at least record individual cases of transwomen's victimisation in fatal intimate partner violence. One such example is the intimate partner femicide of transwoman Christa Leigh Steele-Knudsen, stabbed and beaten to death with a hammer by her husband in her home in Massachusetts in January this year.[6] Claiming the – by now, very familiar – argument that she was 'always belittling' him, her husband told the police that he had 'snapped' before he killed her, entering a not guilty plea to the charge of first-degree murder.[7] While the final judgment is still to be handed down, the

4 Here, I understand 'trans' as an open umbrella category of people whose birth-assigned and legally registered gender is not in line with their gender identity (for example, transgender and transsexual people).

5 The national rules surrounding amendment of legally registered sex vary from country to country.

6 Brammer (2018).

7 Johnson (2018) and Glaun (2018).

misogynist, victim-blaming narrative at play in the defence strategy is chillingly similar to ones used in many other femicide cases depicted in this book. This case, in fact, sheds even further light on how feminist criticism and engagement with the gendered narratives at play in law as depicted in this book are ever so timely and required.

Accordingly, I hope that our book is seen as an open invitation to engage in more discussion and research on the topic of intimate partner femicide in general. In the meantime, while we wait for the transnational culturally inscribed practice of what traditionally was called 'wife-killing' to be taken seriously by politicians, courts and law enforcement, 'femicide' and 'intimate partner femicide' remain useful terms to name very real and pressing problems.

Adrian and Daniela

As we hope this book has demonstrated, feminist campaigns against intimate femicide have met with considerable success, perhaps especially in those Anglophone jurisdictions where law reforms are ensuring that victims are less likely to be blamed for their own deaths and men are no longer getting away with murder. The reforms signify that feminists are achieving one of their central goals, namely elevating intimate partner femicide from its lowly traditional place on the hierarchy of homicides into its rightful assignation – murder, or even aggravated murder in some jurisdictions. But everywhere, the killing continues. The goal for the next generation of feminists is to develop early intervention prevention strategies that contest transnational, culturally mandated excuses for hurting and killing women before sexist views become entrenched, challenging unexamined deeply held beliefs about men's propriety rights over women.

Importantly, devising new strategies will entail more of that essential discursive work that Smart advocated in *Feminism and the Power of Law*. How then, in the final analysis, should the book's impact be assessed today? By 2012, Smart was wondering whether it was still worth reading. In her assessment it is but only because it is 'perhaps' on 'the cusp of remaining a useful text (because we still need to address some of the same issues) and becoming a quaint historical document (which provides evidence of how some second wave feminists used to think)'. She now thinks of the book as 'a phase in an ongoing conversation between feminists and also as part of an interminable discursive struggle which requires constant reformulation'.[8] In our view, she undersells *Feminism and the Power of Law*'s significance by a wide margin. As the contributions to this book attest, the book has remained a touchstone of feminist engagement with law across a wide range of jurisdictions, inspiring two generations of feminists working within common and civil law jurisdictions to think carefully and strategically about how we approach the law question.

8 Smart (2012: 164–165).

It would not do however, to conclude without commenting on Smart's own discursive struggle within feminist circles to get her view of law heard clearly. For hers was a highly controversial book, one that generated a great deal of criticism and even more misunderstanding to this day. Reflecting on the papers published in 2012 in a special issue devoted to assessing *Feminism and the Power of Law*'s legacy, Smart came to realise 'how close' she remained to 'the Smart of 1989'. But she was puzzled as to why some contributors still seemed to misread her position on law and why some thought she had changed her sceptical view of its value for feminism and was now more enamoured of it than in the past. This prompted her to remind them of a 'strong theme' in the book, namely her constantly reiterated argument that law should be conceptualised 'as a site of conflict and dispute and not a place of refuge or of resolution'. Then as now it needed to be said that anyone challenging law and intervening discursively in what she called 'a high profile manner', demonstrating an ability to identify conceptual 'slippage' in legal reasoning and holding courts to account in relation to their principles and practices earned her respect. Such feminist engagement was precisely the sort of 'endlessly valuable' discursive work she had always advocated.[9]

Smart's continuing frustration with feminist misreadings of her work as a 'call for theoretical purity or inaction' and a retreat from law cannot go unremarked. In the past she has read this, accurately in our view, as born of an uninformed view that a poststructuralist approach to law such as she had advocated in *Feminism and the Power of Law* might 'rob us of our politics'. In no uncertain terms, Smart responded that 'those who say that to rob feminism of its certainties and guarantees is to rob it of its purpose' were 'ethically bankrupt'.[10] By 2012 her anger had abated somewhat, but is it any wonder she still gets frustrated? How many times must she repeat her view that decentring law as she explains one last time

> of course, never meant to mean that feminists should ignore the law not indeed that they should never engage with it in its various guises. Indeed law (especially at the levels of both formulating legislation and case law) provides a vital site for the contestation of ideas and values. It provides an opportunity to voice feminist values and concerns, and even possible alternatives.[11]

It followed that any project engaging with actual reported cases would be 'entirely in keeping' with her project of 'encouraging discursive struggle'. That, after all, has been her constant 'strong theme': the importance of concentrating on law's discursive practices in order to encourage 'the emergence of, or more room for, other ways of "thinking" about women and law's relationship'.[12] We can only agree and hope that this book and our contributors have demonstrated an ongoing appreciation of her innovative and remarkably influential approach to the law question.

9 Smart (2012:163–164).
10 Smart (1993: 46–47).
11 Smart (2012: 162).
12 Smart (1995: 223).

References

BBC News 2015 'Vanessa Santillan Murder: Joaquin Gomez Hernandez Jailed' www.bbc.co.uk/news/uk-england-london-34591733

——— 2017 'Jack Williams and Kayleigh Woods Murdered Bethany Hill' www.bbc.com/news/uk-england-coventry-warwickshire-38748599

Brammer, J.P. 2018 'Brutal Murder Highlights Intimate Partner Violence in Transgender Community' *NBC News* www.nbcnews.com/feature/nbc-out/recent-murder-highlights-intimate-partner-violence-trans-community-n837161

Glaun, D. 2018 'Husband Told Police He "Snapped" before Killing Christa Leigh Steele-Knudslien, Founder of Miss Trans America' *Masslive* www.masslive.com/news/index.ssf/2018/01/husband_told_police_he_snapped.html

Johnson, P. 2018 'Husband Charges with Killing Christa Leigh Steele-Knudslien Enters Not Guilty Plea in Berkshire Court Arraignment' *Masslive* www.masslive.com/news/index.ssf/2018/01/husband_charged_with_killing_c.html

Shakespeare, W. 2008 'Othello' in S. Greenblatt et al. (eds.) *The Norton Shakespeare* New York: W.W. Norton and Company.

Smart, C. 1993 'Proscription, Prescription and the Desire for Certainty?' 13 *Studies in Law, Politics and Society* 37.

——— 1995 *Law, Crime and Sexuality: Essays in Feminism* London: Sage Publications.

——— 2012 'Reflection' 20 *Feminist Legal Studies* 65.

Index

For Product Safety Concerns and Information please contact our EU representative GPSR@taylorandfrancis.com Taylor & Francis Verlag GmbH, Kaufingerstraße 24, 80331 München, Germany